Praise for Little Women of Baghlan

". . . the story of a love affair on a number of levels: a woman taking up the story of her friend and making it her own because she felt in a visceral way its importance; a young woman's idealism and her coming of age during a seminal period of US history, and certainly not least, a love affair with Afghanistan itself. Yet *Little Women of Baghlan* is not written with any particular agenda, geopolitical or religious; it is rather, quite simply, the story of how a group of ordinary Americans interacted with the citizens in a village called Baghlan. Fox accomplishes this with attention to detail, sensitivity, and with extraordinary grace."

—Dr. Michael Spath,
Professor of Comparative Religion and Middle East Studies,
Indiana University-Purdue University

"A tonic for cynicism."

—Lawrence F. Lihosit,
author of *South of the Frontera;*
A Peace Corps Memoir

"I think it's important that the word about what Peace Corps Volunteers accomplished in Afghanistan gets the widest possible circulation; it stands in contrast to some of our country's later activities."

—Dr. John Bing, Chairman of the Board,
ITAP International, and former
Peace Corps Volunteer

LITTLE WOMEN OF BAGHLAN

LITTLE WOMEN OF BAGHLAN

*The Story of a Nursing School for Girls in Afghanistan,
the Peace Corps, and Life Before the Taliban*

SUSAN FOX

A PEACE CORPS WRITERS BOOK

Little Women of Baghlan:
The Story of a Nursing School for Girls in Afghanistan,
the Peace Corps, and Life Before the Taliban
A Peace Corps Writers Book
An imprint of Peace Corps Worldwide

Interior Photographs and Cover Images: Courtesy Joanne Carter Bowling.
Private collection. Reproduced with permission.

Epigraphs: Excerpted from *Afghanistan Journal, 1968-70,* Joanne Carter Bowling.
Private collection. Reprinted with permission.

Map of Afghanistan: Courtesy of National Geographic. Used with permission.

Printed in the United States of America
by Peace Corps Writers of Oakland, California.
No part of this book may be used or reproduced in any manner whatsoever
without written permission except in the case of brief quotations contained
in critical articles or reviews.

For more information, contact peacecorpsworldwide@gmail.com.
Peace Corps Writers and the Peace Corps Writers colophon are trademarks of
PeaceCorpsWorldwide.org.

ISBN: 1935925210
ISBN-13: 9781935925217
Library of Congress Control Number: 2013950758
First Peace Corps Writers Edition, September 2013

First Edition
Published in the United States
10 9 8 7 6 5 4 3 2 1

To Peace Corps Volunteers worldwide

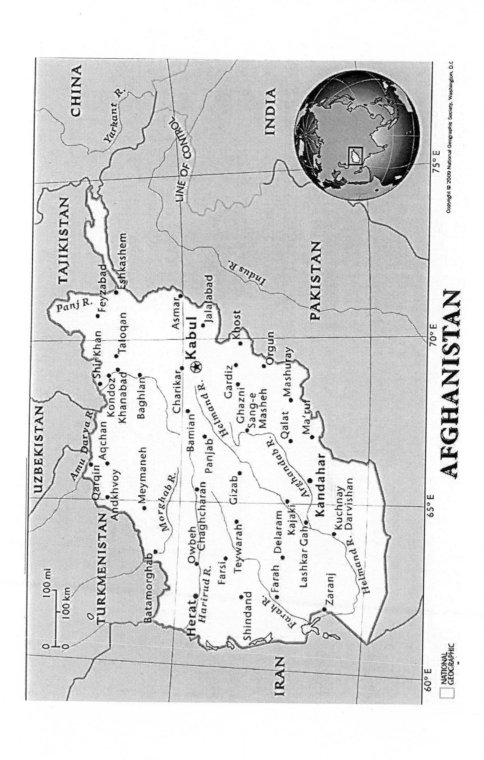

AFGHANISTAN

CHINA

TAJIKISTAN

UZBEKISTAN

TURKMENISTAN

IRAN

PAKISTAN

INDIA

Yarkant R.

LINE OF CONTROL

Panj R.

Indus R.

Amu Darya R.

Morghab R.

Harirud R.

Farah R.

Helmand R.

Arghandab R.

Helmand R.

Eshkashem

Feyzabad

Shir Khan

Taloqan

Asmar

Kondoz

Khanabad

Baghlan

Jalalabad

⊛Kabul

Charikar

Khost

Qarqin

Aqchan

Andkhvoy

Meymaneh

Bamian

Orgun

Gardiz

Mashuray

Batamorghab

Panjab

Ghazni

Sang-e
Masheh

Qalat

Ma'ruf

Owbeh

Chaghcharan

Gizab

Kandahar

Herat

Farsi

Teywarah

Farah

Delaram

Kajaki

Lashkar Gah

Kuchnay
Darvishan

Shindand

Zaranj

100 mi

100 km

60° E

65° E

70° E

75° E

CONTENTS

Foreword..*xi*
Introduction..*xiii*

Chapter 1: The Hindu Kush.................................1
Chapter 2: The Other Side of the Hill...................15
Chapter 3: Group Thirteen................................25
Chapter 4: First Impressions.............................39
Chapter 5: Kandahar Hospital...........................47
Chapter 6: A Little Help from My Friends.............59
Chapter 7: Six Days and Seven Nights.................71
Chapter 8: Jalalabad......................................81
Chapter 9: Exodus...87
Chapter 10: Strangers in a Strange Land...............93
Chapter 11: Mr. Muktar...................................105
Chapter 12: International Relations.....................115
Chapter 13: House for Rent..............................123
Chapter 14: There's No Place Like Home...............133
Chapter 15: Roxanne......................................147
Chapter 16: Curriculum Development..................165
Chapter 17: Baghlan School of Nursing................173
Chapter 18: Lesson Plans.................................181
Chapter 19: Saint Elsewhere.............................193
Chapter 20: Bibi Deeba...................................205
Chapter 21: Autumn Leaves.............................213
Chapter 22: Happy Holidays............................223
Chapter 23: Peshawar.....................................233
Chapter 24: The Long Winter............................243
Chapter 25: Little Women................................255
Chapter 26: Jo's Girls.....................................269

Chapter 27: The Bell Will Crack 283
Chapter 28: Life in Baghlan 291
Chapter 29: Endings and New Beginnings 301

Epilogue 309
Acknowledgments 313
About the Author 315
Appendix: Jo's Girls 317
Bibliography 319
Notes 325

FOREWORD
Joanne Carter Bowling

I want to thank my friend, Susan Fox, for this book. She has labored to make my diary come alive, and every time I read her words, I am transported back to the sights, sounds, and smells of the country I once called home. It was the experience of a lifetime, compressed into the short span of two years. Very few people heard of Afghanistan when I was there, and now the people and their faith are front page news. The Afghans we lived with protected us and took care of us. They made their country my home away from home. Those people are still there. Thanks to Susan's talented writing, the people who embraced us as family, friends, and teachers will not be forgotten.

INTRODUCTION

In spring 2007, I had a conversation with Joanne Bowling, the kind of easy exchange that occurs between two people who have been friends for a very long time. As we chatted, she casually mentioned a box of letters, tapes, and a diary she had saved from her service in Afghanistan with the Peace Corps in the late 1960s.

"I go through the box every couple of years," she said. "And every time, I intend to write a story about what we did—what it was like when we were there."

I had always known about Jo's Peace Corps experience. Unknown to me until that moment, however, was the existence of a diary. I encouraged her to pursue the idea. "Just think of all the things you did, Jo. And you have a record of it all. You should definitely write your story."

Jo nodded in agreement. "Oh, I know. I've tried. At least a half-dozen times."

"And?"

"And I page through the diary, look at the pictures, maybe listen to a couple of tapes. But then what?" She gave me a self-deprecating little shrug. "I don't know where to start. So I pack everything away and put it back on the shelf—until the next time."

I remember that I couldn't help smiling at the abject expression on her face, and before I realized what I was doing, the words were out of my mouth. "I'll write it for you!"

In my enthusiasm, I anticipated a pleasurable and interesting project, a tidy little memoir, and a gift for my friend. I thought it would take a couple of weeks. It took six years, exhaustive research, and resulted in this book.

Just as Jo had done every time she opened her box of memorabilia, I struggled to find a starting point. It was easy enough to piece together a factual account of her experience: the days in training camp, adjustment to life in another culture, and the challenges of getting Afghan girls into a classroom. But as I worked my way through her journal for a second and third time, other perspectives emerged from between the lines.

Nearly a half century later, her diary is a significant historical account. Her words evoke images from the past: black-and-white snapshots of a time and place that has since vanished—a time when Afghanistan was on the cusp of becoming a modern nation. She describes a group of ordinary Americans living in a village called Baghlan, working together despite religious and cultural differences. In a post-9/11 world that increasingly equates different with evil, her narrative is a desperately needed call for mutual respect and understanding.

I queried Jo about the women of Afghanistan, specifically what life was like before the Taliban came to power, for the project soon evolved as a voice for them, indeed, a voice for women everywhere who cannot speak for themselves. At the same time I felt it was imperative to present an accurate and balanced account of that particular time in history. During the 1960s the Afghan government was making the first tentative steps toward recognizing women's rights, a movement tragically cut short by the Russian invasion in 1979.

I investigated the Peace Corps, and President Kennedy's Executive Order to establish a bold new program. I was reminded once again how the Peace Corps continues to reflect the highest ideals of our country, holding an enduring place among all diplomatic efforts initiated by the United States.

Coming full circle, I revisited Jo's diary with a new appreciation of what she had given me: the first-hand account of an ordinary young woman who answers the call to service and adventure during an extraordinary time in world history. Her story unfolds against the backdrop of changing social mores, the Cold War, the Peace Corps, and a country at the crossroads of China, Russia, India, Pakistan, and Iran.

Chapter 1

THE HINDU KUSH

Off in a taxi and made the usual switch in Puli-Khumri. It was an uneventful ride until we came to an avalanche just before the Salang.
—Joanne Carter: Afghanistan Journal, April 21, 1970

"*Taksi!*"

Jo set her bag in the dust, among blades of grass worn thin by countless footsteps. A spindly row of trees cast elongated, early-morning shadows across the taxi bazaar, but already, passengers were queuing up.

A driver waved her forward. "Kabul?" He raised his eyebrows and nodded reflexively, eager for one more fare and a full payload. "*Zut zut shodan!*" —Hurry, hurry! "I have one seat left."

Jo had done this a dozen times. It was another routine trip, but a reprieve nonetheless, a welcome break from teaching five and a half days a week. She climbed into the back seat of a sedan, a dusty, Russian-built Volga.

Three Afghans immediately crowded in after her, and she slid all the way across, to the far door. Three more Afghans fit themselves into the front, the one next to the driver wedged tightly against the gear box.

1

At least there was no one in the trunk. No last-minute traveler had pushed his way through the bazaar, shouting above the noise and confusion to get the driver's attention, wanting to haggle for a reduced fare. Jo had seen it often: passengers climbing into the shadowy recess, their grins reminiscent of a Cheshire cat as they grabbed hold of a little handle on the inside of the trunk lid and pulled it down. But not today. No one was interested in riding to Kabul in the trunk of a car. The trip was five hours at best, and temperatures would be freezing in the high mountain passes.

Jo wore a skirt and sweater in deference to the dress code of a Muslim country and stuffed her coat into the small space by her feet. The men settled in, accepting her presence among them without question. The passenger next to her gathered the folds of a bulky chapan, a wool coat that covered his thin, drawstring tombans much like a heavy bathrobe. Careful not to press uncomfortably close, he maneuvered himself into position. Jo leaned away to give him room, and it occurred to her that if she had been more patient, had waited just a few extra minutes, she could have hired a taxi not yet filled. She could have paid for two fares instead of one—an easy guarantee of extra space. It was a tactic every Peace Corps Volunteer learned by the second day in Afghanistan.

But she had abandoned those little tricks long ago. Over the past two years Jo had become accustomed to Afghan life—the general inconvenience, the pitfalls of navigating a culture that often made no sense, and of course, overcrowded taxis. Just as she had done so many times in the past, she traveled as the only woman and the only American in a carload of Afghan men. She hardly gave it a second thought.

The men in front were businessmen and shop owners. Dressed in tunics and tombans, they had covered their prayer caps with turbans. The driver left his prayer cap exposed, and wore a simple wool jacket. Unencumbered by a heavy chapan, he slid behind the wheel with a self-assured movement, and looked over his shoulder to give Jo a confidential nod. "*Balê*," he said. — Yes. "I will get you to Kabul *zud, zud*."

He reached up and adjusted the rearview mirror, setting in motion a string of colored glass beads that hung as decoration. "*Insha'Allah*," he added. —God willing. Turning around yet again, he looked at Jo and grinned, as if sharing a private joke. "*Shomâ fahmided?*" —Understand?

Jo couldn't help smiling at his cocky, familiar manner. She nodded. "*Man fahmidom.*" —I understand.

Satisfied at her response, he turned back, put the car in gear, and pulled out of the taxi bazaar. With quick surreptitious movements, the Afghan passengers wiped their right hands over their faces and beards to disseminate Allah's blessing: a gesture repeated before every crossing of the Hindu Kush.

Jo understood their concern. "Fast, fast" seemed to be the objective of every driver she had ever hired, and like the Afghans with her, she worried about getting to Kabul safely. How many times had she left Baghlan—a village in northern Afghanistan less than one hundred miles from the Russian border—with a driver who careened through turns so fast it seemed they would fly straight off a cliff? Jo expected the same from today's driver, but when he eased his way around bicycles, donkeys, and horse-drawn carts, she breathed a sigh of relief. Not far from the bazaar he turned onto the only paved road in the village and headed south toward Kabul.

The road would ultimately take them across the vast mountain range that sweeps southwest to northeast across Afghanistan into Pakistan and China. Jo settled into her seat, not bothering to reach for a seat belt. There were none.

"*Asalâmu alaykum.*" Comfortably wrapped in his chapan at last, the Afghan next to her offered the traditional greeting. —Peace on you. With a final tug at his chapan, he introduced himself as a teacher, a mathematics teacher in Baghlan.

"At the Vo-Ag School?" Jo turned as much as space would allow. "Then you must know my friend, Mr. Muktar. He teaches chemistry."

The Afghan inclined his head. "Yes, I know him well. I would be with him today, if I didn't have business in Kabul." He gestured toward the passenger next to him. "This is my brother," he added. "We are traveling together."

Immediately, the brother leaned forward, his inquisitive dark eyes matching those of his sibling. Impatient with their Farsi conversation, the brother spoke in English. "We're going to visit a favorite uncle."

"Ah, yes." Jo tried not to smile at the deliberate switch in language. It was nothing new. On most trips at least one or more passengers wanted to practice English, and in a crowded taxi she was often a captive teacher. She didn't mind; it worked both ways. After all this time in Baghlan, she was still learning the nuances of Farsi. She complimented him on his effort, and teased him slightly by responding in his native language. "*Besyar khub*," she said, —very good, and smiled at the *mazâq*, the little joke.

They chatted, comparing where they lived in Baghlan, and the names of Vo-Ag teachers they knew in common, until Jo was forced to change her position. She turned slightly, easing the pressure on her back where it was pressed against the car door. It was a small adjustment—she stood just over five feet tall and barely tipped the scale at one hundred pounds—but like a pebble thrown into a still pond, it caused a ripple of motion to pass through all four passengers in the back seat.

From her new position Jo surveyed the endless chain of mountains, cresting and plunging steeply to the valleys below. A great upheaval of land mass, the Hindu Kush rises toward the highest peaks in the north of Afghanistan, reaching an altitude of 25,000 feet near the Afghan-Pakistan border. Gazing at the snow-covered summits, she could understand why the Afghans refer to it as the "Roof of the World."

Dwarfed by massive ridges, the taxi appeared as a tiny moving dot, clinging to a pencil-thin line of road etched circuitously into the mountainsides. Occasionally the open side of the road fell away to a deep gorge, with less than a foot of gravel separating the asphalt from a sheer drop to the cavernous space below. There were no barriers, and Jo held her breath each time they skidded around a sharp curve, as if by sitting perfectly rigid and gripping the edge of her seat with both hands she would keep the car from plunging over the brink.

The fact she was the only woman seemed irrelevant when she glimpsed the deep chasms flashing by her window. By comparison, she felt safe in the company of the Afghan men with her, secure in the knowledge they regarded her and the rest of the Peace Corps Volunteers as guests in their country. And she was, after all, an "honorary man."

The peculiar gender distinction was something she had grasped almost as soon as she arrived in Afghanistan. She traveled alone, with her head uncovered. Therefore, she didn't fit the traditional perception of female. She certainly was not male. What was she then, but an entity somewhere in between? And so, out of necessity, the Afghans devised a convenient niche that placed Western women into a category of their own—a third gender—with the rights and privileges of Afghan men. As such, Jo and the other female Peace Corps Volunteers moved about freely in Afghan society.

Of course, there were exceptions to her feeling of security: places not as safe, situations better avoided. She was careful not to get caught in large crowds, for example, where men could take advantage of a noisy throng to bump up against her, pinch and pat, then disappear into the confusion of a tightly packed group of people. If she found herself in a crowd of strange men, perhaps at a particularly large bazaar, she felt trapped, her anger tinged with apprehension, bordering on fear. When she could, she stayed away from large gatherings altogether.

Her friend Nan had more bravado, but all the same, armed herself with a large, heavy purse. Jo had been incredulous the first time she saw it and burst out laughing. "But, Nan," she said, "you can't slug someone with that thing. Either you'll kill him, or start a riot."

Nan's dark Irish eyes had flashed a combination of defiance and amusement. "Just watch me. I'll use it if I have to!"

They both felt safer in their own village of Baghlan, where everyone knew them: the students, neighbors, and shopkeepers at the local bazaar. And to be fair, most Afghan men were courteous—even solicitous of the American Volunteers, just as they had been this morning, when eight people managed to get themselves into a car meant to carry four people comfortably. Acting almost like a host of older brothers, the men had done their best to give Jo as much room as possible. She was grateful. She had her own reason for going to Kabul, yes, even zud, zud.

She would pick up supplies just as she did every time she went to the city, but errands and supplies were not the primary reasons for her trip. She didn't have business at the Peace Corps office, nor was she going to visit friends. She was going to Kabul so she could place a telephone call home to her family.

Home. When Jo tried to picture it, she felt suspended between two countries. After working in Afghanistan for almost two years, Baghlan had become home. She could barely remember a time when she didn't start the day at Baghlan Hospital, teaching her girls in the nursing program. She thought of them with a rush of affection. Her girls. She knew every expression on their young faces: the arch of an eyebrow that said "I don't believe you," the frown that indicated "I don't understand; explain it again." Several of the girls were her neighbors. Jamila, Paregul, and Anorgul were sisters who lived just down the street. The youngest sister, Anorgul, had been only fourteen when she started the program. Now she was a young lady of sixteen.

But when Jo thought of her own family, the one she left behind in the United States, there was a void. She tried to remember little details about her parents and her older sister, Jackie, but in her mind's eye there was a blank emptiness. Their images had begun to blur and fade, disappearing into the shifting sand and swirling dust of Afghanistan.

Then came the carefully worded airmail letter about her father. *Nothing to worry about*, her mother had written. *A few tests ... just to make sure.*

When Jo read it, she had been seized with an irrational fear that something would go terribly wrong before she completed her assignment. Nothing could happen now. Please God, not now, not when she was so close to leaving. She wanted to hear for herself that her father was all right; she wanted the reassurance that when she got home he would be exactly the same as when she saw him last. It was suddenly imperative to hear his voice, even though it meant a five hour taxi ride to Kabul, the only place in Afghanistan with access to an overseas operator.

The businessmen in front eventually exhausted their topic; one of them dropped his chin and closed his eyes. Conversation between the brothers fell into the sporadic, shorthand cadence often heard between close friends or relatives, then ceased altogether. The driver turned on the radio and adjusted the knob, picking up a montage of music and news from Radio Kabul, Radio Moscow, the BBC, and Voice of America. With his other hand draped over the steering wheel, he confidently guided the taxi up the tortuous ascent, following the twists and turns of a pathway nearly two thousand years old.

But unlike the ancient silk merchants and traders who had gone before him, he would not have to negotiate the highest mountain passes. He would simply drive through the mountain itself, courtesy of a tunnel built in 1955 by the Soviet Union. Nearly two miles long, the tunnel passes through the heart of the Hindu Kush, near the *Kotal-e Salang*: the Salang Pass.

It was on the Salang Road that Jo traveled the morning of April 21, 1970.[1]

⌁⌒ᴑᵔᴑ⌒⌁

Radio programs were alternately clear and diminished, as signals were lost, then picked up again with the next turn in the road. The background hiss of static, hardly noticed at first, became louder, and when the snatches of music, the voices in English, Farsi, and Russian disappeared entirely, the driver turned off the radio. The sound of shifting gears, and the laboring whine of the car engine filled the empty silence.

Without a radio for diversion, Jo idly thought of the many trips she had made across the mountains during her time in Afghanistan. She had lost count long ago, the repetitive crossings back and forth blending into a predictable routine. Her alarm at ascending into the Hindu Kush always faded, her uneasiness dulled by the endless turns and switchbacks, mile after tedious mile. And yet, in spite of the boredom and the long hours in a cramped car, there was always that moment of apprehension when they climbed the final steep grade to the tunnel entrance, the claustrophobia at entering the dimly lit chamber, and the long passage through dank and polluted air before emerging on the other side.

Today would be the same, no doubt, and although they were still miles from the tunnel, she anticipated her relief when they were safely on their way down toward Kabul. At 11,000 feet, the Salang Tunnel is at the highest point of the crossing.

At 7,000 feet they encountered the first patches of snow on the northward facing slopes. The areas of snow expanded, gradually covering the mountainsides. At 10,000 feet the taxi emerged from a layer of mid-level clouds into brilliant sunshine and a pristine blanket of white.

Jo blinked, the unexpected brightness making her eyes water. The inside of the car became warm and comfortable in spite of falling temperatures, and she changed her position again. Her thoughts drifted to Kabul—the phone call she would make, and the pleasure of hearing her father's voice.

She became drowsy in the sun and warmth; her head alternately bobbed and jerked. She retrieved her jacket and stuffed it behind her head. Leaning back, she closed her eyes and fell asleep—a welcome respite from homesickness and the worry about her father's health. The miles passed, and she started to dream, a disjointed sequence in which a group of Afghans were talking and arguing. In the dream she couldn't make out what the problem was, and she frowned, wanting them to go away. The voices became louder and more intrusive. Someone spoke loudly right next to her, and with a start she opened her eyes. Her stomach lurched. She had fallen asleep with the car in motion, and now she woke with the dizzying sensation that it had stopped.

She sat up and rubbed her eyes. Squinting, she looked between the turban-covered heads in front of her. She had lost her sunglasses long ago, and now she regretted not replacing them, but sunglasses were hard to come by at the bazaar, even used or broken ones. Her eyes adjusted, and she made out a line of cars and trucks that had stopped in front of them. Shimmering in the distance, a swath of snow obliterated the narrow, two-lane road.

The driver turned around and glanced at Jo. He spoke mainly for her benefit. *"Barf kuch,"* he said. —Avalanche. He killed the engine. Trucks and taxis came up behind them and stopped, the stranded vehicles lined up in a row much like toys on a giant shelf.

Car doors opened and thumped shut in the silence of the mountain-side. A couple of men walked to the front of the line for a better view. Truck drivers climbed down from their cabs, ready to exchange news and have a smoke. Some gathered in small groups alongside the road. Others hunkered in circles, squatting with their haunches up to their heels, elbows hanging down on each side of their knees.

Jo thought about getting out of the car, but even with the "honorary man" status she could not imagine herself hunkered down having a smoke. She smiled. It was a ludicrous image: squatting with the men, her skirt hanging down between her knees, a cigarette dangling from her lips.

She chose instead to remain in the taxi. Two of the Afghans stayed with her: the teacher to her left in the back seat and one of the businessmen in the front.

Beneath a towering summit, the taxi was stopped in the right lane. Jo sat feet away from the mountain face. They had almost made it to the Salang Tunnel, she noticed with a pang of disappointment. The first snow gallery was not more than a hundred yards away.

Little sheds built over the road and supported on each side by pillars, snow galleries were intended to keep the approach road to the tunnel clear of snow and falling rocks. Like covered bridges, she thought the first time she saw them, the kind she had seen in the Midwest.

The men on the roadside talked quietly. The air was still; the silence complete except for the rise and fall of their voices, the sound carried away on wisps of blue cigarette smoke. At two miles above sea level, every rock and ridge had a brilliant edge in the rarefied air.

The Afghans had simply shrugged when they were stopped by the avalanche. *Insha'Allah*, if God willed it, they would be rescued. Jo leaned her head against the back of the seat, as much in frustration at their predicament as the Afghans' acceptance of it. They were stranded, plain and simple, and she was irritated at the delay.

Saber kardan. —Wait. That's all we ever do, she thought. Wait. Wait for something to happen. Wait for things to get better. She resisted looking at her watch. They would be rescued when they were rescued. Impatiently looking at the time wouldn't change a thing. Trying to keep her mind occupied, she mentally reviewed the list of things she would do in Kabul after she made her phone call, the supplies she would pick up, the people she would see. She sighed and absently stretched her legs, taking advantage of the extra room. *Saber kardan.* Wait. How long had it been? An hour?

And then a vague anxiety started to float around the edges of her mind. Uneasiness crept up beside her almost unnoticed until she gave it her full attention.

She brought her head up sharply as it came to her. Within hours, the Salang Road would be closed. Winding its way through the mountains, the road had no guardrails. No lights. Driving the convoluted twists and turns, clinging to the narrow edges of a ravine was dangerous enough in broad daylight. Navigating the road in total darkness would be suicide. In order to ensure drivers enough time to complete the crossing before dark, Afghan authorities closed both entrances by late afternoon.

Jo allowed herself a peek at her watch. It was now midday. What happened if they were still here when the gates closed? They would be stranded overnight. The minute the sun went down, temperatures would plummet. Jo made a quick sweep of the car. She had nothing for protection except the jacket she had grabbed before she left home. She could only hope the body heat of eight people in one car would keep them from freezing to death.

I'm an experienced Volunteer, she thought. *I will cope with this.* And yet, she could not avoid contemplating the seriousness of her situation, and what it would be like to spend a night in the Hindu Kush Mountains at 11,000 feet above sea level. They would be in complete darkness. They would have no food or water. No way of calling for help.[2]

Waiting suddenly took on a new dimension. The window of opportunity for rescue was closing by the minute. Jo had a sudden, fierce longing for the normal, ordinary rituals of everyday life. Once mundane—even tiresome—they were now priceless beyond compare. She wondered how she could have taken it all for granted: the uneventful days of teaching, the cup of tea with Nan and Mary every night before going to bed. Engrossed in her thoughts, she glanced out the car window, watching the men without really seeing them, so preoccupied she almost didn't notice when they all got to their feet. They stood and turned around, facing back toward Baghlan.

Jo twisted in the car seat and looked out the rear window.

A narrow crescent of metallic orange emerged over a snowy ridge. When the bulldozer came into full view, propelled by massive, revolving tracks, she slumped in relief. She had been more frightened than she wanted to admit. After the silence and helplessness of waiting, the industrious chugging of the engine filled the air with a welcome sound. They would get out before dark, after all. The driver revved the engine to full throttle, set the blade down and began to clear the road.

A heavy, ice-crusted snow pack covered the mountainsides. A recent snow squall left a mantle of new powder resting delicately on top. The gun was cocked. In a matter of minutes the vibration from the bulldozer engine would pull the trigger.

Jo didn't register the sound of the muffled explosion. She had sensed an unexpected movement and was turned toward the mountain, wasting a precious second staring in confusion at the undulating wall of snow, mystified when the sunlight disappeared.

With childlike bewilderment, she stared at the closed doors and windows of the taxi, at the snow penetrating through the cracks. She inched back in her seat, terrified by the sudden, sure understanding of a deadly force, the black hugeness of it, pushing against the car. When the taxi shuddered and moved beneath her, a switch tripped in her brain. Adrenaline shot through her.

The man in the front seat was shouting in Farsi. *What?* Jo understood nothing: only the silent scream from the depths of her being, commanding her to escape. The teacher wasn't moving. She clawed past him and pulled on the door handle, leaning into the door with all her strength. When it opened she almost fell into the swirling snow.

The shed seemed to be infinitely far away. She ran as she had never run before, forcing her legs through the rippling drifts, trying to make them move faster as she floundered and struggled to keep her footing. She couldn't fall now. Others were with her, running in a river of snow that swept them forward in a frantic race for survival. At last, she reached the gallery and stood panting. Her mouth was so dry she couldn't swallow. Her chest hurt, and her heart was pounding. She could barely remain standing.

She caught her breath, and when her knees finally stopped trembling uncontrollably, she looked around. Did the teacher next to her get out? The businessman in front? Already, she was filled with regret that she didn't stop to help them. It was an unreasonable expectation, but then Jo was known for placing unreasonable expectations upon herself. No matter that the instinct for survival supersedes every other emotion; it did not assuage her guilt. How could I have left them behind, she wondered, not caring what happened to them? She started to walk through the gallery, hoping to find them, when she heard her name.

"Jo—Joanne … over here!"

Coming toward her was Peggy Cannon, a midwife from Ireland working with the World Health Organization. Jo remembered vividly the time Peggy had come to visit them in Baghlan, her cheerful Irish voice offering advice and support just when they needed it the most, when it seemed the nursing school would never get off the ground.

"Peggy!" Suddenly overcome with emotion, Jo ran to her and hugged her tightly. Why was she crying now? She was safe. It was all over. And yet, it was more than the avalanche and the desperate effort to escape from the car. It was also the worry about her father, the fear nothing would be the same when she got home, and the underlying, nagging terror that for whatever reason, she would never get home at all. The words came out, ragged and incoherent.

"Well then." Peggy hid her own emotion under a brisk, businesslike manner. She led Jo off to the side, away from everyone. They stood arm in arm, Peggy the taller of the two, with a fair Irish complexion and light auburn hair tinged with gray. Next to her, Jo appeared smaller and younger than ever, her dark curly hair cropped short.

They waited until everyone had been accounted for. Thank God. Jo would not have to worry about the businessman or the teacher. The avalanche had not been the massive, lethal event that sometimes occurs in the Hindu Kush, but it had been frightening enough.[3]

The vehicles at the front of the line had escaped the second avalanche, and Peggy located her own car among them. She pointed it out to Jo. "See there? As soon as the road is cleared, we can go." She looked down at her young friend. "And you're coming with us, Jo. We have plenty of room."

"No…" Jo hesitated. "You go ahead without me. I'll stay here."

Peggy frowned, an expression of concern and disbelief on her face. "And what would you be thinking? That I would go off and leave you?"

"I'll be fine. Really."

"And why in God's name would you stay behind?" Peggy surveyed the half-buried cars and taxis, the rounded tops barely visible above the snow. Somewhere among them was Jo's taxi. "It may be hours until you get out."

Jo didn't have an answer. She only knew she felt compelled to finish her trip with the group of men she had started with, the men from her own taxi—the men who left Baghlan with her. How could she explain it? That she would be the one privileged to leave, while they had to wait? It was all too complicated, even in English.

Regardless, her mind was made up. There was nothing Peggy could say to convince her otherwise. Even when the road was cleared and Peggy's driver honked the horn, ready to go, Jo was adamant—she would stay.

But when Peggy's car entered the snow gallery and disappeared, Jo had a moment of doubt. She could have been safely on her way to Kabul. Well, no use second-guessing herself at this point. She had a reason for staying behind. There was something she wanted to do, a question she needed to ask.

She moved between the groups of people along the side of the road, searching for the teacher who had been with her in the car. When she spotted him leaning against one of the gallery pillars having a smoke, she went up to him.

She apologized for climbing over him in her desperate rush to escape. He waved his cigarette. "*Hêch moshkele.*" —No problem. His eyes crinkled at the corners. "How funny we must have looked—running through the snow like scared rabbits." They both laughed in nervous relief. They were all safe, *marsha'Allah*, thanks to God's will. Someone lost a pair of shoes, but what is a pair of shoes? They were from the used clothing bazaar and didn't fit anyway.

Jo recalled the moment of terror when she struggled to get out of the car, and everything seemed to move in slow motion. "I'm positive I heard the businessman in the front seat shouting," she said. "But I was frantic to get out, and I didn't understand a thing." She looked over at the teacher. "What did he say?"

The Afghan took a drag from his cigarette. "He told me to let you go first, because you're the youngest." With a thumb and forefinger, he flicked aside the last few shreds of tobacco wrapped in wrinkled paper, and walked away to help the men who were clearing snow from around the cars and trucks. They dug with whatever makeshift tool they could find: a scrap of cardboard, a broken piece of plastic. Some dug with their bare hands.

Standing by herself in the late afternoon sun, Jo looked out into the distance. The mountains seemed to go on forever, ridge after ridge, covered in snow and ice. She wondered if she would ever completely understand the Afghans, or the code of hospitality they extended to their guests, even to the extent of risking their lives.

The men gave a shout as the first truck was cleared and the engine turned over. The shadows grew longer. Jo moved away from the gallery pillar and pulled her coat collar up around her neck. The sun hovered above the jagged peaks, swelling to emit a last fiery blaze of light before it was extinguished. At that moment, the deepest ravines were plunged into a dusky blue.

The Hindu Kush towered above her, impassive witness to human history.

Chapter 2

THE OTHER SIDE OF THE HILL

Maybe when I come home I will have the roving and restlessness out of my system and will be content to stay at home.

—*December 1968*

Jo's taxi was eventually freed. The men wiped snow from around the engine and brushed more snow from the seats. The passengers crowded back into the car, and once again, Jo found herself next to the window. The driver resumed the trip and passed through the Salang Tunnel almost as if nothing had happened.

The brothers met their uncle in Kabul. The businessmen returned to their shops. Jo made the phone call to her father. He was fine, after all. The connection was good, and he had laughed softly, telling her not to worry so much.

Jo finished her assignment three months later, and returned home in July, 1970. She resumed her career. Married and raised a family. The reminders of the two years she had lived in Baghlan—her diary, letters, tape recordings, and photographs—were stuffed into a box, put away, and forgotten.[4] By the time her family was grown, she found it hard to believe she had ever lived in Afghanistan at all, as if the person who had escaped from the taxi in the Hindu Kush was not really her, but rather someone she once knew very well.

All that changed on September 11, 2001, when al Qaeda terrorists destroyed the World Trade Center in New York City. If Jo thought her Peace Corps experience was no longer relevant, or the town of Baghlan nothing more than a dusty memory, she was mistaken. Prior to 9/11, most Americans would have been hard pressed to find Afghanistan on a map; now it was a household word. *We lived with the Afghans*, she thought. *We shared meals with them, delivered their babies, and taught their children.* She longed for things as they had been, for a time when a little group of Americans thought they could change the world.

Prompted by her memories, Jo retrieved the box of memorabilia. She carried it to her living room and emptied the contents onto a large coffee table. Buried at the bottom, a small, compact journal tumbled out.

She opened the book and thumbed through the pages, stopping at her entry for that April day in the Hindu Kush. She read details she had forgotten; how the phone office in Kabul had been nothing more than a wooden building with a row of phones attached to the wall, and how the overseas operator had placed her call to the States even though it was late and they were about to close.

She turned the page. A snapshot dropped to the floor. Jo picked it up and looked closely. A young woman smiled at her from across the years. The figure in the photograph could have passed as a little girl posing in a nurse's uniform. Short, dark hair framed her oval face, and she stood in a field of scrub brush, holding some books and papers in her arms.

The image was black and white, but the memories associated with it evoked both color and feeling—incredible heat for so early in the day, the intense blue of the Afghan sky, and the taste of dust as she stood in the field. It had been a lifetime ago. Images and sounds flooded Jo's senses: the shouts of *nân* boy as he walked through the streets at dawn, calling out,

"*Nân garm! Nân garm!*" The muezzin calls to prayer, roosters crowing, and the creak of wooden cart wheels.

Warm, whole wheat nân with butter and sweet tea for breakfast. Long walks through the never-ending dust on a dirt road to the bazaar, with the mountain peaks of the Hindu Kush in the distant background. Waiting at the taxi stand while the driver lowered a tin can tied to a string into an underground reservoir of gasoline.

She spread the items from her box across the table, sorting letters, slides, and photos. She found a cassette tape in the original plastic case, bearing an Afghan postage stamp. Did the story begin when she arrived in Afghanistan? She exchanged the tape for a Peace Corps instruction booklet. Perhaps it began with training. But what brought her to the Peace Corps in the first place?

Jo absently tapped the booklet on the table. Before joining the Peace Corps she had worked as a registered nurse. Before that was nursing school. And before that of course, was high school. Her hand stopped moving. High school. Graduation, and the trip she had taken with her family to Washington, D.C., the summer after her senior year.

How could she forget that trip? Looking back, she recognized how significant it had been. Her father had obtained tickets to the United States Senate, she recalled, and they climbed the carpeted stairway to the balcony of the Senate Chambers on a hot July day in 1957. The junior senator from Massachusetts took the floor, prepared to deliver a speech to the Committee on Foreign Relations. Jo had turned to her sister Jackie and whispered, "Look directly across from us. Isn't that his family? Do you see Teddy, Ethel, and Bobby?"

Kennedy's voice rang through the chamber as he began his remarks. "Mr. President, the most powerful single force in the world today is neither communism nor capitalism, neither the H-bomb nor the guided missile. It is man's eternal desire to be free and independent."[5]

His words made a profound impression on Jo. Freedom could be defined in many ways, she thought, but freedom from hunger and ignorance had to lay the foundation for all other freedoms. She was only seventeen, her thoughts half-formed, her vision not yet defined, but the idea had been planted. Someday she would become part of something bigger than herself.

Three years later Kennedy accepted the nomination for president of the United States at the Democratic National Convention in Los Angeles. Toward the end of a long and grueling campaign, he gave a speech in San Francisco, where he used the phrase "peace corps" for the first time.[6]

Kennedy went on to win the election a few days later, on November 8, 1960. On the first full day of his presidency, January 21, 1961, he telephoned Sargent Shriver and asked him to organize a task force that would create a new agency from the ground up.

Jo celebrated her twentieth birthday that same year. She was in nursing school by then, and when she graduated, took her first job with a local hospital. Busy with her own life, she let national politics fade into the background.

Then two events in two years profoundly affected the entire world. John F. Kennedy was assassinated in Dallas, Texas, on November 22, 1963, and the United States sent the first combat troops into Vietnam on March 8, 1965.

As the months passed, Jo felt an increasing desire to become involved. It seemed as if she had known all along—ever since that day in the Senate Chambers—that someday she would do *something*. She just didn't know what.

The Peace Corps or the military? She was drawn to the Peace Corps, and dreamed of travel, foreign countries, and adventure. On the other hand, she felt a nagging responsibility to serve her country as an Army or Marine nurse.

Her sister Jackie had no ambivalence, and no qualms about giving advice.

"Are you nuts, Jo? You *want* to go to Vietnam?"

"No, of course not. But what if that's what I'm supposed to do?" Jo groaned and let her head fall back. "Oh, I don't know! I just feel guilty, that's all."

"Guilty! Why?"

"Because I want to join the Peace Corps for all the wrong reasons. Because I want adventure. The excitement of living in a foreign country."

"So?" Jackie shook her head. "I don't get it. What's wrong with adventure?"

"I mean, what if I just want to see what's on the other side of the hill? Be part of something big?" Jo stopped. "Not that service isn't important."

Jackie laughed at her little sister's transparency. "You don't fool me one bit. Service is just as important to you as all the rest. This is your opportunity, Jo. Take it. The Peace Corps is everything you've always wanted."[7]

A few days later Jo picked up an application at the post office, filled it out, and mailed it to Washington. Although she eventually told her parents about her plans, she didn't tell anyone else, not even her friends or co-workers. What if she didn't get accepted? Why risk the embarrassment of having to go back and explain to everyone she had been passed over?

Indeed, she waited weeks for a response. A month went by. And then one blustery evening in late fall, the doorbell rang. Jo was upstairs and heard her mother greet the neighbor from next door. He stepped inside, and after a few minutes of small talk, casually asked with a little smile, "So, what has Joanne been up to lately?"

Snatches of the conversation drifted up the stairway to her bedroom. "... two men ... the FBI ... asking us questions about Joanne."

Jo was incredulous, excited, and apprehensive, in that order. Her secret was out. Shortly after the neighbor's visit, she received a letter from the Peace Corps office in Washington, D.C. She opened the envelope and read the following:

PEACE CORPS

Washington, D. C. 20525

November 21, 1967

Miss Joanne M. Carter
1093 East Bourbonnais Street
Kankakee, Illinois 60901

Dear Miss Carter:

It gives me great pleasure to invite you to train for Peace Corps service in the program named below and described in the enclosed brochures.

Out of a large number of applicants for the Peace Corps, only a few are invited to enter training. You are among this group because we think you have the background and ability required to work as a Peace Corps Volunteer overseas. The work will be difficult, but there will also be great personal satisfaction from the full use of your capacities where they are most needed. The Peace Corps is a rare opportunity to test and develop your resources and prepare to participate effectively in the life of this country and this world. I hope you will accept it and use it well.

I invite you to read the enclosed Peace Corps Handbook, particularly pages 8-15, which describes our selection and training procedures. Please let us know your answer by completing the enclosed Invitation Acceptance Form and the other required forms within ten days.

If you have any questions concerning your assignment, you should contact Dr. Francis Harding of our Selection Division. Please note your questionnaire number and country assignment on any correspondence.

You have my best wishes for a successful career in the Peace Corps.

Sincerely,

Jack Vaughn
Director

221545

COUNTRY: Afghanistan
ASSIGNMENT: you will be serving on the Nursing Staff of an Afghanistan hospital
TRAINING DATE AND SITE: on or about February 1, 1968 at a site to be announced later

She wasn't going to the other side of the hill; she was going to the other side of the world. [8]

If Jackie had any reservations about losing Jo—her best friend, the one person who understood and accepted her without reservation—she tried not to show it. Instead, she immersed herself in Afghan history, and became so knowledgeable about the country she began to tutor her little sister.

"Okay, Jo, tell me about Afghanistan's government."

Jo responded dutifully that Afghanistan was a neutral country and a member of the UN, ruled by King ... uh ... oh, crap. What was his name?

Jackie gave her a few minutes, then couldn't resist answering. "King Mohammad Zahir, with an elected National Assembly. Now, what countries border Afghanistan?"

Jo visualized the map in her mind. "China, Russia, Pakistan, and ..."

Jackie gave her a hint. "It borders on the west."

"Iran."

The sisters covered a lot of information, but they could not see into a future filled with tragedy for the Afghan people. The little question-and-answer game they played did not include the Soviet invasion in 1979, or the subsequent ten-year war that destroyed farms, irrigation systems, and entire villages. A war that left a million Afghans dead and another five million as refugees.

The books on Jackie's desk did not reveal how the world lost interest after the Russians retreated; how the United States and Europe looked the other way as the Taliban fought for control of the country. It would be up to future historians to write about the attack on the World Trade Center in New York, and yet to be recorded was the response from the United States, not against the Afghan people, but against the extremist groups harbored there.

This was 1968. Afghanistan was an unknown country, even a little exotic, and like her sister, Jo read everything she could find. She spent many late nights traveling with Alexander the Great as he conquered Greece, ancient Troy, Persia (modern Iran), and entered Afghanistan in 330 BCE, establishing cities near present day Herat, Kabul, and Kandahar. She read how Genghis Khan plundered the country in the thirteenth century; how England tried to deny Russia access to India through Afghanistan in the 1800s during the so-called "Great Game," and followed the convoluted rise and fall of Afghan dynasties since then, ending with Zahir's constitutional monarchy.

While Jo studied what she could about her new country, she also worked her way through a list of requirements issued by the Peace Corps. She applied for a special passport that identified her as a guest in Afghanistan, sent on official business by the U.S. government. She completed her physical exam at Chanute Air Force Base in Rantoul, Illinois, and booked her flight from Chicago to Denver, Colorado, for training.

As the day of her departure approached, however, Jo began to have second thoughts about leaving home. Her doubts culminated the morning she got up early to have breakfast alone with her father before he left for work. While they chatted, just the two of them, sitting together at the kitchen table, she studied his features. When did he get the fine gray hair around his temples? How could she have been so oblivious to the droop in his shoulders until now?

He took a last bite of toast and glanced at the clock. "Sorry, Jo. Time for me to go." In the early morning quiet, he smiled at his independent, headstrong daughter, and gave her a long hug. Then he reached for his fedora and settled it on his head—a gesture familiar and endearing to Jo since childhood. She couldn't remember a time when her dad left the house without a hat.

She sat down in the empty kitchen after he left and put her head in her hands. How could she go through with this? Perhaps her obligation was to stay with her family, after all. But then she thought of her sister—the nights Jackie had talked excitedly about Afghanistan, sharing in the adventure almost as if it were her own.

Jo pushed aside an empty plate and took a last sip of cold coffee. She had a swift, clear understanding of Jackie's enthusiasm. Her sister was sending her a message. *Go. Pursue your dream.*

So what was she waiting for? Life to be perfect? Guarantees? There are no guarantees of anything, she thought. There will always be a reason to postpone this. If I don't go now, I'll never go. And with that paradigm shift, she gave herself permission to become excited.

She was scheduled to fly from a little airport near her home in Kankakee, Illinois, to Chicago, and from Chicago to Denver, Colorado. Specially chartered busses would transport the Volunteers from the Denver airport to their training camp in Estes Park.

A week before leaving, she started to envision how events would unfold and what the day would look like, the day she left home. She enjoyed a satisfying sense of the dramatic: a brave young woman climbing into a tiny plane, waving goodbye to her tearful friends and family. In the movie in her mind the plane would disappear into swirling clouds and fog—not unlike the plane that took Ingrid Bergman from Casablanca.

Jo's sensation of seeing herself as part of an adventure was a feeling shared by a large percentage of Peace Corps Volunteers. Such is the poignant vision we all carry deep within ourselves when we dream of leaving our mundane lives and all its problems behind, or when we have the opportunity to start a new and exciting chapter in our lives. Whether the Volunteers saw themselves as teachers in the jungle or working in a remote wilderness, they thought of themselves as part of a big picture, doing something important and historic.

In real life, Jo's adventure started on an overcast winter morning. Yes, she was scheduled to leave on a small plane—a Beech 99 turbo prop, with a passenger load of eight or nine people. And yes, the Kankakee Airport was enveloped in a thick layer of fog when they arrived. And yes, the flight was—what!? Cancelled!? The airport closed? Fogged in?

Jo's Great Adventure vanished into the mist.

The family regrouped. Jo simply would not get to Chicago in time for her original flight; that much was certain. But if her dad could drive her to the airport, and if they hurried, she might catch a later flight to Denver.

In contrast to the sleepy, commuter airport in Kankakee, Chicago's O'Hare was noisy and crowded. The rush of passengers made Jo feel that events were inexorably moving forward and she was powerless to stop them. Her heartbeat accelerated. She gave a round of hugs and kisses, wanting to save her dad for last—no, wanting to save Jackie for last—and then, breaking away, she walked toward her flight.

Comparable scenes played out in thousands of households across the United States. Men and women said goodbye to their families and boarded flights for training camps scattered throughout the nation. The first Peace Corps Volunteers were deployed in 1962, and over the next five decades America would send nearly 200,000 young men and women around the globe to 139 countries, each Volunteer an ambassador of international goodwill.

Jo found her seat and stowed her bags. An attendant locked the doors. The jet engines whined, pressurizing the cabin; Jo fumbled for her seat belt. An ache swelled in her throat. It was too late now to change her mind.

Chapter 3

GROUP THIRTEEN

We are very tired from long classes and no sleep.

—February 20, 1968

During the time that Jo waited for a response from the Peace Corps, while she struggled with self-imposed guilt at leaving her family, a young woman on the east coast also waited for a reply.

Unlike Jo, the young woman—a lab tech named Nan—never heard from Washington. When her application went unanswered, Nan got tired of waiting. She accepted a promotion to research and development at Smith Kline laboratories where she worked, and simply put the idea of the Peace Corps out of her mind. She partied on the weekends with her friends, or made the rounds of her extended Irish family. In the winter she could be found at any one of the Pocono Mountain ski slopes in eastern Pennsylvania.

And so, on an ordinary Sunday morning in January, while Jo shopped for suitable clothes to wear in a Muslim country, Nan was gathering her equipment for a day trip to a nearby resort.

She carried a pair of snow skis to the front hall of her Philadelphia home, balancing the cumbersome equipment with ease. With one deft motion she set them down, then stepped back to examine the rest of the gear, absently running her fingers through her crop of thick black hair. Unlike the efficiency of her earlier movement, it was a futile gesture; her curls defied submission.

A small crease under her eyes made them appear almost crinkled, as if she were perpetually amused at a private joke. The crease deepened at the sound of the front doorbell. It would be her friends, no doubt. They had planned the ski trip just that morning.

She pulled the door open, expecting the familiar group of faces, the close friends who shared her passion for skiing in the winter, and swimming off the Jersey Shore in summer. Instead, a special delivery courier stood on the doorstep, and he gave her a thin, standard-size envelope.

Nan was home alone. Her parents were gone for the day, and if she wondered what kind of letter would be delivered on a Sunday, she had only to look at the Washington, D.C., postmark, and the stenciled "SPECIAL DELIVERY" stamp across the front—a mute exclamation of urgency.

She broke the seal and pulled out a single page. The Peace Corps needed a handful of trained laboratory technicians to go to Afghanistan. One of the applicants had backed out at the last minute, and Nan was first on the reserve list. Could she be ready to start training in Estes Park, Colorado in three weeks?

The words came as a shock. Convinced she had been passed over, Nan had given up waiting for a response weeks ago. At the time she masked her disappointment by pretending it didn't matter, telling herself she didn't care. But now, holding the invitation in her hand, she knew that yes, she did care. She cared very much.

Her thoughts splintered into a thousand directions. Three weeks! How could she be ready with so little time? What to do first?

Respond to the invitation, of course.

Turn in her resignation at work.

Pack.

Tell her parents.

Her knees went weak, and she slid to the floor of the hallway, next to forgotten ski goggles, gloves, and socks.

Her parents.

She had not said a word about the Peace Corps. If her parents didn't know about her application, then neither would they have to know about her disappointment, the sting of rejection if she did not get an invitation. At the time her reasoning seemed perfectly logical. But now—well, now it didn't seem like such a good idea at all.

How would she break the news to them?

Uh, Mom and Dad, I have something to tell you. I'm going halfway around the world to a country you never heard of. Oh, and by the way, I won't be home for two years.

Yeah, right.

She needed some time to clear her head, if only for a couple of hours. She would keep her plans to go skiing, she decided. Wait and see how she felt by the end of the day. Make sure this was what she still wanted, after all.

～⌒ᴏ᷅ʌ⌒～

Knees flexed, ski poles held out to the side, Nan looked over her shoulder. An empty lift chair came around behind her, and she was swept up. She settled back into the seat and dangled her skis, bringing the tips up and down like giant pedals. Yes. No. Right, left. Accept, decline.

Another rider got on. The lift snagged for a moment, then continued with a little jerk. Nan shook her head, as if coming out of a trance. What had she been thinking? Was she crazy? If she had any sense at all, she would forget the whole thing. Why jeopardize a promising career with Smith Kline?

At the top of the lift she pushed off and started down the run, turning from edge to edge. She reached a flat and bent forward, tucking the poles under her arms to pick up speed. The wind bit her face. She felt the excitement of pushing herself to the limit, and knew deep down she had a yearning for adventure. There was nothing she couldn't do, including a stint in the Peace Corps.

On January 31, 1968, Nan said goodbye to her parents at the Philadelphia airport and boarded a flight to Denver. Not until she was buckled into her seat did she realize everything had happened much too fast.

Her mom had helped her shop and pack, had given endless parties for her, and never once complained about having to say goodbye. And now, Nan couldn't remember—did she even tell her mother thank you? That she appreciated everything?

Her dad had been quiet the night she came home from her ski trip and broke the news. When he did speak, he uttered two words: "You're crazy." Nan had laughed and cried at the same time, for she knew exactly what her dad meant to say. He loved her, admired her, and would worry about her. *Wait.*

She felt closer to her parents than she had at any other time in her life, yet she was choosing a separation that would change everything. The plane rushed to the end of the runway and nosed up. Nan was gripped by nostalgia. I can join the Peace Corps, she thought, or I can stay home. I can't do both.

~◠⋆◠~

Jo's departure had been nothing like the dramatic scenario she had imagined. Runway lights twinkled in the darkness when her plane finally touched down in Denver. She caught the last Peace Corps bus to the remote training camp near Estes Park, and by the time she was directed to her cabin—Cedar Lodge—she felt travel weary and disheveled. She could only guess she looked the same.

She gripped her bags and stood outside the door, anticipating a less-than-enthusiastic welcome. She had arrived late and didn't know a single person. What if everyone had already made friends? What if she was left out? What a crummy way to start.

She pushed the door open, and stepped into a scene of half-unpacked suitcases and disorganized bedding. A wave of voices and laughter greeted her. Conversations barely paused; names were exchanged, an empty top bunk found, and just like that, Jo was part of the group, the transition so smooth, the acceptance so complete, she was giddy with relief.

An older woman came forward and introduced herself as Mary. Her light brown hair was threaded with gray and pulled into a severe bun.

Jo extended her hand. "I'm happy to meet you." Mary's appearance prompted Jo to ask the obvious. "Are you one of the teachers? In charge of this building?"

Mary cast a startled glance around the cabin, at the rows of bunk beds and general disarray as the women got ready for bed. "Good heavens. I'm not in charge of anything. I'm just a Volunteer."

Oh, nice, thought Jo. *Offend the very first person I meet.* She apologized. "Sorry. I shouldn't have assumed anything."

But Mary took no offense. She waved a hand dismissively "Don't worry. It's perfectly understandable. Sometimes I wonder myself what possessed me to leave my kids and grandkids to do this."

"You have grandchildren?" Jo's eyebrows went up. "Wasn't it hard to leave them?"

"Sure it was hard, and of course I'll miss them …" Mary regarded Jo for a moment, as if debating whether to go on.

Jo's round blue eyes never left her face, so she continued.

"I was supposed to do this with my husband, and when he died, well, I didn't know what to do. I finally decided this is what he would have wanted—we had talked about it for so long. Anyway, I'm a nurse. I specialize in women's health care." Mary gave Jo a self-deprecating smile. "Sounds like they could use a few of us in Afghanistan."

Impressive, thought Jo, very impressive. But her age! How would Mary get through training? Trying not to stare, Jo took in the tall, robust figure standing before her: a woman with a fair complexion and finely chiseled features. Mary was already unpacked, the bedding on her bunk made up as tight as a drum. It occurred to Jo that maybe the person who should worry about getting through training was herself. Mary looked like she would be just fine.

The Volunteers settled into bed, and Jo hurried to catch up. Her top bunk was missing a pillow, so she folded her jacket and stuffed it under her head. She would worry about a pillow tomorrow. She said goodnight to Mary across the aisle, and then to the bunkmate below her. Lights were turned off. A couple of lingering conversations died away in the darkness, and Cedar Lodge grew quiet.

The moon rose, and a cold wind blew over the tops of the pine trees, their sighing branches the only sound in the silence of the Colorado mountains.

"For real?" Jo raised her voice above the noise, above the hum of conversation, shuffling feet, and scrape of chairs as seventy Volunteers filed into the assembly hall early the next morning. "Peaches?"

The young Volunteer tucked her coat out of the way so Jo could sit down. "Actually, it's Georgia, but everyone calls me Peaches." Before they could say anything else, the Peace Corps director, Ray Feichtmeir, took the podium. He welcomed everyone—Group Thirteen, assigned to Afghanistan. He then opened camp with a review of the mission statement of the Peace Corps.[9]

Jo wanted to stop and savor the moment, the moment she started training, but she did not get the opportunity to reflect on her feelings. Already, teachers were handing out packets of educational material. A new instructor took the podium. "Classes will start at 6 a.m.," he said. "Language class will be in Farsi.[10] You may speak English for one hour after dinner, and then class will resume until 7 p.m. We ask that you do not write home for the first two weeks," he continued. "Unless you'd like to write in Farsi, of course." If his comment was meant to be a joke, no one laughed. He concluded the introduction, and immediately, the teaching staff separated the Volunteers into small groups, directing the groups to individual classrooms. Orientation was over.

Much like the other classrooms, Jo's assigned room had tile floors, a clock on the wall, and desks arranged in a semi-circle. The instructor was

Afghan, dressed in black tombans and a black tunic, layered with a tan vest. His garments produced a faint rustle of fabric as he made his way to the front of the room.

"My name is Tarshi," he said in English. "I am from northern Afghanistan, near the Russian border of Uzbekistan." He wore a black prayer cap trimmed with white ribbon, and his face was clean shaven, his dark eyes almond shaped. He gestured toward the Volunteers. "*Loften* —Please, introduce yourselves."

"Harry." A young African American leaned forward in his seat, his excitement palpable. A slight drawl gave him away as a Southerner before he announced, "I'm from North Carolina."

"Charlotte," offered a shy, soft-spoken Volunteer. "I'm a science teacher."

"Carter," said the person next to her. "I'm from California."

"Peaches." The Volunteer Jo had met in the assembly hall dispensed with her given name.

"Mary." The sixty year old grandmother sat upright in her seat, her bright eyes taking in everyone and everything around her.

"And I'm Nan." A young woman with wild curly hair spoke with a distinctive East Coast accent. "I work as a lab tech."

Tarshi started immediately. "*Asalâmu alaykum.*" —Peace to you. He inclined his head slightly, and answered his own greeting, indicating the Volunteers were to repeat his words.

"*Alaykum assalam.*" —And on you peace.

Over the next six weeks, Jo made a conscious, mental effort to stay with Tarshi, and not let her attention wander as it so often did. She was a visual learner; she knew that much about herself almost from the day she learned how to read. She found it difficult, learning by ear—by immersion.

"*Nâm-e shomâ chist?*" —What is your name?

"*Nâm-e man Jo ast.*" —My name is Jo.

She wanted to stop listening for awhile and take a break. Use her eyes instead of her ears. But much as she wanted to *see* the words, printed on a page, she also knew that Farsi is written from right to left, the words spelled with a modified Arabic alphabet. The only way she could read Farsi was if she had a transliterated version.

Transliteration—taking words written with one alphabet and rewriting them with the closest corresponding letters of a different alphabet—meant the Volunteers learned to read and write using a phonetic version of Farsi.[11]

Some nuances cannot be replicated, however. A handful of Farsi letters simply do not have an equivalent sound in English. The Farsi combination *gh* is one example, a sound produced much like the guttural *r* sound in French.

Jo pressed the palms of her hands against her cheeks to keep from laughing, even as she choked and coughed, emulating Tarshi's "gh."

"… rrrr." The class had turned into growling, gargling lunatics. Or maybe a room filled with deranged French cars that refused to start. "… rrrr." The laughter rose in her throat, and she glanced around. Did no one else find it amusing? Only Nan, who grinned at her from across the room.

Tarshi was relentless, moving through several lessons a day. He listened while the Volunteers repeated phrases over and over, sometimes correcting, but always patient, always encouraging. He gestured, pantomimed, and mimicked words and expressions. He acted out little vignettes, such as the scenario he performed one afternoon when he walked across the front of the classroom.

"*Man tanhâ astom,*" he said, moving from one side of the room to the other. He then called one of the Volunteers to the front, the young woman named Charlotte. He walked across the room again, this time arm in arm with her. "*Ba ham,*" he said. "Charlotte *ba ham.*"

Jo narrowed her eyes in concentration. Nouns were easy, items they could point to and identify, things like fruits and vegetables sold at the bazaar, and *afghanis* or *afs*, the Afghan currency. Even verbs weren't so bad, as long as Tarshi stayed in present tense. But this! This was hard.

Tarshi repeated the exercise. He walked across the room alone.

Alone! That was it! He was alone. *Man tanhâ astom.* —I am alone.

Now he walked again with Charlotte. "Charlotte *ba ham.*" Of course. Charlotte was now *also with* Tarshi.

The Volunteers heard countless Farsi words that day, but "Charlotte ba ham" was one phrase that seemed to stick with everyone. It became a catch phrase throughout camp, the pronunciation corrupted by American accents and less-than-perfect Farsi until it sounded more like *budum* than the original ba ham. Still, "Charlotte budum" had a certain ring to it, and eventually, no one could remember Charlotte's last name. She was, well, she was Charlotte Budum, better known as Budum to her friends.

The Volunteers were becoming immersed in their new language, and now even Charlotte's identity had become intertwined with Farsi. Words and phrases seeped into Jo's mind and psyche, until she felt as if she breathed, lived, ate, slept, and dreamed in Farsi.

But the constant strain of listening to every syllable, the agonizing fumble for words to express every waking thought began to take a toll on everyone. Jo started talking Farsi in her sleep. She developed headaches that lasted for days, and resorted to taking walks in the snow and cold with Budum, hoping to clear her head. The men vented their frustration by clearing snow from a concrete pad to play basketball. Harry, Nan, and Peaches found a way to sneak out of camp one night for a couple of drinks in Estes Park.

And it seemed every time the Volunteers were at their lowest point, they were subjected to another battery of psychological tests. Harry was convinced the tests were a scam, and every question was a trick question. "Seriously?" He tipped his chair back from the dining room table one night. "They really want to know what I think about training?" He brought all four chair legs back to the floor and leaned forward. "If I'm honest and tell them it's awful, they say I'm not committed to the Peace Corps. If I tell them how much I like it, they write in their little notebooks that I'm a nut case. Either way, I'm screwed!"

Everyone laughed, but in fact Volunteers were sent home for any number of reasons. The specter of *deselection* was something they lived with every day.[12]

Training camp itself was a former Bible camp—bare, utilitarian buildings filled with rows of bunk beds. No television. No washers or dryers.

Bitter cold and heavy snows. Concrete floors. Bare light bulbs hanging from the ceilings.

The Peace Corps had chosen the remote area—the spartan facilities—for a reason. The American Volunteers would make Afghanistan their home. They would shop at the local bazaars, eat the same food, and have the same necessities of daily life as the ordinary Afghan citizen. They were expected to become part of the community, not maintain an American lifestyle with imported goods and amenities. The absence of a few luxuries and conveniences in Estes Park hardly compared to what life would be like in their new country; still, it was a way to help them start making the transition.[13]

Jo climbed into her top bunk every night exhausted. She couldn't remember having a previous life. And when classes were expanded to include protocol in a Muslim country, how to bargain in the bazaars, and the ethnic diversity of the Pashtuns, Tajiks, Kutchi nomads, and Hazara peoples, she seriously questioned whether she ever had a previous life at all.

Hydrologists learned how to dig wells. Nan went with the lab techs to the Denver Medical Center to examine slides of bacteria, parasites, and viruses no longer seen in the United States. Jo was told she would teach nursing, and began working with Tarshi to write out a basic curriculum in Farsi—transliterated, of course.

And just when she wondered if it would ever end, they were called into the assembly hall for the last time. Jo could hardly believe it. Where had the time gone? She vaguely heard something about a review and final exam, then cheering and clapping. She looked around. What did she miss? When would she ever learn to pay attention at the right time? She picked up the pieces of information from Mary.

"A bus," Mary was saying. "... the Stanley Hotel. We're going into Estes Park tonight for a dance."

Jo was full of questions as they left the classroom building and walked to the dining hall. "A dance! Really?" She looked over at Mary. "Are you going?"

"I wouldn't miss it."

"Me, neither." Jo skipped a little in the snow, happy that Mary was coming. They opened the door to the dining hall. Nan, Peaches, and Harry were right behind them, and she heard Nan say something, but didn't quite catch it all. Something about packing a party dress at the last minute.

~⌒ᵥ⌒~

The Stanley was upscale by any standard. Compared to Cedar Lodge, it was luxurious.[14] Crystal chandeliers hung from the ceiling. Thick carpeting muffled Jo's footsteps. She wore makeup for the first time in weeks, and in a setting that was beautiful and sparkly, she felt the same herself.

The Volunteers were ushered to a private ballroom where dance lights revolved overhead, showering everyone with little mosaics of color. Jo hopped onto the dance floor with everyone else, including Nan, Charlotte Budum, Harry, and Peaches. Shouting above the music, having a drink, and laughing at shared jokes, she found it hard to believe they had ever been strangers.

She didn't think about Mary until the band took a break, and suddenly realized she had not seen her friend all evening. Where did Mary go? Was she self-conscious among the younger Volunteers? Ill at ease with the loud music, dancing, and drinking?

Jo walked around the perimeter of the ballroom, and spotted Mary seated at one of the tables off to the side. With her gray bun stiffly in place, her carriage erect, Mary had a drink in one hand, and a cigarette in the other, entertaining a constant stream of visitors. Jo watched from a distance, not wanting to interrupt. She hugged the scene to herself and smiled. It would seem that Mary was full of surprises.

The band broke into the second set with their own version of Wilson Pickett's "In the Midnight Hour," and she joined her friends on the dance floor. She did a little spin, and thought she caught a flash of something white from across the room. She stopped and blinked, trying to get a better look. A white ribbon on a black prayer cap bobbed and weaved among the Volunteers. With his arms up slightly, Tarshi danced with the best of them, his tunic rippling in ways it probably never had moved before.

~⌒\⌒~

Training ended as things often do, not with a neat and tidy closure, but with a flurry of activity and last minute details. The teachers scrambled to give final instructions: what to pack for life in their new country, what paperwork to complete. And then, Jo woke up one morning and realized the frantic activity had stopped. What she thought would never end was finally over. She was surprised at the empty, hollow feeling. Six weeks of her life she would not wish on her worst enemy. At the same time, she knew it was an experience she would not trade for anything.

The Volunteers received a last round of immunizations. They started taking quinine as a precaution against malaria, and began a medication regimen to prevent tuberculosis, for they would be living in a country with nearly seventy thousand new cases of TB annually.

Health issues were not the only risks. In 1968, students and workers in Afghanistan were beginning to organize, and their resentment at government restrictions festered just beneath the surface of everyday life. Simultaneously, the Soviet Union was increasing its presence in the country, especially near Mazar-e Sharif and Kabul. In the event violence erupted or the government collapsed, the Volunteers would be evacuated along with diplomats, World Health Organization (WHO) personnel, the United States Agency for International Development (USAID) officials, and lastly, the ambassador. It could not be stressed enough. *Keep your passports safe and accessible if you want to get out safely.*

None of this information found its way into the conversation Jo had with her parents, however. Volunteers stood in line to call home, and when Jo's turn came, it was her mother who answered.

"Mom? It's me. Jo. I'm done. And guess what?"

Without warning, she was overcome with emotion.

"I've been accepted!"

Classes ended on March 12, 1968. Each Volunteer was issued a footlocker, and the next day training camp disbanded.

Along with the rest of Group Thirteen, Jo left Kennedy Airport on a specially chartered KLM jet the night of March 19, 1968. She looked down to see the lights and skyline of New York slip away beneath them, giving way to the darkness of the ocean. As the plane banked and headed due east, Jo silently bid farewell to the United States.

Chapter 4

FIRST IMPRESSIONS

Looking out of the plane all you could see were mountains, snow-covered Hindu Kush and brown vast expanses. All of us were quite excited.
—*March 21, 1968*

Jo traveled nearly seven thousand miles—a journey that encompassed four flights, twenty hours in the air, and one layover in Tehran, Iran. Thirty hours after leaving New York, she was on the last leg of her trip, flying from Tehran into Afghanistan's air space. She pressed her forehead to the plane window, straining for a glimpse of the country she would soon call home.

The land mass beneath her appeared creased and folded: millions of tons of earth and rock that had been crushed and crumpled like so many pieces of discarded paper. The ridges were bleak and unadorned with vegetation; shades of brown deepened to a blue haze in the narrow valleys. She felt a shiver run up her spine, a thrill at being in the presence of the Hindu Kush.

A cluster of raised dots materialized: adobe houses in Braille, made from the same brown earth as the mountains surrounding them. The pilot banked. The camouflaged village silently passed from view.

They headed north and east, deeper into Afghanistan. The mountain peaks became sharper, more defined. Snow appeared on the rocky summits, and the pilot flew at a higher altitude, clearing the massive crests that reached up to them. From the air, Afghanistan was not unlike the surface of the moon: a silent, forbidding expanse of lifeless, sterile rock.

On the ground, Kabul exploded into color and sound. Jo was astounded at the transformation, overwhelmed by noise and commotion. Taxis honked. City buses left trails of dust and diesel fumes. Insistent dings from bicycle bells, sharp and staccato, cut through the air, warning pedestrians to move aside. Motorcycles, trucks, and late-model cars shared the roadway with fat-tailed sheep, their rumps swaying like bustles with every step. Donkeys plodded at their own pace, oblivious of the vehicles swerving around them. Loaded with baskets of produce, the donkeys stopped occasionally to voice their complaints, emitting long-suffering, wailing brays.

A group of young Afghan women in skirts and blouses waited at a bus stop; they were university students, perhaps, their blouses tucked in Western-style, their skirts falling to just below the knee. Two women in burqas passed through, the black fabric of their veils billowing in the wind, their view of the world restricted to what they could see through a mesh opening in front of their eyes.

Gaudies—horse-drawn wooden carts—transported passengers on a little bench that faced backwards. Harness bells jingled in a manner reminiscent of sleigh bells.

A smaller cart came out of a side street: a utility flat-bed loaded with bags of cement. Two Hazara men leaned into a wooden yoke, pulled the cart into an alley, and disappeared into the shadows.[15]

A stinging, pungent odor hung in the air. Infused with notes and colors, it reflected everything about Kabul on a spring afternoon—sweat, dust, animals, wool, waste, and dung, with an occasional hint of rendered fat from a nearby vendor cooking with fat-tailed sheep grease.

Juies, a system of water-filled ditches, flanked the streets, the surface of the water shimmering in the heat. Inundated every spring with melting snow from the Hindu Kush, and narrowing to little rivulets in the countryside with the pleasant sound of gurgling, rushing water, juies are nonetheless convenient receptacles for waste and garbage, comparable to open sewers.[16]

Jo swallowed. She had been thrilled to touch down on Afghan soil at last, amazed at the modern glass-enclosed terminal, hardly able to believe it when the customs agent stamped her passport and greeted her in Farsi. And now, standing on a busy street corner with the rest of Group Thirteen, she cupped a hand to her forehead, shielding her eyes. The sunlight was blinding, and her initial excitement began to fade.

The Volunteers were in front of the Ashraf Hotel in Kabul, milling about as they waited for their room assignments. Jo felt hot and sweaty, queasy with jet lag and sensory overload. Since leaving the skyline of New York, she had seen the sun come up over Ireland, marveled at Amsterdam's network of canals when they stopped to refuel, and witnessed a blazing red sunset in Tehran. It was late afternoon the next day when they got to the Ashraf, and now they waited for the rooms to be sorted, one by one. It seemed to take forever.

Afghan pedestrians stopped and stared at them; drivers slowed down and gawked from car windows. Jo was so tired she didn't care what she looked like, or who saw her. She sat on her suitcase, leaned forward, and put her head on her knees. Just a few more minutes, she told herself. It had to be soon now, and she could finally take a shower and stretch out in bed.

"Joanne Carter! Mary Simpson!"

At last. She picked up her bags and followed Mary up the stairs.

The hotel room was big—much bigger than Jo had expected, but then, what did she expect? She didn't know. Maybe it was the lack of carpeting, the black and white squares of bare linoleum that made it feel so expansive, so echo-y. The two beds, two dressers, and little table seemed disproportionably small. A balcony on the outer wall framed a view of the Hindu Kush. A kerosene heater stood by itself in the middle of the room. The beds were *charpoy* beds, made with four wooden legs and a wooden frame. There were no mattresses. Jute ropes had been stretched across the bed frame, and cotton mats placed over the ropes.

Fifty Volunteers settled into their rooms, unpacked, and looked for showers. Bathrooms were communal, at the end of the hall. New, Western-style toilets lined the wall, although one of the toilets had crashed to the floor. It was left there, broken and abandoned, listing on its side. Shower stalls lined the opposite wall. The water was cold.

Evening shadows had fallen across the balcony of their hotel room when Jo returned from her shower. The air had cooled immediately, and at 6,000 feet above sea level the night would get progressively colder. Mary circled the kerosene heater, eyeing the vent, looking for the pilot light. She got on her hands and knees and moved a lever. The screech of tin scraping against tin filled the air. She struck a match, and bracing herself with one hand, slowly moved the match toward the opening for the pilot light.

A hollow whooshing sound pulled up the hair on Jo's arms. A blue flash blinded her for a moment, and then incandescent circles floated in front of her eyes. She blinked, waiting for her vision to return, and when she could see again, she put her head to the floor, peering into the bottom of the heater, at the pipes, flanges, and opening for the pilot light, knowing full well she had absolutely no idea how to get it started. She had assumed Mary would figure out the intricacies of their little stove, and the irony was not lost on her. At one time she wondered if Mary would survive training. Now, with darkness settling around them, and the hotel room getting colder by the minute, she counted on her older friend to come up with a solution.

She sat up and interlaced her fingers on top of her head, her hair still damp. "So what is this? Some kind of test?"

"Well," said Mary, standing and brushing her hands with a brisk movement, "I don't know. The best idea, I guess, is to sleep in our coats."

Jo contemplated her first day in Afghanistan: the vertigo she felt on the bus ride into Kabul, the modern airport replaced by fields plowed with oxen and wooden plows, the farming method unchanged for a thousand years. The dusty streets of the city, the smells, the animals walking among traffic. The broken toilet, her cold shower, and a heater that didn't work.

She had barely slept in two days, and her bed was made of wood, rope, and a couple of thin mats.

Coming to Afghanistan was by far the craziest thing she had ever done. And the Ashraf Hotel … well, it was laughable. Hilarious. It belongs in a Three Stooges movie, she wanted to say, but her throat constricted and her eyes welled with tears.

Mary rustled about in the shadowy room, opening her trunk and humming under her breath. The movement stopped, and Jo looked over at her roommate.

Mary stood in her coat and muffler, dressed as if she were going to the Arctic Circle.

Jo burst into sleep-deprived peals of laughter, and she continued to laugh, even as the tears spilled down her cheeks.

Mary smiled as she opened her sleeping bag and laid it across the charpoy bed. She climbed on top and zipped herself in, all the way up to her chin.

"You look pitiful!"

"I don't care. I'm warm and toasty." Mary gave Jo a self-satisfied grin.

Unable to come up with a better solution, Jo wiped her eyes, put on her own coat and zipped herself into her sleeping bag. The room was now in total darkness, with a crescent moon shining above the balcony. She burrowed into the lumpy folds and yawned. Then turning as well as she could, hampered by her coat, she raised her head.

"Good night, Mary." As an afterthought, she added, "Welcome to Afghanistan."

⌇⌒◦⌒⌇

Group Thirteen had less than a week in Kabul before they started Provincial Training. It was barely enough time to figure out the maps they had been issued and find their way around the city. They walked the streets, avoided juies, rode gaudies, and explored mosques. They shopped the bazaars and practiced Farsi, stopping at tea bazaars, fruit bazaars, onion bazaars, wooden toy bazaars, rug bazaars, and everything in between. They sampled nân, the Afghan unleavened bread, and ate kebobs, cooked over open fires.

They encountered a group of *Overlanders*, men and women with long hair and dusty backpacks, following the hippie trail through Afghanistan. Dressed in jeans, tie-dyed clothing, headbands and sandals, they were one of many such groups from the United States and Europe, looking for enlightenment and hashish.[17]

They saw Afghan men with a variety of head gear: neatly fitted prayer caps, turbans, and Pakol hats.[18] Young boys who went barefoot. Little kids wearing tiny tombans that resembled pajamas. Women in burqas, hijabs, chadors, and Western dress.[19]

They perused modern shops—a cinema, a library, and a record store. Waited with everyone else when lumbering cows or the occasional camel stalled traffic. Watched in fascination when city buses were filled to over-flowing and passengers sat on the roof. A metal railing, not more than a couple of feet high, enclosed travelers and belongings. No one seemed to worry, not even when the bus turned corners and listed dangerously.

They acclimated to life at the Ashraf, adjusting to cold showers, heaters that exploded, furniture that collapsed, and elevators that didn't work. And finally, thanks to Tarshi, who had followed his charges to Afghanistan, they had the pleasure of more Farsi instruction in a makeshift classroom.

At the end of the week, assignments were posted for Provincial Training. Volunteers crowded up to the roster, and Jo edged her way to the front, for once her diminutive size a distinct advantage. She quickly looked through the list while Mary waited off to the side. Roughly half the Volunteers were being sent to Kandahar, and the rest to Jalalabad. She took another minute to read the instructions. Buses were leaving early the next morning. They had one night to pack. Their Peace Corps trunks would be left in storage at the Ashraf until they returned.

"Kandahar," Jo called out over her shoulder to Mary. She went down the list again. "Both of us ... and Peaches!"

The three women gathered in Jo and Mary's room. They left the door open as they talked, deciding what to pack and what to leave behind.

A knock on the door frame interrupted their conversation. Nan stuck her head in first, followed by Harry.

"Kandahar?" Harry repeated the news. "All three of you are going to Kandahar?" He grinned, and leaned against the doorjamb with his arms folded. "Me, too!"

"What about you, Nan?" Jo hoped they would all stay together. "Are you coming with us?"

Nan shook her head. "Nope. I'm going to Jalalabad with Charlotte Budum. And remember Carter? He'll be coming too."

They compared trips. Nan would be going one hundred miles directly east from Kabul. The Kandahar group would follow a road that stretches almost four hundred miles south, along the eastern side of Afghanistan where it borders Pakistan.

~⌒⋎⌒~

Jo accepted a paper sack as she stepped onto the bus—lunch, compliments of the hotel staff. She took a seat next to Peaches and looked to see what they had. Bread, cheese, one hard-boiled egg, a piece of cake, and an orange.

Mary settled in across the aisle. She struck up a conversation with a married couple, Kathleen and Rick. Kathleen was a nurse, Rick an English teacher.

They left the congestion of the city, driving past the scattered outlying compounds and into the countryside. The pine trees and grassy slopes of northern Afghanistan began to disappear, and the Hindu Kush gradually flattened to broad, semi-desert plains.

Near the walled town of Ghanzi, not quite halfway to Kandahar, the driver crossed over a dry gully and stopped. When several passengers got off, Peaches turned to Jo and whispered, "This may be as good as it gets, you know."

Jo watched the line of people walking along the stony creek bed. One by one they ducked down and disappeared under a small bridge. "Very funny, Peaches, but I can't believe it will be this bad."

"Well, I don't care if the toilets fell out of the wall," said Peaches. "Doesn't this make the *tashnab* at the Ashraf seem luxurious in comparison?"

Jo laughed nervously. She thought about the stories that had circulated before they left, about how primitive conditions would be in the provinces, and how the people of Kandahar—the Pashtuns—were backward and uneducated, suspicious of foreigners.

She was not reassured when the city emerged and the bus stopped in front of a typical Afghan compound, an adobe building enclosed by an imposing ten-foot stone wall. It would be home for the next month.

The women shared a large room, and set their luggage on a cleanly swept concrete floor. Jo found bicycles waiting for them, issued by the Peace Corps.

Peaches called ecstatically from down the hall. "Guess what? We have a tashnab." She came back into the room. "Not just a bathroom, but one with running water!"

So, conditions would not be as primitive as Jo had feared. Other worries still nagged at the back of her mind, however. What would they encounter at the hospital once they started training? And she couldn't help thinking about the Pashtuns in general. They were the most conservative people in Afghanistan, she had heard, and followed a Pashtunwali code of conduct that features hospitality, courage, and revenge. Nothing is forgotten by the Pashtuns, according to rumor, and few debts are left unpaid.[20]

Chapter 5

KANDAHAR HOSPITAL

Got to the hospital and felt at once like a fish out of water. Firstly, because I couldn't understand Pashtu and very little Farsi. Secondly, I didn't have anything to work with—no soap, no running water. Thirdly, I was scared to death.

—*April 1, 1968*

A fly buzzed up around Jo's face. She turned her head and waved it away, but the fly returned, sticky and persistent, making her nose itch. In spite of the heat and stifling air of the hospital ward, she inched closer to Mary and Kathleen.

The women were gathered in a passageway, flanked on either side by rows of hospital beds. The beds had been pushed against opposite walls of the ward much like rows of dominoes, creating an aisle down the middle of the room. A Peace Corps nurse assigned to Kandahar was giving a short orientation, but Jo's attention was on the flies, the heat, and the patients surrounding them. She barely heard a word.

An Afghan physician came toward them. "Welcome," he said in English. "Welcome to Mirwais Hospital in Kandahar."

He left his white lab coat unbuttoned, revealing a collared shirt and Western-style slacks. His face was clean shaven, and he wore a surgical cap. He was about to start rounds, he said, and invited his visitors to accompany him while he worked.

The Volunteers followed him to the bedside of his first patient, a man with a cast that extended from his right wrist past his elbow. "He fell from the roof of his house," explained the physician. "He is very lucky—only a broken arm." The physician bent to examine the cast, while the patient himself stared in curiosity at the three American women standing in such close proximity to his bed. The physician spoke to the patient in Pashtu, and Jo strained to understand the unfamiliar dialect. She was distracted by a movement from the far side of the room and looked up, slightly annoyed at the intrusion.

Two men had come through a set of wooden doors. They were graduate nurses, deeply engrossed in a Pashtu conversation. Their heads were turned toward each other as they talked, their tombans rippling as they quickly moved through the aisle. They passed the small group of Americans without pausing for even a glance, or nod of acknowledgement.

Jo flushed. She suddenly felt foolish in her uniform, her white dress hot and scratchy, the traditional white hose stuck to her legs with perspiration.

The physician seemed unaffected by the Afghan nurses. He moved on. In succession, he examined a man with a concussion from a taxi accident, a newly admitted patient with malaria, and finally, an elderly man with a tubercular cough.

Toward the end of rounds, Jo turned to Mary and whispered, "Where are the women?"

"I don't know," Mary whispered back. "I guess the women don't get sick."

The physician wrote a set of orders for medication and treatments: quinine and IV fluids for the malaria patient, X-rays for the auto accident victim. He spoke with the graduate nurses, shook hands with the Volunteers, and left. There were more patients to see in the next ward.

Jo was sorry to see him go. She had been comfortable in his presence, at ease with his kind and efficient manner, impressed with his knowledge. Now that he was gone, who was in charge? The graduate nurses? They had been rude and dismissive of the Americans, but surely one of them would step forward and organize the staff. Give out assignments. Get everyone to work together.

Instead, the Afghan nurses implemented the physician's orders themselves, delegating tasks to a group of young men who were student nurses. The Peace Corps staff assigned to Kandahar were edged to the periphery of patient care, and even more discouraging, it appeared they had adapted to the hierarchy of power, for they took on the menial tasks of the hospital ward as if it were a matter of course.

Jo felt awkward and out of place, not knowing what to do. She had left her family, come all this way, and endured training for what? To be treated like this? She appraised the patients in the ward. If the Afghans expect me to stand around all day and wait to be recognized, they're sadly mistaken, she thought. Her eyes fell on a young man with dressings on his arms and chest.

It wasn't hard to understand what had happened. With gestures, and speaking in a mixture of Pashtu and broken Farsi, he explained. He had been working on his father's truck. An open can of gasoline had caught fire.

Initially, the burned areas on his arms and chest had oozed a watery drainage streaked with pink. When the serosanguinous fluid dried, the gauze dressings crusted over, adhering to the raw tissue underneath.

Jo explained to the student nurses that she wished to bathe the patients and change dressings. She pointed to the burn patient. She would start with him.

Their heads moving in unison, the students turned from Jo to the patient, and back again to Jo. Why should they care about impressing a Peace Corps worker—an American who was here today and gone tomorrow?

She waited for them to decide, and noticed the graduate nurses in the background. They also waited, watching to see what would happen next.

Sweat trickled from the hollow area under her arms and slid down her rib cage.

Seconds ticked by. When a couple of students finally stepped forward to help, Jo was absurdly relieved, as if she had passed some sort of test, or won a contest when she didn't know the rules.

She asked them for a liter of sterile normal saline.

The students were confused. "Normal saline for an IV?"

"No," said Jo. "Sterile salt water."

She could not imagine cleaning the burns with contaminated water. She wanted to soak the dressings with a sterile isotonic solution of 0.9 percent sodium chloride. Remove the dirty bandages and black eschar—the crusted scabs—without tearing the fragile, healing tissue underneath. Dress the area with antibiotic ointment. Give pain medication. Make arrangements for a skin graft to avoid scars and contractures.

The best she had was boiled water, and if not sterile, then at least clean dressings. She was vaguely aware of how quickly she was willing to compromise her standard of care; how the lack of supplies dictated what she could, or could not do. She soon became absorbed in her task, explaining the procedure to the students while she worked. When the last piece of soaked gauze had been gently peeled away, she glanced up reflexively.

The graduate nurses stood with their arms folded, watching her every move. Jo didn't need to understand Pashtu to interpret their body language. They were amused at her efforts. For the second time that morning, she flushed. Hot and self-conscious, she lowered her head and applied the clean dressings, not wanting to appear inept in front of them.

Next she approached the elderly TB patient. She told the students she needed supplies: towels, washcloths, and soap.

They stared at her blankly. A couple of them shrugged.

Jo felt her heart speed up. What was she supposed to do? The Afghan nurses were back at work, talking among themselves in Pashtu. Already the Americans had been forgotten as nothing more than a nuisance.

Her heart pounding now, her lips dry, Jo filled a basin with water and returned to the old man's bedside. She improvised, washing his face with the top of an old pair of pajamas. It was nothing more than a stupid, ineffectual gesture, but then the entire morning had been a string of useless gestures, a colossal waste of time and energy. She might as well leave. Go back home.

In the hot, oppressive ward, her blood turned to ice. Never, not once in all the weeks of training, had she entertained even the slightest notion of quitting. Homesickness gripped her like a physical illness. Home. She would simply go home, that's all.

But how? How would she get out of this hell-hole the Afghans called a hospital? She had an overwhelming urge to sit on the floor right were she was. First, she would have to find a way back to Kabul—another six-hour bus ride. Complete the paperwork and official forms to process out of the Peace Corps. Make arrangements for a flight out of Afghanistan. And once she got home, she would have to explain to everyone why she quit on the very first day.

That night after dinner, she found a quiet, recessed area within the compound walls. Kathleen joined her, and it was not quite dusk when Mary slipped into the little alcove.

"Things are worse than I expected." Kathleen started the conversation. "The hospital's filthy. Patients are crowded together—"

Jo cut her short. "Forget the hospital. It's all about the graduate nurses, and I get it loud and clear. We're not welcome."

Kathleen shook her head. "Well, I *don't* get it. I thought the Afghans would be glad to have us here."

"Apparently not. And what if ..." Jo stopped, not sure she wanted to reveal her greatest fear. "I mean, what if conditions are like this everywhere?"

"So what are you saying?" Kathleen tried to make out Jo's features, partially hidden in the shadow of the compound wall. "Is this what we can expect when we get our own assignments?"

"Yeah. I guess that's what I'm asking." Jo didn't add what seemed to be the logical conclusion. *If so, why should we stay? Why not quit now, before going any further?*

Kathleen sat back against the stone and concrete wall. "None of it makes any sense. The Afghans are offended by the Peace Corps, in my opinion. And the Volunteers who work here—well, they're walking on eggs, afraid to say anything."

"But why?" Jo pulled at her sweater in the coolness of the desert evening. "What have we done to offend them?"

Mary spoke for the first time, her voice coming out of the gathering twilight. "We have new ideas. They're used to being in charge and knowing it all, and now we come in and know more than they do. We've upset their apple cart."

The clip-clop of a horse-drawn gaudie could be heard outside the compound walls, the sound of bells fading as it passed by.

Mary continued. "Actually, the graduate nurses don't bother me at all. They do their thing, and I do mine."

"Oh, sure—that's because you're ..." Jo caught herself in time. "Uh, because you're a *muy safad*—a white hair, a person of respect."

Mary saved Jo from further embarrassment. "It's because I have kids older than most of them."

The women's laughter rose into the night air and softly died away.

Kathleen broke the ensuing silence. "Is it just me, or was everyone more friendly in Kabul? Maybe it's because everyone there spoke Farsi."

"I think it's more than a language difference," said Jo. "The people here seem more ..." She stopped, groping for the right word.

"More set in their ways," Mary finished for her.

"Suspicious," added Kathleen.[21]

The Afghan nurses saw things from a very different perspective. It was the Americans who were insensitive, coming in with their pretentious acts of kindness—the touch on a shoulder, hand on a brow, and words of encouragement—behavior that was interpreted as a judgment on the Afghan health care system. The Afghan nurses were not inclined to exhibit such behavior, for they were surrounded by poverty, disease, and unrelieved misery every day. Besides, Afghan women who touched men, even to give care, were considered little better than prostitutes. Obviously, the Americans didn't understand that, either.

And yet, the Afghan nurses watched the Peace Corps Volunteers carefully, barely able to conceal their curiosity. More than once, Jo caught them quietly observing her as she worked.

"The best advice I can give you is to change your definition of success." John Bing, the Peace Corps project director in Afghanistan, had stopped in Kandahar to speak with the Volunteers. He knew first-hand what Provincial Training was like, for he had served as a Volunteer himself, teaching in the village of Baghlan.

"No one can make changes overnight," he continued. "So let go of your expectations—the fantasies of what you thought you might accomplish. You can't measure success by American standards. You have to measure it by Afghan standards."

Jo was relieved to hear his words, to hear that yes, making the adjustment from classroom training to the real world of Afghanistan was a difficult transition. She felt validated, knowing her frustrations were shared by others, and yet … *I came to change someone else*, she thought. *No one ever said anything about changing myself.* But that's exactly what Bing was asking her to do—surrender the American virtue, or vice, of expecting instant results.

She reflected on the day she had wanted to go home so badly, the day she came close to quitting. Now she understood what was at stake. It wasn't just the months of training she would have lost, although that was significant enough. She would have quit before she really got started, before she knew what she was capable of doing.

That night, she wrote in her diary: *Have decided if I leave now I'll be as immature as I was when I first came over.*

It was during this time Jo made an unrelated and surprising discovery about herself. She loved the bazaar. She had always considered herself a rather quiet person, a reader, and prone to introspection. Drawn to adventure, but not necessarily to things that were frenzied, loud, and chaotic, yet Bazaar Street in Kandahar was all those things and more.

The labyrinth of small wooden stalls, each one a bazaar unto itself, was a world she had never seen before. Tea bazaars offered rows of tiny ceramic teapots; vegetable bazaars had asparagus and red-streaked stalks of rhubarb, the first of the early spring produce. Eggs were stacked in pyramids; burlap sacks of seed wheat stood on end, the top opened to display grain ready for spring planting. Each item of cookware, pottery, and furniture was hand-crafted and unique. Nothing was made by machine, with the exception of donated clothing from the United States, Canada, and Europe, sold at the used clothing bazaar.

The rug bazaar lured shoppers with an array of tightly woven wool carpets, and although the colors and patterns were exquisite—seemingly without a blemish—Jo knew each carpet had one flaw hidden within the design, for only Allah is perfect.

Kebobs sizzled over small fires, and flat, oval pieces of hot nân were stacked like plates, the savory aroma of food mingling with the musky scent of hashish.

A whistle flute musician played to the rhythm and clamor of the marketplace as buyers and sellers shouted for attention. Nothing was standardized; weights and measures changed arbitrarily, prices were negotiable, and goods varied depending on the day. It was organized bedlam: noisy, confusing, and exciting.

Jo stopped at a spice bazaar, intrigued by the ginger-lemon scent from a display of small, green pods. She gave the shopkeeper a questioning look.

"Cardamom," he responded.

She nodded. Turning around, she intended to move on, but was stopped by a wall of at least twenty people staring at her. She wondered if she would ever get used to it—regarded as strange, the one who was odd, the foreigner. Then one day a man "accidentally" bumped up against her. She turned to confront him, but he had disappeared into the crowd. The incident made her distinctly uneasy, and she decided from then on she would not come alone.

And so, when she wanted to shop for a particular item one afternoon, she pestered Mary to go with her. She explained what she hoped to find as they walked out of the hotel compound.

Mary looked at her with amusement. "You mean we're walking all this way for a hat?"

"Come on, Mary, it's for my dad."

"And why do you think your dad wants a hat?"

Jo remembered the morning before she left for training, the morning she had gotten up early to have breakfast with him. "He never leaves the house without something on his head." Jo raised her shoulders. "That's just my dad."

"And you expect your dad to wear a turban?"

Jo shot Mary an exasperated look, only to see Mary smiling at her own joke.

"No." Jo tried not to sound petulant. "Actually, I was thinking of a Karakul hat."[22]

"Ah. Good choice."

They made their way deeper into the crowd and stopped in front of a bazaar filled with Karakul lambskins. Jo fingered the curly wool, displayed in every color from black to dark brown to silver. It felt like silk. Recognizing the interest in her eyes, the shopkeeper was at her elbow immediately. A small crowd gathered to watch.

Jo made her selection: a silver gray skin. They haggled back and forth. He made a show of exasperation by coming down a couple of afghanis in price; she ran her hand over the soft wool and finally agreed. Before she could pay for it, however, one of the spectators stepped forward. "*Nê!*" He shook his head vehemently. "You are cheating the foreign woman, charging an inflated price."

The shopkeeper denied the charge, and the two men raised their voices, making Jo the subject of a heated argument. The noise escalated with each offer and counteroffer on her behalf until everyone was shouting at once. A police officer came up. Irritated at the disturbance, he dispersed the crowd, chasing away Jo and Mary as well, but not before Jo bought her lambswool, and gave the shopkeeper her dad's hat size.

Walking back to the compound, she reflected on the massive amount of time and energy that went into the simple acts of daily living. "All that commotion, just for a hat."

"And you still don't have it," said Mary.

"But I bet it's beautiful when it's finished," said Jo with a little skip. "My dad will love it."

~∩⁖∩~

Things were looking up. Jo had her Karakul lambskin, and over the past weeks the tension between the graduate nurses and the new Volunteers had settled into an uneasy truce. If the Afghans didn't applaud her efforts, at least they didn't interfere, gradually accepting her work as a normal part of the daily routine. A small victory, but gratefully accepted none-theless.

It was April in Kandahar, the days sunny and warm. Birds chirped in the hotel compound. Jo was filled with such a sense of well-being, she wrote in her journal: *I woke up to another beautiful spring morning. We had fried eggs, nân and coffee. It was delightful.*

Less than eight hours later she was sick with dysentery. She was astounded at how quickly the symptoms appeared, and how rapidly she progressed from feeling perfectly fine to desperately ill. She went to bed with a temperature of 102 degrees Fahrenheit. Her head felt as if it was going to explode; her joints ached. A taste of fat-tailed sheep grease rose in the back of her throat, and soon her nausea gave way to painful abdominal cramps, vomiting, and spasms of watery diarrhea.

She heard Mary and Peaches talking sometime during the night, their voices sounding strange and far away, as if from the end of a long tunnel. She thought Peaches said something about five o'clock in the morning—or was she dreaming? A door closed. Then Mary was at her bedside, giving her a tablet of Lomotil.

She woke again; only now it was broad daylight. Peaches and Mary offered her a cup of powdered milk, some crackers, and a can of tomato soup. It was all they could find, even after scavenging every room in the hotel.

Jo took the packet of crackers. It was an enormous effort to hold up her head and open the cellophane. Her limbs felt heavy as lead. Someone knocked; she barely heard it.

Still discussing with Peaches whether or not it was safe to reconstitute the powdered milk, Mary crossed the room and opened the door. Standing in the doorway was John Bing, holding a loaf of white bread.

"I think you better slice this for Jo," said Bing with a little smile. "She looks green from fat-tailed sheep grease." And although he handed the bread over to Mary, he looked directly at Jo, his expression one of commiseration.

The tears were like needle pricks against her feverish lids. The only place that had soft, imported white bread was the USAID compound in Kandahar. Jo knew immediately that Bing had ignored the Peace Corps mandate to live off the bazaar, and had gone there to buy the bread, just for her.

Over the next two years dysentery became a fact of life. Everyone got it, no matter how many precautions they took. They soaked fruits and vegetables in iodine water, cooked meat in a pressure cooker, and boiled water to wash dishes. If they ate in a restaurant, they swished out teacups with scalding tea, poured the tea into a bowl to be discarded, and refilled the cup. None of it made any difference. Sooner or later, every single Volunteer became sick. There was only one guaranteed way of escaping amoebic dysentery—if the Volunteers closed their mouths, and did not open them to eat or drink until they left Afghanistan.

It was so pervasive Jo got tired of writing about it in her diary, and began to cast about for innovative ways to slip it in among her entries. She was discreet at first: *Under the weather today*. When that got boring she wrote: *Rotten egg syndrome again*. She finally ran out of creative ideas and put it bluntly: *Have diarrhea today*. Even that got tiresome, so in succession, she had the trots, the runs, and—oh, what the hell—the poops.

By the time she returned to work, the Volunteers were making plans to explore the area. The majority wanted to see the ruins of the old city of Kandahar, said to have been founded by Alexander the Great. Others, including Harry, wanted to ride a camel. "I'm not leaving Afghanistan until I've done it at least once," he insisted.

They held a little meeting and voted to do both, choosing to see the ruins first.

Chapter 6

A LITTLE HELP FROM MY FRIENDS

We proceeded to bike to the old city and scaled to the top. As always, the other kids were helping me out. And on the top the dust and wind storm started and pelted us with stones and pebbles for over an hour.
—April 5, 1968

No signs. No shops selling souvenirs. It was simply there: the exposed foundations and broken down stubs of compound walls, the remains of a city that had flourished two thousand years ago—the old city of Kandahar, four miles west of its present location.

The guide pointed out a citadel, not quite one hundred feet high. "The steps to the top are cut from solid limestone," he said. And like every good Afghan, he was convinced it was on those very steps that Alexander the Great married the Bactrian princess Roxanne in 300 BCE. A stone rampart encircled the ruins, and he showed the Americans a way to the top, indicating where a series of indentations had been worn into the fortress over hundreds of years.

The men went up first, feet splayed in toe-holds, fingertips grasping for ledges. Jo tried not to laugh; she didn't expect to make a graceful ascent herself. When her turn came she hugged the stone formation, pushing her toes into crevices, pulling herself up with whatever protrusion she could find. She awkwardly brought one leg up over the lip and grasped Rick's hand as he reached down to help her. She hoisted herself onto the broad parapet and crawled away from the edge, a little surprised at how high she was. But when she looked out, the effort of scaling the wall was forgotten. From her vantage point she had a spectacular view of the old city.

She imagined how the enclosed area might have appeared in antiquity: the metallic chink of soldiers in armor, the stamping and neighing of horses, dogs barking. She envisioned smoke from cooking fires, and the celebration and pageantry of a marriage ceremony twenty centuries ago.

Leaning against a bulwark and drawing her knees up to her chest, she came back to the present. Images of a vibrant city faded; sounds from the past were hushed. Occasional wisps of sand blew across the deserted, empty spaces. The Volunteers had breached a massive stone wall that once deterred ancient enemies; now it stood guard over half-buried streets and the ghosts of Alexander's army.

She turned away from the city, toward the semi-arid plains of Kandahar Province. The fields had turned faintly green in the early spring, and the Hindu Kush appeared as a double row of hills, brown against a deep blue sky. The colors and contours reminded her of the biblical pictures she had seen as a child in Sunday school.

A light wind came from across the open land, bearing an earthy, loamy scent. Capricious, the breeze ruffled Jo's hair, and chased little whirlwinds of dust along the ground. The whirlwinds expanded, spinning faster and higher, rising almost even with the top of the wall. A forgotten jacket, carelessly tossed to the side, was caught by a strong gust and sent tumbling across the plains, gone forever.

A cold draft swept across the wall and Jo shivered involuntarily. Air that had been warm and clear suddenly filled with sand and choking dust. A pebble struck her cheek, the sting unexpected and sharp. She let out a yelp of pain, but the words were snatched from her lips by the increasing, howling wind. She brought the neckline of her t-shirt up over her nose and mouth, and wedged herself into a crevice next to Peaches. Rick huddled beneath an overhanging rock; Kathleen buried her face in his chest. Harry's head disappeared inside his sweatshirt.

For over an hour, the wind scoured the landscape, picking up sand and whipping it through the air before hurling it back to the ground. The high-pitched whistle was deafening, wave after wave, until it seemed even the stone fortress would be picked up and carried away.

And then, as quickly and inexplicably as it started, the wind died down and was still.[23] Jo raised her head. Dust hung in the air; an eerie, sallow twilight dimmed the afternoon sun.

She climbed back down, stumbling when her feet touched the ground. Her hands trembled as she worked the sand and dirt out of her bicycle chains. If she abandoned her bike there, she wondered, how long before it vanished permanently, buried under dust and sand? Years? Days?

Never before had Jo experienced anything like the dust storm. The wind had been so ferocious it brought her to her knees. And yet, there had been something about the wildness of it, the spectacular, untamed display of raw power that was exhilarating, a pure adrenaline rush. In the aftermath, Jo was left so weak she could barely move.

She straddled the bike and willed her fingers to grip the handlebars, but her muscles refused to respond. She pushed off and stood to put her weight on the pedals. Moving the wheels of the old coaster bike was like trying to move through molasses.

The Volunteers weaved and wobbled, riding two and three abreast. They dropped into single file when a truck came up behind them, and Jo bent her head over the handlebars to avoid yet another blast of sand and dirt.

She lifted her head when the truck had passed, standing once again on the pedals. But wait. Was the driver slowing down? Was he really leaning out of his cab, waving them forward? She got off her bike and half walked, half ran toward him, not caring how awkward she looked, afraid he would change his mind if he had to wait for them.

Harry and Rick loaded the bikes onto the truck bed, and everyone fit themselves around wheels and handlebars. Jo rested her forehead on her arms. She would be forever grateful to the driver—a random stranger who just happened to stop.

Windblown and dirty, they straggled into the compound. Jo's hair was matted and gummed to her scalp. She felt sand gritting between her teeth and wanted to spit, but didn't have enough saliva. She wiped her face with her hands; her skin felt like sandpaper.

She lathered in the shower and shampooed her hair, the dirt, dust, and sand swirling in little eddies of water by her feet. She rinsed and soaped again, and yet a third time before she felt clean. She then turned her attention to her clothes. Sand was ground into her white t-shirt, imbued into the cotton fiber, and although she rinsed it until the water ran clear, it remained permanently brown, a dusty dun color, the color of Afghanistan.

A shower never felt so wonderful, and a hot meal never tasted so good. She had never known a group of people more congenial than the group with her in this compound, on this night in Kandahar. She reveled in the knowledge she was part of it all, and felt lighthearted, happy, and accepted.

And precisely when everything seemed so clear and straightforward, she found a way to circumvent her enjoyment of the moment. True to her headstrong, sometimes contrary nature, she announced that perhaps she would review some Farsi lecture notes.

"I don't want to hear it." Peaches momentarily covered her ears. "Oh, come on, Jo. Lose the guilt trip for once. Party with us tonight. Besides, you can't study in our room—Mary has plans for a bridge game."

Jo hesitated, and Peaches pressed her case. "Good grief. Everybody's up for a good time, even Tarshi."

"You don't leave me an option, do you?" Jo's smile was rueful, perhaps hiding an emotion she found hard to articulate. Acceptance? A sense of belonging? Outwardly, she made a show of protest; inwardly she embraced the warmth of being wanted. She eventually allowed herself to be talked into partying—all she needed was a little encouragement from her friends.

The two women started with a visit to a group of Volunteers trained as surveyors. They laughed and joked with the men, flirted a little, then moved on to Rick and Kathleen's room where another group of Volunteers had gathered. From there they went to a party in Harry's room.

Mary was putting away the cards when they got back. Her cheeks were flushed, her eyes sparkling. "Well, it was a hot card game, let me tell you!"

Jo laughed and exchanged a look with Peaches. It was easy to see who won.

The women closed their door for the night and compared parties while they got ready for bed. Jo plugged in her shortwave radio, something she did every evening. Reception was always better at night, and she relished the little bit of down time when she listened to Voice of America before falling asleep. Of all the things she brought with her to Afghanistan, her radio was perhaps her most valued possession.

It was the evening of April 5, 1968—Friday—the Muslim Holy Day of the week. Jo put her head on the pillow with a sigh. It had been a long day: bike rides, dust storms, and parties late into the night. She reached over to adjust the volume, anticipating the final news broadcast of the night.

The top story was a recap—not of the day's events, but those of the previous day. Martin Luther King had been assassinated on April 4 while standing on the balcony of his room at the Lorraine Motel in Memphis, Tennessee.

Mary's sharp intake of breath was audible. Peaches threw off her blanket and went over to sit on Jo's bed. They listened to the details, the follow-up stories of looting and riots in Washington and Chicago.

Not knowing what else to do, the women went from door to door in the hotel. They knocked softly on each one; not to party, but to share the news with those who were still awake. They returned to their own room and climbed back into bed, talking after the light was turned off.

"It's a loss, no doubt about it," said Mary. "For his family, of course, and for a peaceful civil rights movement."

"It's a loss for everyone—the entire United States." Jo turned over, feeling very far from home. The hotel room was quiet. She thought about

Kandahar Hospital and the day ahead of them. Tomorrow would be an ordinary work day, no different from any other day. She pulled the blanket tightly around her, certain that Mary and Peaches were also wide awake in the darkness.

Jo's assessment that King's death would make little difference in Afghanistan proved to be accurate. The student nurses were already making rounds with the physician when she arrived the next morning. She caught up with them at the bedside of a patient about to be discharged. The physician was giving final instructions.

Jo was familiar with the case: a man with severe frostbite in both feet. Today he was sitting up and animated, talking rapidly in Pashtu. After spending many weeks in the hospital, he was happy to be going home. The ordeal was behind him, and he smiled, regardless of the fact he had lost several toes. The pain was better, he said. Better than those first few days, when the white areas had turned black and sloughed off. Better than the weeks on morphine, while the doctors waited for a demarcation line to form—the line separating living and dead tissue—indicating where to amputate.

Frostbite was not unusual, considering adults and even children sometimes walked barefoot in the snow. Jo looked at his bandaged feet. He was fortunate; he could have died from sepsis or gangrene.

She accompanied the physician as he continued rounds, her mind preoccupied with dark thoughts. The medical care in Afghanistan was heartbreaking, but there was a limit to what she could do. She couldn't change history. She couldn't stop the snow and freezing temperatures of winter. She couldn't supply shoes and socks to every Afghan. And she couldn't force them to change their ways.

She had more empathy for the Peace Corps workers in Kandahar. They were expected to bring improvements to Afghanistan, yet not pass judgment on what they saw every day.

~◌⟡◌~

"Are we still up for the camel ride?" Harry looked around at the group.

Jo made a pretense of thinking it over. "Hmmm." She tapped her upper lip with her index finger. "You mean like our trip to the old city? The little bike ride that turned into a dust storm?"

"Okay, okay!" Harry grinned. "Think positive. We may never have a chance like this again."

"But Harry—the camels are in Lashkar Gah." Peaches threw up her hands. "That's almost eighty miles from here."

Everyone started talking at once. It would be a long bus ride. They would need a driver. And how would they contact a camel owner?

"That's a lot of planning," said Jo. "Do you really think we can arrange it?"

"Don't worry," said Harry. "What could go wrong?"

Halfway to Lashkar Gah, the bus lost a muffler.

"Not to worry," shouted Harry above the sound of the engine. "It happens all the time!"

Jo was laughing. "Sure, Harry," she shouted back. "Think positive!"

In Lashkar Gah they hired a driver with a station wagon, the blistered wood panels peeling at the edges and covered with dust. "*Hêch moshkele,*" he said. —No problem. He would take them to the camel owner. Not only that, but as a special favor, he would wait for them until they came back from their ride. He waved a hand as if the amount was insignificant. "For only a small extra fee, of course."

By that afternoon, Jo was standing before the camel she would ride. She assessed the height of the saddle nestled up against the camel's hump. She could barely reach the blanket that hung down between the saddle horns. The camel shifted and bawled. She jumped back.

The owner gave a command and brought all six animals to the ground. At close range, they mesmerized Jo with their soft, doe-like eyes, their long, curling double lashes, and the knowing, Mona Lisa smiles on their lips. She tried to work out in her mind exactly how she would get on, for the saddles were still at least four feet from the ground. The nearest camel turned toward her, jaws moving around a piece of cud. Again, she backed up several paces, and sought out Harry. Perhaps they should ride together.

Everyone promptly agreed. They would double up: Kathleen and Rick, Mary and Peaches, Jo and Harry.

Harry straddled the camel first, and gave Jo a hand, settling her in front. When everyone was ready, the owner gave another command. The animals rose on their back legs. Jo pitched forward, clinging to the blanket to keep from falling. It was like riding a bronco. She tightened her grip, a little frightened at how high she was when the camel's front legs came up and her perch evened out.

The camels walked single file into the Helmand Valley, plodding through crumbling dirt, dust, and sand. The fine, porous ground was almost white, as if bleached by the sun, and extended to a line in the distance where it met the sky. There were no trails, buildings, or compounds, only the Helmand River in the distance and a bit of green around the irrigation canals.[24]

She and Harry talked for a while, but as they moved across the barren landscape, riding to a rhythm of undulating dips and sways, they fell into a companionable silence. Jo could feel him behind her, and she occasionally leaned back into his chest for support as the platform beneath her rolled and shifted. She wondered if his quiet mood had anything to do with Dr. King's assassination.

She turned her head sideways. "What was it like, Harry? What was it like for you growing up?"

Harry spoke softly when he answered, his deep voice right behind her. "The times with my family were great, but my parents—you know, they carry a lot of baggage." He was quiet for a moment. "They saw things and heard things. Things they whispered about at night, thinking us kids were asleep and wouldn't hear. The Ku Klux Klan. Lynchings. But we heard anyway. I was barely a teenager when Emmett Till was murdered."

For a reason she couldn't name, Jo was glad Harry couldn't see her face. It was easier to talk that way. She thought about the civil rights movement—the Freedom Rides in 1961, the fire hoses and police dogs used against black demonstrators in Birmingham that same year. She had seen it all on TV, and while she was affected by what she saw, she didn't really understand what was at stake; it was too far removed from her world.

Now she saw it all through Harry's eyes: a world she hadn't known existed, or perhaps she knew all along, but didn't want to acknowledge the possibility such a dark place in human history was possible.

"My parents will carry their past with them to their graves," Harry continued. "But I always thought the next generation would be different. That I would be different. Martin Luther King gave us the freedom to hope. And his voice is gone."[25]

The desert stillness was like a presence that surrounded them, as if every sentient being stood silent, and every inanimate object rested in the fullness of being. Jo had a sense of stepping outside herself to become the observer of this moment in her life, a moment that never was before, and would never come again. She heard the camel's steps, barely audible, the leathery pads between their hooves imploding softly in the dust.

Eventually Jo and Harry went on to talk of other things, and as the hours passed without a familiar landmark, they began joking again, wondering if they were destined to ride the desert sands forever. Harry kept his eye on the horizon, staining to see through waves of heat. When the blurry outline of a station wagon came into view, he shouted to the riders behind them. "It's still there! I see it!"

The animals had been slow and lumbering through the desert, but coming back to the owner, they stretched their necks forward and picked up speed. Rick and Kathleen's camel caught up with Jo and Harry; Peaches and Mary were helpless to stop their camel as it nosed up even with the other two. The animals came to the owner three abreast.

Jo pitched forward and back again as the camel lowered its front and back legs respectively. She awkwardly slid off the saddle, happy to have her feet on solid ground.

The owner had been waiting patiently and now he was ready to be paid. "Six camels at twenty afghanis each," he said. "That's 120 afs."

"But we rode three camels," said Harry. "Sixty afs."

The owner waved his arm. *"Parwâ na dâra!"* —It doesn't matter. "You asked for six camels. 120 afs."

His insistence sparked a flash of anger in Jo. Our Peace Corps salary is a pittance, she thought. Just because we're American doesn't mean we can afford everything. "Three camels," she said. "Sixty afs."

The driver stood by his station wagon, ready for the return trip to Lashkar Gah. While everyone was arguing, he quietly opened the car door on the driver's side. He slid in behind the wheel, and watched the scene unfold through the front windshield. Now Mary was talking, almost even with the owner in height. Her gray bun bobbed up and down. The moment she handed over a wad of afs, he reached down and switched on the ignition.

The Americans turned and walked a few paces toward the station wagon. When they broke into a run, he put the car in gear. The Volunteers jumped in, laughing and landing in a heap. The camel owner shouted and grabbed a camel to chase after them, but he was too late. The driver had already pressed the accelerator, spinning tires and churning sand. The station wagon fish-tailed away with Harry still pulling the car door closed behind him.

The Volunteers may have gotten a bargain, but they paid for their experience in other ways. That evening, Jo wrote in her diary. *April 12: Still have diarrhea. Mary has a saddle sore.*

The trainees were down to the last few days in Kandahar. Jo found time to visit the bazaar and pick up the Karakul hat for her dad. It was beautifully crafted and neatly folded. She couldn't wait to ship it home.

On the last morning, everyone lingered over breakfast. For the past three weeks they had lived together, worked together, depended on each other, and taken care of each other when sick. Now that Provincial Training was finished, they were free to travel anywhere in Afghanistan, as long as they got themselves to Kabul by the end of the week.

Jo, Mary, and Peaches drew up plans to see as much of the country as possible in six days. First they would visit Herat, three hundred miles west of Kandahar, near the border of Iran. From there they would travel north to Mazar-e Sharif, and complete the circuit by coming back south to Kabul.

Jo intended to have an early night, for the bus was leaving at 5 a.m., and she was already having qualms about an eight-hour ride through the desert. Once again however, doors were left open and people stopped in to visit for the last time. Harry came with several friends to say goodbye; he would not be going to Herat with them, but he would see them in Kabul.

They went down the list of Volunteers. Nan was leaving Jalalabad to go up north, someone heard, and Carter planned to meet up with Jo and Mary when they got to Mazar-e Sharif.

Once again, Jo felt everyone was scattering to the four winds. It was a strange lifestyle, with people constantly moving in and out of her life. She looked forward to getting her permanent assignment. Maybe then she could finally settle down.

Late that night, she got out her journal. Although she had already recorded the events of her experience in Kandahar, she wanted to add a conclusion, a reflection of all she had done. It occurred to her the pivotal entries were not about her work in the hospital at all, but rather about how close she had come to quitting, the acceptance of help from her friends, and how much she loved the bazaar. She thought about her conversation with Harry and wondered if someone could truly walk in anyone else's shoes.

She looked at her watch. Midnight, and she had not written a thing. They were leaving in five hours. She simply could not capture it all, so she picked up her pen and made her entry. *April 19, 1968: Crammed everything into a suitcase and Peaches cut my hair.*

Chapter 7

SIX DAYS AND SEVEN NIGHTS

Woke up at 4:45 am and started out on a crowded Afghan bus to Herat. Everyone was coughing (probably TB) and as the ride went on the women took off their burqas and talked to us.

—April 20, 1968

A blazing red crescent broke over the horizon. It spoke wordlessly to desert rock and sand. The hills replied, bathed in pink and gold reflected light. A bird twittered once from the compound wall and flew away.

Jo picked up her suitcase and stood in line behind Peaches and Mary, unconsciously gripping the handle more tightly than necessary. The road to Herat meandered for three hundred miles through a hot, stony, and unforgiving desert. She regarded the approaching bus with skepticism. It would not have air conditioning, she was certain of that much, and as it rattled to a stop she closed her eyes, waiting for the swirling cloud of dust behind it to billow forward and dissipate. She nervously wondered who would contact her parents not if, but when the worst happened—when they all died of thirst somewhere in the unmarked expanse of southern Afghanistan.

The door opened. Peaches stepped inside, then quickly backed out, bumping into Mary, who stood behind her. Mary stepped back and almost knocked Jo over.

Jo craned her head and peered into the bus. Every seat was filled, but the Afghans cheerfully waved them inside. "*Dâkhel shawêd*," they said. — Come in. Already they were moving to make room for the Americans, shoving belongings into piles, picking up toddlers, and stacking wooden crates filled with live birds, mostly quail.

Dâkhel shawêd! Come in! Come in! The Farsi words were as welcome to Jo as English. No more pantomimes trying to communicate. No more stumbling over unintelligible Pashtu. She squeezed into a seat next to Mary, behind an Afghan man, his three wives, nine children, and one bird.

One of the children, a toddler with a round face and huge brown eyes, turned and stared at the strange women behind him.

Mary smiled and raised her eyebrows, coaxing him to smile in return.

"*Nam-e shomâ chist?*" asked Jo. —What's your name?

The brown eyes soberly moved from Mary to Jo. "Abdul."

"Well, Abdul, *shomâ chand sâl dârêd?*" —How old are you?

"*Panj.*" —Five.

That was enough conversation for Abdul; he turned to the safety of his mother, hiding his face in the folds of her burqa. However, curiosity and the boredom of a long trip meant that inevitably he peeked over the seat again. Mary gave him another engaging smile and held out her hands. This time Abdul lifted his arms to be picked up. He was barefoot and wore a little tunic and miniature tombans.

"*Asalâmu alaykum.*" Jo greeted the mother as she turned around to help lift Abdul over the back of the seat.

A disembodied voice came from under the burqa. "*Alaykum asalâm.*"

Jo averted her eyes from the intricately crocheted opening, aware that she had been staring. The latticed panel was smaller than the size of a post-card, and Jo couldn't tell if the young mother was smiling or fearful as she handed her son over to the *khareji* —the foreigners.

The physical impediments to a woman in a burqa are obvious. She is confined, the air hot and suffocating under layers of fabric. The cap fits tightly around her head, often causing massive headaches. She has no peripheral vision—dangerous enough when crossing streets and walking through the bazaar, but there are other, insidious consequences. She can see only what is in front of her. If she hears a voice from the side and turns to identify the speaker, her intentions are revealed. She cannot look at anything or anyone freely. She never knows who may be watching.

The bus continued west, past Lashkar Gah and into the desert, through a monotonous panorama of spiny tamarisk shrubs and tufts of camel grass dotting a parched landscape. The odor of sweat and dust mingled with a faint bird smell from the quail, the wooden crates stacked three and four high. Abdul returned to his mother. A baby started to cry. Open windows brought in drafts of hot air. The sun blazed unimpeded in a cerulean sky until it seemed they traveled in a heated tin box.

A hundred miles past Lashkar Gah, near the town of Delaram, the road turns north toward Herat. At that juncture the driver pulled over and stopped. They were at a *chai-khana* —a teahouse.

Jo would have overlooked the place entirely. There was nothing to indicate the one-room adobe building was inhabited, much less open for business. An overhang had been added to the structure, supported by thin wooden poles. Extending from the flat roof, it cast a small area of shade in the dust.

The men rose from their seats and filed off the bus. They would have their food and tea, and when they had finished, they would return with something for their wives and children. Denied access to a *chai-khana*, the women were left to deal with crying babies and squirming toddlers.

As Westerners and as honorary men, the American women were free to do as they pleased, but Jo found the situation untenable. Until now, she had been vigilant at keeping herself emotionally detached, unwilling to jeopardize the fierce grip she had on her own independence. She would never be subservient or inferior, less important simply because she was a woman.

Anticipating her nursing school, she thought about the Afghan students in Kabul, the women in Western dress getting on a city bus, and wondered what it would be like—if she would teach a new generation of young women who no longer wore the burqa, or even the chador, for that matter.

Mary and Peaches stood to follow the men into the teahouse, but Jo couldn't move, feeling as if she had been caught in a terrible quandary. If she sat with the men, did it mean she had abandoned the women? If she stayed on the bus, would she simply condone the men's behavior? Still conflicted, she slowly got to her feet.

The American women joined the Afghan men around the perimeter of a dusty carpet. They sat on the ground, in the little square of shade from the mats and branches that covered the flimsy overhang. The men were solicitous of the Americans, but Jo couldn't help thinking about the arbitrary twist of fate that governed every woman in Afghanistan; how the happenstance of birth dictated whether she was free or restricted; whether she ate with the men or waited on a hot bus.

The Afghan women were eventually served their food and tea. In preparation for their own meal, and in order to feed the children, they flipped the shorter, front part of their burqas up over their caps much like a wedding veil, and left the fabric draped over their shoulders. Individual faces materialized. Personalities emerged. Some of the women were openly curious, asking the Americans questions; others hid bashful smiles behind a hand.

The trip resumed. The wives left their veils off, facilitating conversation with the Americans. The two groups of women entertained the kids for hours. They played games with them, listened to their little songs in Farsi, and laughed as the younger ones showed off for a new audience. The Americans held the babies. The wives pointed out which of the children were theirs.

The Afghan women were distinct individuals. And yet, when the bus roared through the city gates of Herat that evening, they lowered their veils once again, and stepped off as anonymous black or blue-shrouded figures.

~ひ~

Herat was an oasis. A least that's how Jo viewed her surroundings. The Volunteers were in a gaudie first thing the next morning, riding on a wide avenue lined on both sides with a double row of trees. The branches almost touched overhead, the leaves rustling as sunlight danced between them, dappling carriage and horse with shifting patterns of light and shade. The clip-clop of hooves rang out a staccato rhythm, the horse's head reaching forward and up with every prancing step.

Before the sun went down that evening, the Volunteers had seen ancient Islamic tombs, watched ceramic tile craftsmen at work, toured mosques, shopped bazaars, and walked through modern city parks.

"Herat in a day," whispered Peaches as they climbed into their gaudie for the last time. Enchanted with the city, she impulsively decided she would stay, and not move on with the rest of the group.

Jo and Mary elected to keep their original plans. They would continue on to Mazar-e Sharif, where Carter would be waiting for them. They also agreed to fly this time, booking a flight on Ariana Airlines.[26]

They traveled in a Convair two-engine plane, and as they headed northeast, almost to the Russian border, they left the gentle rolling plains of Herat behind them. The landscape changed yet again, the terrain becoming rugged and untamed, with low-lying brush partially covering the jagged talus and rock at the base of the Hindu Kush.

Other differences became evident on the ride to the hotel. For the first time since arriving in Afghanistan, Jo saw new construction. They passed road crews, the men working alongside massive earth moving equipment and Soviet military trucks. The modern buildings, new infrastructure, and ribbons of black asphalt looked out of place in the ancient landscape.

Carter met them as soon as the driver pulled in. He reached for Mary's bag and took it from her hand. "How are you? And Kandahar? How was it?"

They gathered in his room, where the exchange of questions and answers continued. Jo told him a little about the hospital, and their struggles with Pashtu and the graduate nurses. They laughed over the Camel Incident.

Mary wanted to know about Jalalabad. "And what about Nan? Did she like it? Were the people friendly?"

"Nan loved it all." Carter laughed. "She will have some great stories when we get to Kabul. Remind her to tell you what it was like to meet a village mullah."

"I can't wait," said Jo. "We all have a story, that's for sure. But what's going on around here?" She glanced toward the door, as if someone might be listening. "The Soviet trucks? The construction?"

The smile faded somewhat from Carter's face. "I'm not sure what it means, exactly. The Afghans don't talk about it much. Everybody seems to be conducting business as usual."

He regarded the women closely, gauging their reaction. "I don't see any reason to change our plans. If you're up for it, I made arrangements for a tour of the Blue Mosque tomorrow, and the ruins at Balk the day after that. I'm sure we'll be safe with our guide."

~⌒◦⌒~

Built in AD 1136, the Friday Blue Mosque in Mazar-e Sharif is believed to be the burial place of Ali ibn Abi Talib, the son-in-law of the Prophet Muhammad. Jo crossed the courtyard, her eyes drawn to the domes and arches, covered with thousands of hand-painted turquoise and cobalt-blue tiles, the colors stunning in the Afghan sun. The Volunteers followed their guide through antechambers and tomb chambers—everywhere but the main prayer room. As non-Muslims, they were not permitted to enter. Jo listened as the guide spoke.

"An ordinary businessman," he said. "The Prophet Muhammad was an ordinary businessman who lived in Mecca over a thousand years ago." The guide went on to explain that in 610 AD, Muhammad fasted and prayed, reflecting on the fact that his tribe, the Quraysh, had become wealthy from decades of trading. But instead of looking after the weaker members of the tribe, as the nomadic code prescribed, the Quraysh were intent on making money at the expense of the poorer families.

After praying, Muhammad fell asleep. He woke to an overwhelming presence, a spirit so powerful he heard the first words of a new scripture pouring forth from his own lips. Muhammad could not read or write, so he kept quiet about his experience until AD 612, when he began teaching his new scripture, the Quran.

According to the Quran, it is wrong to build a private fortune; rather, men are called to share wealth and create a society where the weak and vulnerable are treated with respect.

"The new sect would be called Islam," the guide concluded. "*Islam* means "surrender," and a Muslim is a man or woman who submits to Allah's demand that human beings treat one another with justice, equity, and compassion."[27]

Jo emerged from the mosque, and surveyed the rows of shoes awaiting them. We are the same, she thought, as she found hers and put them on. East or West, Christian or Muslim, we have the same core values. And yet, there seemed to be a gap, a piece missing from the moral principles of compassion, justice, and equity. *What about the women?*[28]

She walked through a final archway and into the courtyard. A few worshippers walked slowly across the stone; a little girl and her brother played with flash cubes from a camera, carelessly discarded by a tourist. A couple of white doves fluttered in front of her. Then without warning, birds from everywhere rose into the air with a massive whoosh, startled by a droning sound in the distance.

Jo looked up. Three planes flew abreast, advancing directly toward the mosque. The planes expanded as they came closer, filling the sky, flying so low she could make out the USSR insignia on each aircraft. She stood rooted to the spot, paralyzed by the noise, the swiftness of their appearance, and her own fear. The planes were Soviet MIGs, and she instinctively ducked at the last minute when they buzzed the courtyard with a deafening roar, pulled up steeply, and disappeared into the sky.

It took several minutes for the ordinary street sounds to resurface: traffic, conversation, and the occasional birdsong. The afternoon sun shrouded

Mazar-e Sharif in a soft hazy light, accentuated by the ever-present dust in the air. It was as if the planes had never appeared.

The city returned to normal, everyday life on that particular afternoon in 1968, but the Soviet presence foreshadowed disaster for Afghanistan. Within a few years the airport in Mazar-e Sharif would become a strategic air base for the Soviet military.[29]

Long after they returned to the hotel and had dinner, Jo was still unnerved. She slept fitfully, turning from side to side, trying to recall the tree-lined streets of Herat, or the brilliance of the Friday Blue Mosque, but the images would not come to her. Instead, the MIGs appeared again and again in her dreams, flying closer each time, until it seemed she could make out the dimpled lines of rivets in the fuselage. Not until the shadowy grayness of early dawn filtered through the windows did she fall into a quiet and dreamless sleep.

She woke to a room flooded with sunlight. A dull ache throbbed in her temples. Her eyes felt puffy and she rubbed them, trying to clear her head. In broad daylight, she wondered if the show of military force had been nothing more than her imagination. She looked over at Mary's bed. It was empty.

She dressed quickly, knowing they had planned another day of sightseeing. Another day, another adventure, she thought sardonically. But maybe today would be less exciting. Maybe their trip to Balk, trekking through forgotten ruins—supposedly the site of the oldest city in the world—would be less eventful.

Mary and Carter were on their second cup of coffee and deep in conversation when Jo sat down to join them. She listened as she poured her own coffee and buttered a piece of nân.

"I heard there's not much left except piles of stone and rubble," Carter was saying. "I hope we're not disappointed."

"Well, what do you expect?" Jo sipped her coffee. "After all, it's how old?" She set down her cup. "Four thousand years?"[30]

The driver picked them up in his Jeep shortly after breakfast and took them to an uninhabited area in the countryside. He stopped by a nondescript, abandoned field. The Volunteers got out and wandered in the empty space, not sure which way to go. Jo climbed over a ridge. Her foot slipped on some loose rock, and she almost fell. Carter was right, she thought. There's nothing here but a mass of ruin and rubble. Weather-beaten walls encircled a field of dry scrub plants, and she found it hard to believe the walls had enclosed a city of 200,000 inhabitants in the Middle Ages, or that the mounds of debris had been Buddhist shrines during the seventh century.

The Volunteers walked through the field for hours, taking advantage of the privacy and a chance to talk freely. They discussed the Soviet presence in Afghanistan, what it meant to the average Afghan, and whether it would jeopardize the role of the Peace Corps. They talked about their return to Kabul, the exams awaiting them, the final selection board, and possible assignments. Occasionally, they sifted through a few bits of rubble, hoping to find a broken piece of pottery.[31]

The driver waited without complaint, giving no indication he was in a hurry or impatient for the Volunteers to finish their exploration. When they returned to the Jeep and thanked him for his understanding, he merely shrugged. Why worry? "*Parwâ na dâra*," he said. —It doesn't matter.

On the way back to the hotel, Jo watched the passing landscape from the open sides of the Jeep, the vast foothills and steppes, the immense sky, and the peaks of the Hindu Kush in the background. With the wind in her face as the driver picked up speed, she thought about Balk and its history of four thousand years. No wonder the Afghans never complained about waiting. In comparison, a few hours were insignificant. We're all tiny specks on the continuum of history, she mused. A lifetime is a moment. Eventually every living person follows the journey of the ancients.

Jo had almost completed her circuit of the country. A short jog east to Kunduz, and the next day she was in a taxi heading south toward Kabul. She sat with four Peace Corps Volunteers in the back seat. Three Russians and the driver sat in the front. They drove through Baghlan Valley, the town of

Baghlan itself, and the smaller village of Fabrika. Jo wondered aloud if any of the Volunteers might be so lucky as to get an assignment in this area. It was a beautiful valley, she noted. Someone asked about the fields, the rows of small plants just peeking above the ground. What were they?

"Beets," the driver told them. *Bôra.* —Sugar beets.

Once past Baghlan they entered the foothills of the Hindu Kush. The temperature had been close to 100 degrees Fahrenheit on the valley floor; by 11,000 feet, they were driving among snow-covered peaks.

They passed through the Salang Tunnel, and started the descent into Kabul, finally entering the city in a light, misty rain. Jo wiped the fog and moisture from her window to get a better look. The streets and buildings had changed, or perhaps she was seeing them differently. In either case it seemed Kabul had become cleaner and more welcoming during her absence. The Ashraf Hotel had the familiarity of an old friend, and taking her bags up the stairs to her room, Jo felt as if she were coming home. She heard voices down the hall.

"Nan!" she called out. "Peaches! Is that you!?"

Chapter 8

JALALABAD

... The rest of the day was spent bumming and talking over experiences with the other people, some of whom we hadn't seen for over a month.
—April 26, 1968

Nan sat on the checkered linoleum floor of the hotel room, propped up against Jo's dresser. Mary sat on her charpoy bed, with Charlotte Budum next to her. Jo refrained from bouncing on her own bed, thinking how comfortable the room felt, how different it was from her first night in Afghanistan, when she and Mary slept in their coats and sleeping bags.

Final exams were the next day, and although Jo thought briefly about studying, she was more interested in talking. If she hadn't learned anything else in Kandahar, she learned how important her friends were.

Harry was sprawled on the floor, leaning back on his elbows. He listened as Jo described the bazaar in Kandahar, and the day she turned around from a display of cardamom to face a crowd of Afghans, staring at her in curiosity.

"I know!" Harry came up to a sitting position. "I know exactly what you mean. Just wait until you hear what happened to me." He gestured toward Nan. "She was behind me, and saw it all. We were taking a bike ride, minding our own business, when this Afghan kid pedaled his bike right up and joined us. He rode next to me with his head sideways, staring at me." Harry's eyes opened wide at the memory. "He came so close we almost bumped handlebars."

Jo couldn't help herself. "And?"

"And then he disappeared. I heard a thunk, a splash, and he was gone." Harry allowed himself a grin. "He ran smack into a street sign and fell into the juie. I turned around and there he was—waist deep in water, fishing out his prayer cap and turban."

Even though Nan had seen the incident first-hand, she laughed all over again, entertained by Harry's rendition. "There's so much to remember," she said. "All the things we saw in Jalalabad. The places we went. The things we did."

"The trip we took to see the Kuchies, for one thing," said Budum. "Remember the nomad camps? The tents pitched across the fields? And the camels!"[32]

"How could I forget?" Nan laughed again. "One of the Kutchie men picked me up like I was a little kid and hoisted me onto a saddle." She stopped, then continued in a subdued tone, almost as if talking to herself. Her voice held a note of wonder, and she described the scene as if describing a painting. "The surrounding landscape was so green. It looked like a garden with mountains in the background—like biblical times. The Kutchie men had robes and turbans. The women wore dresses over turquoise tombans. They left their faces uncovered, and wore silver bracelets on their arms. They had such a proud carriage, and their eyes were so intense—oh, maybe it was their weathered features that made it seem that way, but they were magnificent, in my opinion." Nan unconsciously straightened her shoulders. "I could feel the heat and smell the dust," she blurted out. "I do love this place."

The words had come uncensored, but Nan recovered quickly, and turned the conversation away from herself.

"Okay, Jo—so tell us about Kandahar."

Jo shook her head, not wanting to spoil the mood. "You first," she countered. "What about Jalalabad? The lab? The hospital?"

"Well …" Nan settled back against the dresser. Like everyone else in the room that day, she struggled to make sense of what she had seen. "It was terrible, and sad, and funny, all at the same time. A comedy of errors. Like a Peter Sellers movie, or a Keystone Kops comedy."

She leaned forward. "Okay. Here's a perfect example. One of the nurse's aides took an OB patient to the delivery room one day, and zigzagged down the hall so out of control he ran the cart into the wall. But that's not all. He backed up to get a running start for the delivery room, but didn't bother to check if the swinging door was locked." Nan ran her hands through her hair as if that would keep her from laughing. "He banged into the door so hard the patient bounced off the cart and onto the floor."

Even Mary, with her vested interest in obstetrics, was caught between a horrified expression and a stifled laugh, suppressed with her fingertips. "So what happened then?"

"We got her back onto the cart, unlocked the door, and went into the delivery room. We were putting her feet in stirrups when the doc came in, gloved and ready to go." Nan shook her head. "I guess he wanted to be a nice guy. He took off one of his gloves, stuffed it into his pocket and helped us position the patient. All fine—except he didn't bother to get another sterile glove for the delivery. He pulled the contaminated glove out of his pocket!"

Jo commiserated. "I'm not surprised. The docs go through the motions for sterile technique, but I don't think they really get it."

"They're just starting out," said Nan. "I mean, they're doing the best they can. They have no money and no education. Anyway, believe it or not, our patient ended up with a healthy baby girl."

"It's complicated, isn't it?" Jo thought about her struggles with the graduate nurses, and how close she had come to quitting. "While we were in Kandahar, I thought it was awful, but looking back, there was so much to learn … and it went by so fast!"

There was a general chorus of agreement.

"Even the week of travel flew by," said Nan. "All of a sudden it was over and we were in a taxi, riding through Baghlan and back to Kabul."

"You went through Baghlan?" Jo was immediately curious to hear Nan's impression of the area. "Isn't it beautiful?"

"Oh, it is," agreed Nan. "Our taxi stopped outside the village for a picnic lunch, and a couple of students came round to practice English. And do you know what they asked us? If we knew Mr. Bing."

"Oh, my God!" Jo sat straight up on her bed. "He saved my life! I was sick—really sick with dysentery, and he brought me some white bread from the USAID compound."

"Well, it has to be years since he taught in Baghlan, and that's all the students talked about. Like his time in their village was the most important event in the history of Afghanistan."

Nan leaned back against the dresser and folded her arms. "And me? I hope I never have to go back."

Budum explained. "The village mullah came to meet us, and well, no surprise. Nan had to be the first one to step up and put out her hand."

"Who knew?" Nan arched an eyebrow. "Who knew as a woman you don't touch a mullah? He covered his knuckles with the sleeve of his robe and barely made contact with my hand as a sort of handshake. It was very embarrassing."

Budum started to laugh. "Nan couldn't wait to get out of there. Our taxi was parked on the other side of the juie, but she was in such a hurry she didn't bother walking to the nearest crossing. Instead, she jumped."

"I didn't quite make it." Nan smiled at herself. "I landed on the other side all right, but in the thickest, sloppiest mud you ever saw. It almost sucked both shoes off my feet when I crawled up the bank. And of course everyone was watching. Thank God they'll never see me again!"

Even as she laughed with the rest of the group, Jo had a flash of insight. Nan always seemed to see the positive—often comic—side of things, no matter what the situation. Jo listened as Nan continued her description of Jalalabad, talking about the bazaars, and how cute the little kids were, speaking in Farsi with their tiny voices.

She was beguiled by Nan's storytelling. They all were, but at the same time, a part of Jo's mind processed a fundamental truth: they each coped with the hardships of Afghanistan in their own way. Some were better equipped than others, and as she observed Nan, she concluded there was more to her friend than a gregarious personality and a sense of humor.

I can learn a lot from Nan, she thought. Instead of struggling to change things, Nan accepts things for what they are and makes the best of them.

~✦~

The soft murmur of voices seeped through closed hotel room doors that night, creating a hushed atmosphere in the hallway. The Volunteers were somber as they prepared for the next day, but Mary especially looked tired, a little older, withdrawing into herself as if preparing for the inevitability of bad news.

"You'll be fine, Mary." Jo sounded more confident than she felt. "Just remember, you know midwifery and women's health better than any one of us."

There was a knock at the door, and Peaches stepped in to say good night. "I can't study one more minute."

Jo agreed. "I know. The more I read, the more I second-guess everything. But no matter what happens tomorrow, I'll never forget these past few weeks. Besides, I can't wrap my head around it—living here for two years. And where will I go?"

"That's the easy part for me," said Peaches. "Just like I thought, I'll be at the Peace Corps office here in Kabul."

"How can you be so sure?"

"Well, the Peace Corps staff gave me a tour of the office yesterday, so I take that as a pretty good sign. You should see how busy they are—Volunteers come and go like it's a revolving door. The nurses and secretaries are constantly on the go, dispensing malaria medicine, giving advice, helping with exit physicals and paperwork, you name it."

Peaches lowered her voice. "They do everything there. And I do mean *everything*, if you know what I mean. The adjoining medical suite is the depository for stool specimens—they go to the American Embassy twice a week to be tested for parasites. Anyway, yesterday was a pickup day, and there were about a dozen stool cups lined up in front of the door. When the Volunteer unlocked the office, she looked at me and said, 'See? Every other secretary in the world gets flowers. All I ever get is shit!'"

Jo went to bed laughing, but with Peaches back in her own room, it suddenly got very quiet. She lay awake in the dark, wondering what the next day would bring.

Board exams for Group Thirteen were given on April 29, 1968. Jo wrote the last answer, and leaned back in the chair, stretching her back. Training was over.

Some Volunteers went to bed that night with confidence; others agonized over real and imagined wrong answers. Every possibility flitted through Jo's mind. She tried to imagine Peaches behind a desk at the Peace Corps office. Then she tried to imagine herself working somewhere in Afghanistan, and wondered who would be assigned with her. She tried not to think about the possibility of failing the test and being sent home.

Chapter 9

EXODUS

Received my letter of acceptance from the Peace Corps, but eight train-ees were deselected and two more left voluntarily. … It's a day of mixed emotions.

—April 30, 1968

The classroom at the Ashraf erupted with shouts and cheers. Volunteers ran in circles, calling out names, looking for one another. They had frenetic, disjointed conversations to compare assignments and exchange information. *Where are you going? Who's going with you?*

Mary stood quietly while the activity swarmed around her, lips pursed, her blue eyes glittering with unshed tears. She had been accepted. Her assignment: Baghlan.

"I knew it!" Jo impulsively stood on tiptoes and threw her arms around the older woman. "I knew you could do it."

Then she looked for Nan, shouting as she made her way through the constantly moving clusters of people. "Nan!"

"Over here!" Nan waved her letter in the air. "Well, wouldn't you know," she said, laughing. "I'm going to Baghlan, after all!"

Jo hopped a little in excitement. "Me, too." Before there was time to say anything else, Peaches came up to them, clutching her own letter.

"No surprises for me. I'll be at the Peace Corps office right here in Kabul."

"Great." Nan grinned at her. "We'll count on you to keep us up to date—you know—with all the news from headquarters. And you can visit us. Come to Baghlan as soon as we get settled."

Jo's racing thoughts came to an immediate stop. With Nan's offhand remark, euphoria collided with reality. *As soon as we get settled.* They were truly going to live in Afghanistan for the next two years. From a sudden maelstrom of emotion came thoughts of her family, and the compelling desire to let them know she had been accepted. The voices around her began to spin to the periphery of her consciousness. She wanted to get away and be alone for a little while. She would write to her folks. No—she would make a tape; that way she could tell them everything.

Acceptance letters went out that day to almost everyone who was still left in Group Thirteen—approximately fifty Volunteers out of the original seventy. Not included were the few individuals who had been deselected after the final test. They had been notified privately, and had a very different conversation as they packed to leave Afghanistan. Their voices carried down the hall, and Jo could not avoid hearing them as she came up the stairs.

"Now!? They're telling us *now?*" Jo heard something thrown onto the floor; a drawer slammed shut. "Deselection—I hate that word! You know what? I'm done. Yeah, I'm glad it's over. I wouldn't stay now if they begged me."

Deselection. It had haunted them from the very first day of training. When the Volunteers had arrived in Estes Park, it had been with a sense they were called to do something vitally important. Most of them had been regarded as celebrities when they left home: heroes and adventurers. They were under enormous pressure to live up to the expectation they would be successful. No one wanted the stigma of having to go back and explain to family and friends they would not be serving in the Peace Corps, after all.

Jo let herself into her room and closed the door, wondering what she would say to her own parents, and how she would tell them about her final acceptance. She retrieved her tape player from under the bed and inserted a blank cassette, then dragged a chair out to the balcony. She was alone at last.

No one was there to see how she brought both hands up to her eyes, as if the pressure could stop hot tears from seeping between her fingers. In the few hours since receiving the letter, her emotions had taken her on a wild ride, swinging from elation at being accepted to panic at the commitment she was about to make. Things were suddenly out of control. She thought about the trainees who had been deselected at the last minute, and although she was relieved not to be one of them, she also knew they would be going home, and a small part of her wanted to go with them.

Thoughts of home seemed incongruous with the view of the Hindu Kush and the Afghan rooftops below her. The air was cool and pleasant on the balcony, and birds chirped nearby. How could she have been here only seven weeks? When she considered all she had seen, it seemed she had been in Afghanistan forever.

She pressed the "Record" button and brought the reels of tape spinning to life. "*Asalâmu alaykum!*" Her voice was clear, youthful, and a little breathless.

A tapestry of sound accompanied her narrative: chittering birds and the rush of city traffic—trucks shifting gears, cars honking, and the ring of bicycle bells. She read her acceptance letter into the microphone, and when she came to the end, she hastily turned off the tape, not to collect her thoughts, but to control her emotions. She still had a great deal she wanted to say, and didn't want her voice to betray her.

There wasn't much time. Within days they would be leaving Kabul. Turning on the tape once again, she reported with a steady voice, "I am being sent to Baghlan, which is a fantastic opportunity. I'll be going with a medical team to set up a rural health clinic and provide public health teaching."

She explained the Peace Corps would be working with resources from the World Health Organization and the Afghan government to establish a demonstration project in the Baghlan Valley. The local hospital would serve as the nucleus for the project, and she would be instrumental in starting a nursing school for young Afghan women. She spoke with more confidence about the impending move and what she would take with her: kerosene lanterns, an electric hot plate, supplies, books, and personal effects. After living out of a suitcase for the past six weeks, they were all impatient for a place of their own, she said, a place to call home, where they could settle down and get to know the community.

"Five of us are going to Baghlan," she reported. "Mary, Nan, and myself. And a married couple. They're coming too. Kathleen's a nurse. Rick teaches English."

She went on to ask about various family members and friends back home—her grandmother's health, her sister Jackie's new job. She asked about her dog, the Yorkshire terrier she had to leave behind. "I miss him," she said. "The dogs here are juie dogs. They run wild, and scavenge for any scrap of food they can find. Someone rescued a juie puppy, and I'm taking him with me to Baghlan. You should see him! His face is white with brown ears, and there's a little brown spot beneath each eye. I've named him Alex."

She was almost to the end of the tape and felt that even though she had related a great deal of information to her family, she still had not done justice to her experience, or to the Afghan people. With the exception of the Afghan nurses in Kandahar, everyone had been friendly and welcoming.

A couple of Afghans passed beneath the balcony and looked up at the sound of her voice. Aware of how odd she must appear to them, talking out loud with no one else around, Jo turned off the microphone.

I might as well add curious, she thought, waiting for them to pass by. Insatiably curious. She wondered if she could explain that part to her family, how they sometimes stared openly, their eyes traveling from the shoes on her feet to the top of her head and back down again. And yet, the Afghans have gone out of their way to make us feel at home, she mused.

Her words tumbled out as she turned on the tape recorder for the last time and described how the Volunteers had been received.

"The people are so friendly and hospitable. They bend over backwards for you. They feel you have put yourself out to be here in the first place and are always asking, 'Are you happy? What can I do to make you happier?'"

She felt intensely the exchange of knowledge went both ways, and the Afghans had much to offer. She continued. "At home, we don't even notice what kind of day it is, or what the weather is like. But the Afghans live right off the earth. They live with the elements and are very, very close to God. They live their religion. They live a simple life yet have so much to share. Two things we can learn from them: Don't be in such a hurry to get nowhere, and have confidence things will work out over time."

In the last remaining minutes on the tape, she talked about the letters she had received from home and how much she appreciated hearing from everyone. She related how the handwriting on each envelope was as distinctive as individual voices. "I save them until I'm alone," she said, "and then I read them, and read them again."

With her final remarks, she reassured her family that she would be okay. To her sister especially, she pleaded, "Jackie, don't worry about me. Sure, I'm a little homesick. I look at my watch and think—what time is it at home? What are they doing now? But I haven't cried yet. It will be better when we get our own house. So please, don't worry. Really, I'm fine."[33]

Jo stopped the tape and finally allowed the tears to flow. She didn't know why she was crying. It was not one single thing she could name, and at the same time it was everything. She cried with relief because she had been accepted; she cried because she was homesick and afraid of the unknown. For the Volunteers who were going home, and the Afghans who had so little. For no one and everyone.

Within hours the Volunteers were back in the classroom at the Ashraf, attending meetings and receiving final instructions. Jo was introduced to Ken, the medical director of the Peace Corps in Afghanistan, the person who would be her immediate supervisor. She had seen him around the Peace Corps office, and now, shaking his hand, she assessed his friendly, outgoing personality. He would be their link to Kabul—their lifeline—the person they would count on if they needed help. His fair complexion was sunburned from the Afghan sun, his sandy hair tousled as he moved among the Volunteers, answering questions and helping them prepare for the move to their assignments. He would escort some of the Volunteers himself, he said, those going north to Baghlan and Kunduz.

That afternoon they were officially sworn in at the home of Robert G. Newman, United States Ambassador to Afghanistan. After months of arduous training, Jo was surprised at the informality of the ceremony. A simple oath, with no fanfare. She raised her right hand and spoke these words:

> I, Joanne Carter, do solemnly swear or affirm that I will support and defend the Constitution of the United States against all enemies, domestic and foreign, that I take this obligation freely and without any mental reservation or purpose of evasion, and that I will well and faithfully discharge my duty to the Peace Corps by working with the people of Afghanistan as partners in friendship and peace.

Over the next week, Volunteers were deployed to villages and hamlets all over Afghanistan, effectively splitting up Group Thirteen for the last time.[34]

Those Volunteers going to Puli-Khumri, Kunduz, and Baghlan were combined into one group for the exodus from Kabul. Led by Ken, they drove out of the city in two station wagons and one pickup truck, heading north across the Hindu Kush Mountains. The vehicles followed each other in a tiny caravan, vulnerable and insignificant against the vast expanse of the Afghan landscape: eleven people, three dogs, bicycles, furniture, trunks, belongings, and equipment.

Chapter 10

STRANGERS IN A STRANGE LAND

You wouldn't believe the poor housing structures here. There are no window panes on the window openings and no wells or electricity. Rick and Kathleen's house looks like a palace compared to what we've seen.
—May 5, 1968

The owner shook his head. There was no well.

"*Barq?*" asked Nan. —Electricity?

"*Nê.*" No electricity either.

Jo bowed her head in disappointment. At the same time she felt like a snob, dismissing the Afghan homes as if she were too good to live in them.

The women pressed on. Perhaps the next house would be better. And when they walked through the doorway into an unusually large room, Nan raised her arms expansively. She turned in a little circle and grinned at Jo, teasing her. "Well, we'd have plenty of space."

Jo took in the dirt floor and remnants of straw, the faint outline of adobe brick on the walls. She thought she had seen everything, but evidently not. They were inspecting a building that had once housed livestock. She glanced over at the landlord.

He nodded, his turban moving up and down, his bright eyes riveted on her every move.

Jo gave him a weak, apologetic smile. "*Mota' asefam.*" —I'm sorry. "We're not going to rent your house."

The owner shrewdly looked at all three women, his eyebrows furrowed. Suddenly he brightened again. "*Hazâr afghanis,*" he offered. —One thousand afghanis.

Nan held up her hand, but the owner preempted her answer. "*Noh sad afghanis.*" —Nine hundred afghanis.

Nan spoke sotto voce. "How can we leave? I don't want to offend him."

By way of reply, Mary settled a wide-brimmed hat on her head and stepped forward. "*Bâmâni khodâ!*" —Goodbye! She gave the owner a little bow and vigorously pumped his hand. "*Tashakor.*" —Thank you.

The women emerged from the house and Mary adjusted her brim, pulling it forward to protect her sunburned nose and cheeks. Jo and Nan had teased her about the oversized hat, but now, almost blinded by the Afghan sun, Jo thought perhaps Mary had the right idea. What happened to the spring rains they had been warned about in training? It was the first week of May, and already it felt like summer.

They crossed a small juie and fell into step along a dirt road. Walking three abreast, they were quiet. No one had expected that finding a place to live would be such an issue, or that they would be stuck in temporary housing for so long.

Rick and Kathleen had been fortunate. They had simply taken over the lease on John Bing's old house. Jo, Nan, and Mary had moved into the only hotel in Baghlan—the Sugar Hotel, named for the sugar beet refinery in nearby Fabrika.

The women walked in silence across town. Three shadows moved in tandem beside them as if in empathy, the outline of Mary's hat rippling over stones, brush, and juie.

"I think I've changed my mind about the real estate market here," said Nan finally. "Remember what we thought of Rick and Kathleen's house?"

"I remember," said Jo. She remembered only too well how excited they had been to unload the truck and station wagons; how Ken's sandy red hair had been more disheveled than usual, his fair complexion flushed with exertion as he and Rick wrestled with the heavy Peace Corps trunks. And then she had carried an armload of bedding into the house and saw it for herself: the dusty windows, soot-covered walls, and concrete floors littered with sand, dried mud, and bits of ash.

"We thought it was awful," she said. "And *now* ... Well, now it's a palace compared to what we've seen."

A gaudie passed them, the clip-clop of hooves muted by dust, the bells fading into the distance. Gone were the sounds of Kabul, the buses, trucks, honking horns, and throngs of humanity. Gone too, were the tree-lined avenues of Herat. All had been replaced by dirt roads and the quiet sounds of the village. An occasional rooster crow and the sporadic bark of a juie dog underscored the emptiness and isolation surrounding them. A group of barefoot children dressed in little tunics and tombans played in a nearby field, interrupting their game to stare at the foreigners—three women in Western dress looking out of place in the mostly deserted road.

⚬⚬⚬

The women elected to have dinner on the balcony of their hotel room that evening. The platform was not much more than a concrete ledge with a small railing, but still, it provided a view of the open fields behind the building, and a chance to get out of a stuffy room. Mary served their meal out of a tin can while they gathered around a small table.

"Just a minor setback, that's all." Nan accepted her plate from Mary.

Jo took her own plate. "A minor setback? We don't have a place to live, for God's sake. All we have is a hotel room without running water. And we're eating canned stew that's been warmed over a hot plate. Face it. We're homeless."

"Not exactly *homeless*," said Nan. "We have each other. And you can't tell me there's not a house for us somewhere in this town."

"And in the meantime," said Mary, "nothing says we can't start to work."

Work? Jo pushed aside her plate of congealed food. This was all wrong. They weren't supposed to start their assignments—her nursing school, Mary's clinic, and Nan's lab—like this. They were supposed to be settled first, in a home of their own, not living in a hotel.

On the other hand, how long could they wait? Nan and Mary were already talking about a plan of action, and she allowed herself to be drawn into the conversation. Yes, they would pay a visit to the hospital, they decided. Meet with Dr. Ali, the medical chief of staff. Start plans for the nursing school. Check out the lab. Lay the groundwork for Mary's clinic.

～◠ᵛ◠～

Dr. Ali wore a black Western-style suit, with a white shirt and narrow black tie. He extended a hand first to Mary, then to Jo and Nan, the sleeves of his jacket barely coming to the end of his long arms. His straight, coal-black hair was combed back from his forehead, bringing the features of his cleanly shaven face into stark relief.

"*Khosh âmadêd,*" he said. —Welcome.

He gestured to the chairs in his office, then took a seat behind his desk. Wasting no time on preliminaries, he came straight to the point. "*Injâ,*" he said, looking at the women. —Here. He tapped the top of his desk. "I need nurses to work here."

Mary spoke the least Farsi, and yet it was Mary who responded first. "*Nê, nê … ghalat,*" she said, almost choking on the *gh*, the French *r* sound, the sound Jo had found so amusing in training. It was not so amusing now.

"No," repeated Mary in English. "You are mistaken. We are not here to work. We are here so that we can teach. Set up a clinic."

Dr. Ali stood abruptly, perhaps choosing not to understand her words, but in any case, effectively ending any further discussion. "Come," he said in heavily accented English. "I show you hospital."

From the outside, Baghlan Hospital reflected the architectural style typical for buildings constructed in the 1950s and 1960s. Much like the Sugar Hotel, the lines of concrete and steel were straight and functional, not graced with adornments or flourishes of any kind.

Inside, there was little to soften the concrete walls. Patient rooms were four-bed wards with a wood or coal-burning *bokhari* in each. A corridor led to the only operating room, which also served as the delivery room. Glass panes in the windows cranked open with a handle. There were no screens. Sinks and Western-style commodes were impressive, but useful only when there was electricity to run the water pump. No one ever heard of a hospital cafeteria. Central supply was a closet.

The classroom was on the second floor, with window openings that overlooked the main entrance of the hospital. Rows of student desks filled the room, and a free-standing chalkboard stood toward the front, next to a table for the teacher. Jo wanted to start immediately, impatient to see the desks filled with young women.

On the way back to the main level, Nan asked Dr. Ali about her lab.

"Oh, yes," he responded. "Yes, of course there is a lab."

The women almost trotted to keep up with his long, quick strides, catching up with him when he stopped at the doorway of a small room.

"Here you are," he said. "Here is your lab."

Nan assessed the equipment: a hand-cranked centrifuge, one antiquated microscope, a tiny sterilizer, and beakers covered with dust. She glanced at Jo as she turned to leave, the usual amusement in her eyes gone, replaced by a thoughtful, somber expression.

They finished the tour in Dr. Ali's office. Once again, he positioned himself behind his desk. He reached for a cigarette and left it dangling from his lips while he struck a match, then lowered his head toward the flame and inhaled. Holding his breath, he leaned back and crossed his legs, appraising the women before he exhaled.

He knows exactly what he's doing, thought Jo. He's in charge, and he wants to make sure we understand.

After another long drag on his cigarette, Dr. Ali spoke in a mixture of rapid Farsi and broken English, the words shooting out on little puffs of smoke. He reiterated the same point in both languages. It could not be misunderstood this time. He wanted the women to begin working immediately. He desperately needed nurses and someone to manage the lab. The Volunteers could live at the hospital.

Nan flushed, and with an effort to keep her voice steady, she said, "My purpose is not to work alone, Dr. Ali. The Peace Corps sent me here so I can work with students. Train lab technicians."

Mary added a last comment. "And we cannot live at the hospital."

Dr. Ali remained impassive. He stood and thanked the women for coming, making it clear they were dismissed. Then, with an imperial wave of his hand, he simply concluded the interview.

Jo left his office not exactly sure of the final outcome. Was he indicating they could teach after all? Or did he plan to ignore them until he got his way?

Mary turned on the hot plate and made tea as soon as they got back to the hotel, and once again they sat out on the balcony, gathered around the table. Thickening clouds dimmed the afternoon light, and a gray fog swirled around the peaks of the Hindu Kush. An early twilight fell softly over the countryside, but they hardly noticed. They were deep in a discussion about Dr. Ali's behavior and ulterior motives.

"I don't know." Jo rubbed her forehead. "Living at the hospital isn't exactly what we had in mind, but how long can we wait to find a house? Maybe we *should* accept Dr. Ali's offer. Live at the hospital and start working. It would be better than staying here with nothing to do all day."

Mary shook her head. "But what happens then? We'll never teach. And we'll never get a home of our own."

"I agree," said Nan. "If we live at the hospital, we lose any leverage we have. It would be too easy for Dr. Ali to forget all about the nursing school. He would have exactly what he wants. Three convenient live-in additions to his hospital staff."

An unexpected flash of lightning startled them all, followed a few seconds later by a clap of thunder from across the valley. Large drops of rain spattered the dust, and the women went inside, the discussion ended for the moment.

Jo listened to the soft, rustling sound of rain as she burrowed under her blanket that night. It was not unpleasant—soothing, actually—and tomorrow was another day. Nan was right. These were minor setbacks. A good night's sleep would put everything in perspective. They would sort it all out tomorrow.

She woke to a steady downpour. Had it rained all night? There would be no breakfast tea or coffee on the balcony, and no trips to the hospital or the bazaar. Their "minor setback" would not be resolved today, it seemed, and she resigned herself to passing the time by playing cards and reading.

At the end of the day, Nan turned on the light switch. It clicked ineffectively in the gathering dusk. She flipped it up and down a second time. Still nothing. Faced with the prospect of a night without electricity, the women quickly ate a cold dinner while they could still see. When the room became completely dark, there was nothing else to do but go to bed.

Once again, Jo fell asleep to the sound of a waterfall pouring over the balcony, and woke to yet another morning of gray clouds and more rain. The torrential downpour continued for days, sometimes abating to light showers and drizzle, only to become another deluge a few hours later.

A thin, slick film of moisture collected on the concrete floor. Clothing felt perpetually damp; bedding was cold and clammy. A forgotten container of mulberries grew a fuzzy halo of mold, and the dirt road in front of the building turned to a river of mud.

Confined to a musty, cheerless hotel room with nothing to do, the women were bored and on edge. Jo slept poorly, unable to turn off her thoughts. She replayed random conversations and events with her family back home, then turned over in bed to visualize the houses they had seen in Baghlan. Some nights she couldn't get song lyrics out of her mind, the words and melodies looping endlessly over and over, keeping her awake for hours. Other nights she remembered the first line to a song, then stared into the darkness, trying to remember what came next. She began to have nightmares, once dreaming a tornado had destroyed her parents' home in Illinois.

By the second week, the women were squirming in their beds at night, constantly waking to scratch at tiny, peculiar red dots on their arms and ankles. Jo was convinced the rash was directly related to stress, made worse by the everlasting dampness. Her theory held up until Mary announced over breakfast one morning that she had solved the mystery.

"And?" Jo rubbed her ankles together under the table.

"We have fleas."

"Fleas!?"

She jumped up and approached her bed. Gingerly, she picked up the edge of the blanket and turned it over, bending down to examine the sheet more closely. Horrors! Tiny moving dots covered the surface.

Her bedtime ritual that evening included a careful examination of her bedding before she got beneath the top sheet. She didn't know what to do. With no screens on the windows she had gotten into the habit of sleeping with the sheet over her head—a way to avoid waking up in the morning with unnamed insects buzzing around her face. But she had no desire to put her head under the sheet and share her sleeping quarters with fleas, either. She finally compromised with the sheet over her mouth, and fell asleep.

She woke sometime during the night as usual, scratching her arms and legs, frantic for relief. In desperation, she kicked off the blanket, got up, and quietly felt her way around the room. She dragged three chairs into a row, pulled the blanket from her bed, and positioned herself across the chair seats.

A reprieve. She sighed hugely. Closed her eyes and fell into a deep, lovely sleep. Minutes passed in the quiet hotel room—or was it hours? Jo stretched, turned over, and fell onto the floor with a thump.

Startled awake instantly, she got up on her hands and knees, listening in the darkness. Nan stirred, but did not wake. Mary didn't move. Jo got back into bed, this time pulling the blanket over her head, wanting to shut out the rain, the boredom, and the damp; but most of all wanting to shut out the oppressive, black depression that oozed from every corner of the room.

By morning something was different. Jo felt the change even before she was fully awake: an unaccustomed brightness that pressed against her closed eyelids. She kept them closed and listened. The steady thrum of rain was gone. A bird chirped from the balcony. The weather pattern had finally shifted. The rainy season was over.

The women moved their little table to the balcony and had breakfast there, taking deep breaths of the dry, sweet air. Jo marveled at the changes all around them, the fleas forgotten. She observed the Hindu Kush in the distance. "It's amazing," she said. "The air is so clear I can see the different greens on the mountains, and even the snow-capped peaks."

Nan stood and put her hands on the balcony railing so she could take in the shimmering landscape. "This takes me completely by surprise. Look—the wild roses are beginning to bloom. The fields are turning green. And the mountains beyond the fields—well, can't you *feel* their beauty? And how do you convey the smell of the land after a rain, or the sound of frogs croaking? A picture is only a little square, after all!" She turned and went in to retrieve an airmail sheet and a pen, calling over her shoulder, "I have to describe this in a letter for my folks."

She came back, sat at the table, and began writing furiously, glancing up occasionally at the wild roses, blooming pink and fresh against the dark green foliage. "I'm telling my mom I'll pick a rose just for her."

Nan didn't have to explain her remark. It was Sunday, May 12, Mother's Day. "I'm letting her know I'll put the rose on my dresser," she continued, "so I can see it and be reminded of her."

Jo was quiet for a moment. "I think I'll write home and ask my mom for some flea powder."

The pools of mud disappeared, bedding dried out, and roads reverted to dust. Instead of waking to the sound of rain, the women woke to clear, sunny days, without a single cloud in the sky. And although the hotel room changed from damp and miserable to hot and oppressive almost overnight, one thing remained the same—the search for housing had come to a dead end.

The women explored every possibility. They requested a meeting with the governor of Baghlan and explained their dilemma. They talked to the shop owners in the bazaar, and finally, drafted a letter to Ken. If ever they needed someone from the Peace Corps office to intervene, it was now. Then, in a moment of inspiration, it came to Nan. She almost knocked over the breakfast table in her enthusiasm.

"Of course! Why didn't we think of it sooner? What about Rick? He's been teaching at the Vo-Ag School ever since we got here. He knows every teacher in Baghlan. Surely somebody at the school knows of a house for rent."

Jo looked at Nan in amazement. "The teachers at the Vo-Ag School," she repeated. "Of course. Rick talks about them all the time." She ticked off the names on her fingers. "Mr. Monier, Mr. Areff, and somebody named Mr. Muktar."

Nan laughed and ran her hands through her hair. "We'll get our own home yet," she said. "Just wait and see."

There might have been any number of reasons to explain why the women couldn't find suitable housing, but one issue overshadowed all the rest. The fact they were foreigners was not the problem. Even the fact they were women didn't make a difference. The explanation for not finding a place to live was simple. Baghlan was a small, rural community with only a handful of homes to rent, and the few that were available did not have a well or electricity.

The inability to do a single thing to help themselves was maddening. Jo lost count of the times she wanted to jump up and walk to the corner store, buy a newspaper, and peruse the real estate section. And each time, she was reminded: there was no store. No one bought newspapers, because no one could read.

There was nothing to do but wait. *Saber kardan* —Wait for someone to come forward with a suitable property. Jo felt like a bird in a cage, beating her wings against the invisible constraint of a culture that is defined by patience and resignation. She was tired of the hotel room, tired of playing cards, the heat, the four walls, and, most of all, tired of no running water.

Fed up with boredom, the women cleaned, hauling water from a spigot in the hotel lobby. They visited Rick and Kathleen. They cooked. They ate.

They shopped the bazaar for something to do, picking up a teapot or a little dish—items for the house they hoped to find.

The hotel was no place for a dog, and Jo was forced to accept Kathleen and Rick's offer to keep Alex. She went to visit him almost daily and often wandered through the bazaar stalls on her way home. The day she found herself next to an outdoor pen was the day she saw almost thirty donkeys tethered to a rope.

The memory of her first day in Kabul came back to her in a flash: the donkeys loaded with produce, and their mournful wails of protest. These animals were standing quietly, but if she could get them to bray, what a sound it would make! Like Nan, she wanted to share Afghanistan with her family, and if she made a tape for her parents—included all the sounds of the bazaar—at least they could hear what it was like, even if they couldn't see it.

She returned the next day with a tape recorder tucked under her arm, and made her way to the pen of donkeys. She stopped. Looking in both directions, she scanned the bazaar stalls and shoppers.

A few men watched in curiosity. They seemed friendly enough, a couple of them nodding, recognizing her presence. With nothing better to do, they waited for her to make the first move.

Jo stood indecisively.

The men hunkered down and had a smoke. She could take as long as she liked; they had all day.

Jo fingered the buttons on her little machine, hesitant to take that first step. What a stupid idea, she thought. I'm the only non-Afghan in the entire bazaar, and I want to hear a bunch of donkeys bray. No wonder the Afghans think we're crazy.

Tethered to ropes, the donkeys patiently endured the sun, heat, and swarms of flies. Occasionally, with ripples of flesh, the animals repelled ordinary household flies. Flat camel flies were more persistent, and buried themselves within the bristles of each donkey's coat.

Jo glanced over at the men. They were still watching, still waiting. What the hell, she decided suddenly. I've come too far to back out now.

She approached the nearest Afghan and explained her idea well enough, or so she thought, until he posed to have his picture taken. A group of men rushed to surround them, all talking at once. They waved their arms at each other and raised their voices.

"*Nê, nê! Na kamra!*" one of them shouted. "*Kaset! … Kaset!*" He repeated it in exasperation. —Cassette! With the last man convinced, the argument was settled, and they turned their attention back to Jo. Now it was a game, Jo realized, the best entertainment these men had seen in months. A middle-aged Afghan wearing a turban grinned hugely as he let one donkey loose. The corners of his eyes wrinkled in amusement, and he sought Jo's approval. "*Balê?*" He gave the donkey a little push. —Yes?

Jo laughed in anticipation. She could only nod.

The animal stood still for a few minutes, then moved among the other donkeys, bumping up against one of them, causing it to bray. Like an adolescent boy's voice beginning to change, the sound broke from high to low and back again, squeaking with an ear-splitting intensity between octaves. It was answered by another donkey, then another and another until all thirty donkeys were braying.

The uproar drew a small crowd of spectators, and they clapped with enjoyment. The men shouted above the commotion. "*Bashe?*" They asked. —Okay?

Jo's voice was lost in the escalating din. She pantomimed *balê, balê* — yes, yes, and got it all on tape: the donkeys, the men shouting, and her own distinctive peals of high-pitched laughter. She couldn't wait to get back to the hotel and play the tape for Nan and Mary. She was still laughing when she opened the door to their room.

Chapter 11

MR. MUKTAR

Walked to Ghulam Bay village about one mile west of Baghlan for a mêhmâni—a party—and played cards and chess and ate chalaw, qorma and candy with 25 Afghan teachers.

—*May 24, 1968*

She stopped at the doorway in surprise. They had company. Rick and Kathleen were there—not unusual—but this time they had a guest with them.

He stood politely at Jo's entrance, and in that moment the bazaar, the tape, the donkeys—all were forgotten. She gazed into the face of a man only slightly taller than herself, and although she never quite understood the term *neat* as a physical attribute, it seemed to have been coined for the person who stood before her. He was small and compact, with fine, even features, inquisitive light brown eyes, and a little scar above one eyebrow. All this passed through her mind within the first few seconds of seeing him. He wore a suit and tie, and bowing slightly, introduced himself as Mr. Muktar, one of the teachers at the Vo-Ag School, the *lycee* or high school in Baghlan.[35]

He was grateful to Rick and the Peace Corps for helping the Vo-Ag teachers learn better English, he said, and the sound of his voice opened a new dimension of attributes for Jo to consider. Unhurried and polite, he spoke with a quiet self-assurance, explaining the reason for his visit. Quite simply, he wanted to repay the Peace Corps Volunteers, and so, he had come to issue an invitation.

His eyes, almost hazel, Jo decided, held her own, and although she had no reason in the world for jumping to such a conclusion, she interpreted his demeanor as kind and gentle. She became so busy taking in the measure of the man, she missed the message.

"Sorry," she said. "A what? A picnic?"

Yes, he was hosting a picnic, he said, and they were all invited: the Volunteers and the entire lycee teaching staff, almost twenty-five teachers.

Jo was thrilled. They finally had somewhere to go and something to do.

~〇ⅰ〇~

It was an easy walk to Mr. Muktar's compound. A mile from Baghlan, his home was part of a small community of adobe houses enclosed by the traditional stone and concrete wall. A plentiful supply of juie water meant that gardens flourished and roses bloomed within the compound; beyond the walls were the distant peaks of the Hindu Kush.

On the day of his picnic, Mr. Muktar covered a flat area of the compound yard with rugs and blankets. As the guests arrived, they arranged themselves in a large circle around the patchwork of carpets and ground coverings, leaving an open space in the middle. Some of the Afghans sat cross-legged; others lounged against *toshaks*, or cushions. When the Americans arrived, Mr. Muktar insisted they take a place of honor beneath the shade of a small mulberry tree.

Jo wore long trousers, and as she lowered herself to the ground she tugged at the skirt she wore over them. Unless the skirt covered her legs completely—slacks notwithstanding—she could not sit cross-legged without offending her Muslim hosts. She angled to the ground sideways.

"Side-saddle," whispered Nan as they settled on a cushion.

The first order of business as usual, was tea.[36] The Volunteers had become accustomed to the practice of rinsing a cup with hot water or tea before filling it to drink, and as a gesture of hospitality, the Afghans rinsed the Volunteers' cups for them.

"Do you drink tea at home?" someone asked. "I hear Americans only drink coffee."

"And Coca-Cola!" Another teacher—Mr. Monier—joined them.

Jo and Nan laughed. "No—I mean, yes," said Jo. "We drink both … and tea."

Mr. Monier smiled and raised his cup. "*Salâmat bashed!*" —Health to you!

The questions continued. "What is your house like at home?" Mr. Areff, the school principal, leaned in toward Jo. "Do you have brothers and sisters? Wasn't it hard to leave them?"

When Jo answered that her house was made of wood and brick, and that she had one sister, there was a flurry of conversation in Farsi: astonishment at having so much wood, enough for an entire house! But only one sister—a pity.

Mr. Areff explained. "It's hard for us to understand how you can be so far away from your family." He quickly amended his remark. "But we're glad you came to Afghanistan."

The teacups were filled by Mr. Muktar a second time, and then a third time before he brought out an array of games, the boxes worn smooth. Mary joined a card game along with Rick and Kathleen. Nan accepted the challenge to a chess match, and Jo found herself across a checkerboard from Mr. Areff.

She wondered what would be considered proper etiquette. Be gracious and let her opponent win? She made the first move, tentatively pushing her red checker diagonally one square. She had barely lifted her finger when Mr. Areff decisively countered her move. He sat hunched over the board, eyes bright with concentration. Well, that answered her question, she thought. It would be an insult to hand over a meaningless victory. She gave the game her full attention, until eventually he was forced to crown her king. Letting down her guard, she fell into a trap and lost two pieces at once. Another half dozen moves each and it was over. Jo conceded.

They set the board for a rematch, while the competition escalated around them. Winners rubbed their hands and shouted with glee; losers groaned in defeat. Jo stopped herself from laughing out loud, not wanting to offend anyone, yet enthralled by the abandon with which the Afghans played.

She bent her head over the checkerboard, ready to start the second game. A breeze tousled her hair. The air cooled slightly. The shadows lengthened. Shade from the mulberry tree moved across the yard, creeping to the base of the far compound wall. It fingered its way up the uneven surface of stone and concrete, and when it fell across the top of the wall, the players finished their games. The women came out of the house.

Mr. Muktar's mother came first, bearing a pitcher of water. The younger women followed with shallow basins. Older children ran ahead with drying towels. Toddlers hung back, suddenly shy, hiding behind chador folds.

Like her son, Mrs. Muktar was small and graceful, her weathered face wizened and fine featured. Still, it was a handsome face, with high cheekbones and lively dark eyes. She knelt in the dust and poured water over Mary's outstretched hands. Mr. Monier's wife held a basin to catch the water. One of the children offered a drying towel. The hand-washing ceremony extended to the rest of the Americans, the teachers, and lastly, to Mr. Muktar.

Immediately, a staggering amount of food appeared on the carpet. The women set down platters of *chalaw* —plain rice, *pilau* —rice with meat and vegetables, and finally *aushak* —a sort of Afghan ravioli made with leeks, swimming in meat sauce and yogurt. There were side dishes of cucumbers, more yogurt, and *bulani* —vegetable and meat patties covered with flour and fried in oil.

Jo bit into a piece of nutty, whole grain nân. She turned to Mr. Areff, who sat next to her. "This is so good. How exactly do you make it?"

Mr. Areff held his own piece of nân, poised to scoop some pilau from a communal platter. He stopped, considering Jo's question, then turned and regarded her thoughtfully.

"*Âyâ.*" —Well. "First you have a hole in the ground." He indicated with his hands it needed to be several feet deep.

"*Kam-o bêsh*," offered Mr. Monier —More or less. "You light a fire at the bottom of the hole and wait until the flames are gone."

"But it is still hot," continued Mr. Areff. "You mix up the dough, and you pat, pat, like this, on the side of the hole." Mr. Areff made a motion to indicate the dough was placed directly onto the earthen sides of the underground oven. "And when it's done, it looks like this!" Grinning, he reached over and picked up a flat piece of nân, perfectly toasted and shaped almost like a snowshoe.

Right. Jo raised one eyebrow. She looked from Mr. Areff to the circle of faces around the carpet. The women did all the work of making nân, but the men were quick to take credit for the procedure.

Conversation and laughter subsided as the Afghans turned their attention to the array of food. Some leaned forward to scoop pilau and chalaw from communal platters with pieces of nân; others picked up morsels of food directly from the serving dishes, using the first two fingers and thumb of their right hand—to use all their fingers would be greedy. The Americans ate with plates and spoons, courtesy of Mr. Muktar.

Dessert completed the meal: dried apricots, pastries, and sugar-coated almonds, served with yet more tea. The women came out with bowls and pitchers of water for the final hand-washing ceremony, and only after everything was cleared away did they retire to the house to have their own meal from what was left

The last few crumbs of food were brushed from the rug. A couple of chittering birds alighted on the compound wall, waiting to flutter down and peck at whatever they could glean from the dust.

One of the teachers picked up his *dhol*, an upright Afghan drum. He introduced the music quietly, his fingers tapping lightly on the membrane. The bird flew away, leaving the drum beat as the only sound in the stillness of the early evening. The musician's cadence was unhurried, the beats precise and subdivided. A predictable string of steady, even pulses came from his expert hands—then, the pleasure of unexpected syncopation with its percussive explosion just after the beat. He laid out the pattern smoothly, never rushing, always in control, until the beats seemed to fall without effort. He allowed the cadence to build gradually—the crescendo still hours away—and quickened the rhythm in increments so small as to be hardly noticed.

When he reached a pre-determined point, the men stood and formed a circle. Holding their arms above their heads, they moved with deliberate, intricate steps, turning and twisting to the uneven meter. The pace accelerated and they began to sing, clapping and snapping their fingers. Several of the men stepped aside to make an opening in the circle, indicating the Americans should join them.

Jo laughed and shook her head.

Nan jumped up immediately, and tried to copy the complex pattern of steps, faltering and laughing, caught up in the frenzy of the music. Jo smiled, wondering what the Afghans thought of the new moves being introduced to their national dance.[37]

The sun dropped behind the peaks of the Hindu Kush, leaving a fiery glow that extended across the heavens. The tempo of the drum beat increased, the men appearing as black silhouettes, moving against the background of a red-streaked sky.

Jo shifted on her blanket. She wondered how much longer the party would last. Her legs were numb, and her stomach rumbled from the Afghan food, especially the aushak, the leek-filled pasta and yogurt. She didn't want to appear ungrateful for the Afghans' hospitality, but on the other hand, she thought it best to leave. Better that she appear rude for leaving early than falling asleep on the spot, or worse—she swallowed, the taste of leeks rising in her throat—getting sick on the unaccustomed food.

She went into the house to thank Mrs. Muktar and the wives, then walked back to the hotel alone. The first stars were barely visible, and strains of music gradually faded into the distance. The breeze picked up, and she felt better already, stretching her legs in the coolness of the evening.

She wanted to remember the night and the boundless hospitality of the Afghans, but like the syncopation of the music, her mind erratically entertained one random thought after another.

The Afghan generosity was overwhelming. She had been treated like royalty, but at what cost? The Afghan women had prepared and served a massive amount of food, and as thanks for their effort, they ate by themselves, confined to the house. The practice was so accepted, so normal … Jo almost stopped walking. So normal, no one questioned it.

She resumed her pace. Conventional wisdom—that was it. That was it exactly. An accepted way of thinking. She had come across the term years ago, in one of her college classes, and had all but forgotten it until now. At the time she had dismissed the idea, not really interested in the instructor's explanation, or his archaic example of Christopher Columbus. Who cared if conventional wisdom in the fifteenth century maintained that the world was flat? Interesting concept, but what relevance did it have to her own life? Walking the dusty path back to the hotel, she now understood that it was a concept of enormous consequence. To a great extent, conventional wisdom condemned Afghan women to a life of subservience.

She thought of her conversation with Harry. For many white folks growing up in the South in the 1950s and 1960s, segregation was right and moral: it, too, had been conventional wisdom, accepted by the majority, and everyone simply went along with it. Soon the only sound was the soft, steady pat of her footsteps in the dust, interspersed by the occasional croak of a frog from the juie.

The picnic gave the women something new to talk about for days, but when they had exhausted the topic, Mary became increasingly restless. She was impatient to set up her clinic for young pregnant mothers, but she needed supplies and equipment. She would make a trip to Kabul, she declared, and meet with Ken. As their medical director, he would be the one who could help her.

She returned to Baghlan a few days later with news. Ken had received their letter and was coming for a visit—as early as next week. And he was bringing John Bing with him to address the housing situation.

It was now June. The Volunteers had been in Baghlan for one month. All their ideas about finding housing had come to nothing.

June 5, 1968, dawned clear and bright, much like every other summer morning in Afghanistan. A lone bird chirped once in the pre-dawn darkness. From somewhere within the branches of thick juie brush a lark stirred, then answered with a distinctive, melodious whistle and churr. The shadowy outline of trees and shrubs slowly materialized; swallows chirped and twittered. Sparrows added their voices, followed by wrens, thrushes, and magpies, until birdsong from every species swelled to a cacophony of sound, announcing a blazing sunrise in a cloudless sky.

Jo was up early, working while it was still cool. Already, she had made dozens of trips up and down the stairs of the Sugar Hotel, hauling water from a communal spigot. She had postponed this particular job for as long as possible, knowing it would be labor intensive, but she needed clean clothes, and had to start sometime. Today was the day. The day she would do laundry.

She filled containers and pans with water and soap, laundered a few items at a time, then refilled the containers to rinse. Doing laundry by hand was a long and drawn-out process, but with humidity levels hovering at twenty percent, everything dried quickly, even pegged to a little string in the hotel room. By lunch time, she was folding clean clothes.

She took down a blouse and shook it smartly with a little snap. Before smoothing out the wrinkles, she turned up the volume on her shortwave, happy to have found Radio Ceylon, a station that played hours of uninterrupted classical music. The afternoon heat had not yet settled into the room, and Mary took advantage of the time to write a letter home. Nan was engrossed in a book.

Jo hummed along to the selection for the day—Vivaldi's "The Four Seasons." Her spirits lifted by the opening strains, she took down another blouse. She was folding a collar when the music stopped, abruptly cut off in the middle of a phrase. Panicked, unrehearsed voices took over the broadcast. Nan looked up from the book she was reading. Mary stopped writing her letter home. A white silence swirled in Jo's brain.

"Senator Kennedy has been shot! Senator Kennedy has been shot; is that possible? Is that possible? … not only Senator Kennedy, oh my God. Senator Kennedy has been shot, and another man, a Kennedy campaign manager, and possibly shot in the head."[38]

Nan was talking over the radio. "… terrible … Rick and Kathleen … have to let them know—"

Jo didn't remember the walk across town, or how she had unplugged her radio and carried it with her, or even how they broke the news to Rick and Kathleen. She only remembered that as she plugged it back in, she had an expectation it was all a terrible mistake. They had misunderstood, that's all. Her program of music would still be on, because nothing had happened.

But it was no mistake. The five Americans listened as more information became available. Robert Kennedy had delivered a rousing speech to a crowd of exuberant campaign supporters in the ballroom of the Ambassador Hotel in Los Angeles, California, thanking them for helping him win the California Democratic primary for president. Minutes later he was shot three times as he walked through the kitchen pantry of the hotel.[39]

Jo kept a vigil by her radio, along with millions of other Americans listening and watching television in the United States.

Kennedy died at 1:44 a.m. the next morning, Thursday, June 6, 1968. He was 42 years old. The announcement was made at 2:00 a.m. Pacific Time, exactly noon in Baghlan.

Following the announcement, the Volunteers talked for hours about the Kennedy family, the assassination of his brother, and the promise of a "new frontier." They spoke of Martin Luther King's crusade for a peaceful civil rights movement, and the profound loss of three men who had served the common good.

They discussed the ideals of the Peace Corps, the state of humanity, and the decline of the human race. Even as they argued over ideological and philosophical differences, they were united as Americans in a foreign land, far from home and grieving over yet another shooting, another senseless tragedy.

Jo speculated whether the news would affect the ordinary Afghan. "It would have to," she said. "The Kennedy name is known around the world."

"I don't think so," argued Rick. "Oh, maybe the teachers at the Vo-Ag School. Yeah, I'll grant you that. They might know who Bobby Kennedy is, but the average Afghan? Think about it. No one has a radio or TV. How would they find out? By reading the newspaper?"

He's right, thought Jo. Apart from the Vo-Ag teachers, most Afghans couldn't read a newspaper even if they had one. Nor did they have the time or energy to become involved in a news story halfway around the world. It was all they could do to survive from day to day.

And besides, there was plenty of turmoil in the political landscape of Afghanistan. It was common knowledge the Soviets had a compound in Baghlan Valley, and she wondered how the Afghans felt about the increasing presence of the Soviet military. At the same time, rumors circulated constantly about a revolution. Was Afghanistan capable of changing peacefully from within? And what was the probability change would come from outside its borders, forced by violence upon the Afghan people? The day Jo saw a convoy of trucks taking Russian soldiers to Puli-Khumri was the day she wondered how long the Afghans would have control over their own destiny—or if they ever had control at all.

She felt small and powerless, adrift, buffeted forward by the inexorable movement of history. What recourse did the ordinary citizen have? And yet, she mused, violence begets violence.

Her dream of playing a role in the grand scheme of things seemed tarnished and faded. What could she possibly do? She couldn't even find a place to live, for God's sake. She thought about the impending visit from Ken and John Bing. They couldn't get to Baghlan soon enough.

Chapter 12

INTERNATIONAL RELATIONS

Slept only a few hours during the night because of the pressing, never-ending heat. Woke up feeling rather desperate about no work and boredom.

—June 17, 1968

The shadow of Kennedy's death cast a pall over the Volunteers, and Jo began to question her purpose in Afghanistan. She found it difficult to concentrate, wondering if her efforts at writing out lesson plans were pointless. How could they foster understanding between peoples from different nations when in their own country, a passionate voice for peace and justice had been silenced with a bullet?

Discouraged, she felt as if she did nothing more than shuffle stacks of papers, some in English, some in Farsi. How much progress had she made? Not much. How many students did she have? None. Zero. They had offered an entrance examination at the hospital, and not a single prospective student came to take it. Jo felt a hot wave of embarrassment just thinking about it. And then there was the curriculum. It was barely half finished. She missed Tarshi, her teacher from training in Estes Park. Without his help, writing even the simplest translation seemed to take forever.

She spent hours on it every day, and when the hotel room became hot and stuffy, she moved her books and papers to the balcony. Nan and Mary often sat with her, helping organize the morass of half-translated lectures and scribbled notes she euphemistically called her lesson plans.

Most days Kathleen joined them at the hotel. Other days they worked at Kathleen and Rick's house, and when Rick came home from his teaching job at the Vo-Ag School, they had dinner together.

"Be grateful you're working," said Jo one night as they sat down at the table. "At least you have a school. You have a curriculum. Students."

"I wish I could help you." Rick filled his plate. "But I do have some news that might interest you."

"Oh?" Jo looked up.

He grinned and tantalized her by giving a hint. "On the social front."

"Come on, Rick—what is it?"

Rick made sure he had everyone's attention before he relented. "Well, I found out there's another group of Volunteers stationed here in Baghlan Province. A group of young men, for your information."

Jo blinked in surprise. "You're kidding."

"I'm perfectly serious."

"How can that be? Surely we would know about it, don't you think?"

"Not if they're from Germany."

"Germany!" Everyone said it at once.

"West Germany, actually, and they work as accountants at the sugar refinery in Fabrika. And ..." Rick reached for a piece of nân. "They were quite interested to hear of three single American women." He looked at Mary, hoping to get a rise out of her. She didn't give him the satisfaction. Instead she put her lips together and shook her head.

"Wow." Nan was almost speechless, but she recovered quickly. "We'll issue an invitation. Oh, wait. On second thought, we should let them invite *us*. No, that won't work. They don't know who we are." She turned to Rick for more information. "How did you find out about this?"

Rick was laughing. "Easy. A few of the Vo-Ag teachers have connections to the sugar refinery. Trust me. It's no problem getting the word out. All you have to do is pick the day and I guarantee they'll be knocking on your door."

〜◠⋆◠〜

The German Volunteers in Fabrika wasted no time in making contact with the Americans, sending Hans and Gunther to the Sugar Hotel as emissaries. The men were part of the Deutsche Welle, the German Peace Corps. They stood politely in the doorway, and in a mixture of English, German, and Farsi, introduced themselves.[40]

The connection was instant, the laugher immediate as they stumbled over the first words of introduction: *welcome, guten tag, khôsh âmadêd, hallo.* Within minutes they were exchanging information about their respective assignments in Afghanistan, the women interested in the sugar refinery, the men asking about the nursing school.

Mary boiled water for tea, and they carried their cups to the balcony, where they sat around the little table. The Americans wanted to know what life was like in Germany. The Germans wanted to know what it was like to grow up in the United States. They compared first impressions of Afghanistan, amazed at how similar their reactions were to almost everything, from the juies, gaudies, and bargaining at the bazaar, to the friendliness of the Afghan people. They laughed at each other's stories: Nan dancing at Mr. Muktar's picnic, the Afghan accounting system at the refinery.

The afternoon passed quickly, and when sun slipped behind the peaks of the Hindu Kush, they were taken by surprise. The men got up from the table, thanking the women for a great afternoon.

"But we can't leave before we ask you a question," said Gunther. He shifted his weight, suddenly shy. "Would you be interested in ... ummm, would you consider ... Well, do you want to come to a party?"

Jo stared. A party!? Was she interested? Of course she was interested. She could hardly get the words out fast enough. "Oh, yes." She didn't care where it was, or who was going. "*Balê*," she added, laughing. "*Ja.*"

Gunther continued. “How about a date to go swimming?”

Nan repeated the word as if she couldn’t believe it. “Swimming? In Afghanistan?”

“Sure,” said Hans. “The Russians have a pool in their compound near Puli-Khumri. We’d be happy to take you as our guests.”[41]

Less than a week later, Jo dove into a clear, chlorinated pool. She swam underwater as long as she could, taking pleasure in the current of clean water flowing past her body, then surfaced and stroked to the side. She held her face to the sun, amazed at how good it felt. It was hard to believe this was the same Afghan sun that wilted weeds and gardens alike, beating down on adobe houses, dirt roads, and fields of dust.

Hans and Gunther finished their swim and sat with Nan at the far side of the pool, but Jo lingered in the water, kicking her legs to stay afloat. She observed Nan and the German Volunteers, how they had casually flipped towels over their shoulders and sat next to each other, warming themselves in the sun. She heard their voices, an interweaving cadence of masculine and feminine, German and American, and the occasional laughter at a shared joke.

These were not high-level communications between governments, they were ordinary conversations between ordinary people. Here she was, an American in Afghanistan during the Cold War—a guest of German Volunteers, swimming in a Russian pool. She ducked under the water one last time, smiling with her mouth closed. No one would believe it.

That evening Hans and Gunther took the women to their compound, where fifteen German Volunteers waited to entertain them. Unlike the Americans who lived off the bazaar, the Germans had their own commissary privileges, including access to Western food and alcohol. They prepared and served the women a feast of roast turkey and champagne. After the meal, everyone had another drink, listened to music, and took turns playing Ping-Pong.

Just past midnight Hans and Gunther safely delivered the women back to the hotel. After they left, Jo sat on her bed without the slightest care about fleas. She sighed with contentment. "What a ball!"

It had been a good time, but more than that, the enthusiasm of the German Volunteers rekindled her own. She remembered the feeling she had when she first thought about joining the Peace Corps, how she wanted to be part of something big. Well, she was. She was part of a worldwide movement.

The World Health Organization pledged its support for the Peace Corps project, and sent a representative to visit the women a few days later. Her name was Peggy Cannon, and she was a nurse-midwife from Ireland. Nearly the same age as Mary, she was also regarded as a *muy safad* —a white hair, a person of respect.

The women entertained Peggy as well as they could in a hotel room with no air conditioning. They purchased ingredients for dinner from the bazaar, and cooked over a kerosene stove and an electric hot plate. Still, they enjoyed a satisfying meal of nân, scrambled eggs, and dried apricots, with mulberry pie for dessert, thanks to the almost daily gift of fresh mulberries from Rick's students.

Peggy settled back with a cup of tea when they had finished and talked about her work with the World Health Organization. Her primary job was caring for young mothers, she said, mothers who were young girls themselves, children having children, with the obstetrical complications and infant mortality that accompany such high-risk pregnancies.

"It's the little things that make a difference," she noted. "Pre-natal vitamins. Early detection of breech presentations. Vitamin D for girls who don't get enough sunshine behind compound walls."

Mary was listening avidly. "I know. We're ready to start, but Dr. Ali has other ideas. He thinks we're here to work at the hospital."

"Be patient." Peggy made a small, cautionary gesture. "Don't be so quick to give in to his demands." She turned to Jo and Nan. "Remember, Mary and I can do only so much with our clinics. When we leave, we take our skills with us. But if you can teach some of these young girls—get them on the path to midwifery school in Kabul, or train them as lab techs—well, they can work here long after we're gone."

The hotel room went quiet. Peggy's ringing endorsement of education dangled in the silence.

Mary looked down at her hands, folded in her lap. Nan cleared her throat.

Peggy set her teacup down with a little chink and looked at the three women in turn, waiting for an explanation.

Jo rested her head against the back of the chair and stared at the ceiling. "It's not that easy." She rubbed her forehead, as if she could erase her conflicting emotions: confusion, hurt, and most of all, indignation. "We gave an entrance exam. We thought it would be a good way to start." She sat up and folded her arms. "No one came to take it."

"We did everything we could," said Nan. "We visited schools and talked to the girls. Met with the teachers at the Vo-Ag School and asked them to spread the word. We told everyone at the hospital. We set up the classroom as a testing center, and well, Jo's right. Not a single prospective student came."

Strangely enough, Jo was relieved to have the issue out in the open. What a stupid, stupid mistake she had made. In retrospect, it had been a glaring oversight. How could she have taken such a critical aspect of her preparation for granted? What had she been thinking, for God's sake? That Dr. Ali would wave a magic wand and supply rows of bright, shining faces in her classroom?

From her own experience, Peggy knew that platitudes were useless. She responded carefully. "Keep at it. The Afghans won't jump into anything new without thinking it over, especially if it involves their young daughters. But don't give up. You might be surprised if you offer it again."

In essence, the Americans and Afghans were reading from different scripts. The Volunteers had no doubt they were providing a fabulous opportunity to the young students. The Afghans viewed the Americans as meddlesome, disrupting the traditional social order with unwelcome change.

Peggy stayed two days, and when she left, her cheery Irish lilt hung in the air like a tinkling chime. When it eventually faded, the hotel room seemed to contract, becoming even smaller and more tiresome than before, the nursing school a distant, perhaps impossible goal.

The women were bored. Hot. Nothing was convenient or easy. Everything was a chore.

Chapter 13

HOUSE FOR RENT

We moved out of the hotel, tin bathtub and all.

—June 21, 1968

Water was the worst, or the lack of water, to be more precise: the treks up and down the hotel stairs with every container they could find—buckets, pans, crockery—anything they could fill with water from the communal spigot. Then there was the inconvenience of boiling it, adding iodine tablets before using it for cooking, washing dishes, making tea, or brushing their teeth. The only water they didn't boil was what they used for bathing. It was more like washing up, thought Jo, done standing and using a basin. Oh—and the bucket of water they carried up every day to flush the commode. They didn't boil that, either.

They tried not to complain, but pure running water was only one deprivation among an entire inventory: air conditioning, a real stove, a refrigerator filled with gallons of cold milk. "Forget air conditioning," said Nan. "I'd be happy with a fan, or better yet, a day at the beach, the Jersey Shore." Jo developed a craving for soda, the fizz, the bubbles of carbonation rising in a glass filled with ice. She dreamed about hamburgers, and crisp, salted French fries. Collectively, they spent hours going down the list, until finally Mary offered a suggestion. "We'll have a contest. See who can go the longest without expressing her unfulfilled wishes and desires."

Jo and Nan accepted the challenge, but as early as the second day into the contest, Nan ran into a difficulty. She had an idea. A great idea, actually, but how could she broach the subject without losing? "I'm not complaining," she was quick to point out, "but aren't we all tired of washing up out of a saucepan?"

Yes, everyone certainly could agree to that.

"So, what are we waiting for?" Nan folded her arms, inordinately pleased with herself.

"I don't get it." Jo wondered if Nan had finally gone a little crazy. "Waiting for what?"

"The tin bazaar!" Nan almost shouted with excitement.

"I still don't get it," said Mary.

"The tin bazaar. We can have a bathtub made at the tin bazaar!"

It was such a good idea Jo wondered why they hadn't thought of it sooner. They discussed shape and dimensions. How long? How high? Mary, as the tallest of them, sat on the floor and bent her knees. If it fit her, it would fit all of them. Jo measured the space around the pretend bathtub and called out the numbers to Nan, who drew a sketch. Was it really possible? Could the tinsmith in Baghlan make one?

No, they decided. They would have a better chance in Kunduz, where the bazaar was three times the size of the one in Baghlan. It would be worth the trip, even though it meant a fifty-mile taxi ride. Jo and Nan offered to take the drawing first thing in the morning.

Jo pushed her way through the crowd, turning around periodically to make sure Nan was still behind her. If they got separated, they would never find each other among the mass of humanity, or hear each other above the deafening noise. Groups of Afghan women moved from stall to stall comparing prices, their chadors and burqas fluttering in the breeze. Men had the luxury of shopping alone if they wished, but most of them perused the shops in groups of two or three, sometimes with their arms draped over each other's shoulders. Jo had become accustomed to the casual, overt displays of friendship between Afghan men. It seemed to be a fact of life everywhere in Afghanistan.[42]

She came to the open area set aside for craftsmen and waited for Nan to catch up. They walked past carpenters, tailors, and finally stopped in front of a tin bazaar where a tinsmith displayed his handiwork.

He ran a blackened index finger over the bathtub drawing. Making a pretense of scrutinizing it carefully, he glanced at the women, assessing their interest.

Jo watched him intently.

He lowered his head as if to look at the sketch again, hiding a smile of satisfaction. He allowed several minutes to pass. Finally he shook his head. "I make small items," he said. "This is big. Very big."

"But it can be done, right?" Jo nodded, imploring him to agree with her.

"Perhaps. But I would have to charge you three thousand afghanis."

Jo gasped; it was half a month's salary.

Nan started laughing and spoke for both of them. "One thousand."

He shrugged, feigning indifference. "Two thousand."

The women hesitated, and the shopkeeper folded the paper, making it clear he was not interested.

Jo saw the bathtub slipping away. "*Mowâfeq!*" —Okay! "Two thousand afghanis."

The tinsmith gazed at the two women, then unfolded the paper, reconsidering. He wagged his head back and forth, thinking it over. "For two thousand afghanis, I will do it for you," he said. "Come back in three days. I will have it done."

Jo had buyer's remorse the minute they walked away. "I'm sorry, Nan. That was a mistake. I just spent a lot of our money."

"Don't worry—if you hadn't accepted his price, I would have. You beat me to it, that's all!"

Jo could hardly wait to get back to Baghlan and give Mary the news. Just knowing the bathtub would be theirs in a matter of days made the heat, the dust, the un-airconditioned hotel room bearable.

Jo and Nan were at the taxi bazaar in Baghlan early on the appointed day, and in their excitement, told the driver why they were going to Kunduz. He smiled and nodded agreeably, guiding the taxi onto the road.

"And what is this thing called a bathtub?" he asked.

"A container," said Jo. "Big." —*bozorg*. She expanded her arms. "*Besyâr bozorg.*" —Very big.

"To wash," Nan added. She made a motion of washing herself. "*Shostan.*"

"Oh."

The driver was still curious. "And will you bring it back to Baghlan?"

"Yes."

"And will you bring it back in this taxi so I can see it?"

"*Yaqinan,*" said Nan. —Of course. "If you wait for us, we will come back in your taxi."

Jo loved it the minute she saw it. No matter that it was made of ordinary tinplate—she could almost feel herself immersed in cool, soapy water. She envisioned putting her head under and coming up refreshed. It was worth every afghani the shopkeeper had charged them.

She and Nan made a movement to pick up their new purchase, but a tall, imposing Afghan stepped in front of them. Without a word he grasped the unwieldy tub and swung it high above his head, his bearing regal when he turned around. Shoppers parted to make room for him, and he processed through the crowd, ceremoniously taking it to the waiting taxi.

He helped the driver push it into the trunk as far as it would go, and when the lid still wouldn't close, they tied it down with string. Jo tried not to smile, filled with glee at getting their tub at long last. She was in such a good mood she wanted to laugh at everything: the tinsmith who had displayed it so proudly, the puzzled Afghans who stuck their heads inside, and the man who had carried it through the crowd as if it were something rare and priceless. She noticed the crease under Nan's eyes deepening, and as soon as they settled into the back seat and closed the door, they burst into laughter.

"Did you see the reaction of the crowd when the tinsmith told them what it was for?" Nan wiped her eyes. "They must think we're completely nuts!"

The taxi driver knew a few English words, but not enough to understand what was so funny. He laughed because the women laughed, but at the same time, his eyes were questioning. Were the women making fun of him? The tinsmith?

Jo glanced up. Her eyes locked with his, framed in the rearview mirror. How easily their behavior could be misinterpreted! How offensive their laughter must appear to him.

Nan caught the exchange, and for the rest of the trip, the women smothered waves of mirth that welled up and threatened to explode. Jo sucked in her top lip. Nan suffered from several bouts of unexplained coughing. They stared out the window to avoid looking at each other. They barely spoke, and when they did, they didn't mention the *you-know-what* until they were safely back in the hotel.

It was shiny. Oval. Just the right size. Watertight, it did not leak. Not one drop.

~⌒⌒⌒~

The simple pleasure of a bath was more than getting clean, it was a luxury—the shampoo and soap, the rinsing off and toweling dry, the smooth sensation of clean, taut skin afterwards, of hair slightly fragrant, damp and combed back. Jo had not felt this good since the day she had gone swimming in the Russian compound.

The entire process put her in a hopeful frame of mind. Maybe this will be the day, she thought, as she dried off and put on a set of clean clothes. Maybe the person who was coming to see them—this Mr. Hyatullah, or whatever his name was—would have a lead on another house.

"So how do you think he found out about us?" Jo dragged the tub to the balcony and tipped it over the side. "Do you think he heard about us from one of the Vo-Ag teachers?" She leaned the tub against the railing to dry. "Or maybe it has something to do with the visit from John Bing and Ken. Remember the meeting we had with the governor while they were here?"

"Oh, could be," answered Nan. She was bent over her bed, pulling at the edge of her blanket to smooth out the wrinkles. "Actually I thought the meeting didn't accomplish a thing, but who knows? Maybe the word got out somehow." Satisfied with her bed, she stood up and put her hands on her hips. "Who can figure out how the communication system works here?"

No kidding, thought Jo. There was a mysterious, invisible pathway of information among the Afghans that was intuitive, even scary. Looking back, she remembered that Dr. Ali had been prepared for their visit to the hospital, and had greeted them as if he had been expecting them all along. The hotel staff had grinned knowingly when she came back from the bazaar with her tape recorder; they had nodded the day of Mr. Muktar's picnic as if to say, "Have a good time."

But then, perhaps it was not so different from anywhere else in the world. The Peace Corps Volunteers stuck out as odd and peculiar in the little community of Baghlan. Their comings and goings were talked about in homes, the bazaar, and teahouses much the same way news and gossip travels in Small Town, USA.

⌒⌒⚚⌒⌒

Mr. Hyatullah's presence filled the hotel room as soon as he stepped through the doorway. He wore a Western suit and tie, and his English was impeccable. Like Dr. Ali, Mr. Hyatullah was tall, but unlike the doctor, he had a compact, muscular build. His tightly curled hair was clipped short. He was a businessman, educated in the United States. An elected public official in Afghanistan, he worked for the Ministry of Public Roads in Baghlan.

He settled into a chair and accepted a cup of tea, and while they all spoke, it was Mr. Hyatullah who dominated the meeting, not because of an overbearing, arrogant attitude, but quite the opposite. He gave the women his complete attention. By listening carefully, he became the focal point of the little group, asking questions and assessing the situation. He was interested in everything they had to say: why they were in Afghanistan, the nursing school, the inability to find housing.

He responded that he wanted to offer his services. "If I help you, I help Afghanistan," he said. "As for a house, I have a friend who is an electrician. He has a house to rent, if you're interested." He leaned back and crossed his legs, as if housing was a minor issue and could be solved easily.

Mary voiced her primary concern. "Does it have a well?"

As long as they were listing requirements, Jo added her own. "Glass in the windows?"

Mr. Hyatullah laughed. It was a deep, hearty sound that seemed a natural extension of his physical appearance. "Yes, it has both. My Jeep is downstairs if you want to see it."

Just like that, thought Jo. A snap of the fingers. It must be the same the world over. It doesn't matter what you know, it's who you know that counts.

Mr. Hyatullah led the way, and the women followed him down the stairs and through the lobby. Jo turned around to look at the hotel staff as they left. From the way the men smiled and nodded smugly, she was certain they already knew all about the purpose of Mr. Hyatullah's visit. She hooked arms with Nan as they walked out of the hotel. Bending her head so that she would not be overheard, Jo whispered, "Sometimes I think the Afghans know what we're going to do before we know we're going to do it."

Mr. Hyatullah gave them more information as he drove his Jeep across town. The landlord was Mr. Arsala, and he lived next door to the property with his two wives and five children.

The house was adobe. It had a flat roof, and small, concrete stoops, front and back. Like the other houses they had seen, it was surrounded by a stone and concrete wall nearly five feet high. Inside, there were two large bedrooms, a kitchen, and a sitting room with windows on three sides. The panes of glass were unbroken.

Mr. Arsala leaned against a doorway and watched without comment while the women walked through the house and inspected the grounds.

His Karakul hat was pulled to the side at a slight angle, and a cigarette dangled from one hand. Jo didn't want to stare, but she had never known a man with two wives. A quick glance told her he was of medium height, and had a small, neat mustache. Other than that, there was nothing remarkable about his appearance. She wondered what she had expected.

When he did speak, it was in Farsi, and he called their attention to the sitting room, pointing out how pleasant it was with all the windows. He would repair a section of the compound wall where it had started to crumble, he said, but made it clear the cost of labor and cement would be added to the cost of the lease. Still, the property had everything they needed: two bedrooms, a well, and electricity.

~◠◡◠~

Rent a truck at the bazaar. Load the few personal items they had at the hotel room in one or two trips down the stairs. Pick up their Peace Corps trunks at Rick and Kathleen's house. Pet Alex—ruffle his fur, and tell him she would come back for him as soon as they were settled. Jo anticipated that with an early start they would be moved by lunch time.

The truck was a massive 1930s Bedford truck decorated in the Afghan tradition, with red, blue, and yellow geometric designs painted across the hood and side panels. Thin wooden slats enclosed the open truck bed. A crank handle protruded from above the front bumper. The wide bench seat accommodated all three women plus the driver, although Jo ended up with the gearshift between her knees.

A half-dozen men and boys, including hotel staff, Vo-Ag teachers, and kids from the neighborhood, climbed onto the truck bed for the short trip to Rick and Kathleen's house. The driver threw his weight into the crank handle, and when the engine caught, he ran back and hopped in next to Jo. Depressing the clutch, he dropped the gear stick into first, apologized for hitting her knee, and they were off, the truck chassis trembling so violently that Jo put her hand on the dash to steady herself.

They came to a stop in front of Rick and Kathleen's house, and the men jumped down. They enthusiastically handed up trunks, charpoy beds,

130

dishware, and boxes. Heavy items got dumped on top of light items, chair legs stuck out at all angles, and a bookcase balanced precariously. With everything loaded, Jo climbed up to make sure nothing fell off.

It was not quite mid-morning, but already the day was hot, the sun blinding. It was stifling among the boxes, and she felt light-headed from the heat. Spots danced in front of her eyes. She wiped the sweat from her forehead, impatient to be moving. At least then she would get a breeze.

Thankfully, they started forward. Jo closed her eyes and leaned her head against a bookcase. The driver revved the engine. He was about to shift into second gear when the truck bed dropped and bounced beneath her. Dishes rattled, and the unexpected jolt banged her head against a book shelf. She rubbed the knot already forming and scrambled down to see what happened.

One of the back wheels had slipped into a deep rut, making the truck bed uneven. Jo glanced with alarm at their belongings, listing to one side. The driver pressed the accelerator. Tires squealed, spinning in place, throwing dust and dirt into the air. He quickly stopped, and slid the gear shift into neutral. The men lined up against the back panel and pushed, rocking the vehicle back and forth. The back wheel came up higher with each push, until it hovered on the forward lip, held in place by groaning, straining Afghans. They put their heads down and pushed harder, feet slipping on loose gravel, but the initial momentum was lost, and the tire dropped back into the hole—and kept on going, out of the rut and backwards, slowly turning toward the juie.

Nan and Mary were still in the front seat, their faces receding, their eyes wide with fear. Jo screamed. At the last minute, the men jumped out of the way. The motor was silent. The only sound was that of tires crunching on dust and gravel.

The truck came to rest with one front wheel on the bank, the other front wheel up in the air, and the two back wheels submerged in juie water. The front seat listed at a steep angle. Nan gingerly scooted across. She fell to her knees when she got out, in spite of the waiting arms of the men. They turned toward Mary next, catching her as she tumbled out.

Everyone was safe, *marsha'Allah*, although Mary's face was white. She wandered crookedly down the road. From a distance she could be seen walking in circles and talking to herself, fanning her face with her hat.

They waited two hours for a truck to come and pull them out, another two hours while the driver removed the gas line and carburetor, cleaned the parts, and reassembled the engine. He wiped his hands with an oily rag and cranked the handle. The motor backfired once and started. They continued down the road, coming to a stop in front of their new home. It had taken four hours to go the equivalent of five city blocks.

The truck was unloaded in the same manner it had been loaded, with everything piled in the front room. The driver stayed behind, waiting to be paid. He grinned brashly at the women. See? Thanks to God's will, they were moved. Why worry?

Still smiling, he pocketed his afs. He left and walked down the path, passing two young girls coming toward the house.

The girls were dressed in tunics and loose-fitting trousers. One wore a hijab securely on her head; the other had allowed her scarf to slip, and left it draped over her shoulders. They carried platters of food, and as they approached the Volunteers, they echoed each other. "*Man Mêrman Arsala*," said one of the young women. "*Man Mêrman Arsala*," repeated the other. With nods, bows, and bashful smiles, they handed over plates of pilau and chalaw. "*Khôsh âmadêd*," they said in unison. —Welcome.

My God, thought Jo. Mr. Arsala's wives. They are adorable. And so young! They look like little girls playing house.

"*Dâkhel shawêd*," the Volunteers insisted. —Come in.

"*Nê, nê.*" The wives shook their heads and backed up a step or two, as if terrified at the thought.

Jo inhaled the savory aroma of rice, meat, and vegetables. "*Tashakor*," she said. —Thank you.

The wives nodded, and not knowing what else to do or say, bobbed awkwardly in a little curtsey and left.

Chapter 14

THERE'S NO PLACE LIKE HOME

We cleaned like mad and moved the furniture into our bedrooms. ...
The swallows in the nest on the kitchen ceiling are big and almost ready
to leave.

—*June 22, 1968*

Mary's paintbrush dripped with whitewash. She held it with the bristles
pointed away from her face and bent her wrist to wipe a bead of perspiration trickling down her temple, inadvertently pushing her glasses askew.
She lifted her chin and squinted through smeared lenses.

"Can you see, Jo? It sounds like our mother bird wants out."

Jo was on her knees, scrubbing the concrete kitchen floor. She sat back
on her heels and looked up at the ceiling. Sure enough, a swallow twittered
softly, peeking out from a mud nest almost hidden in the logs and branches
that served as rafters.

She got to her feet and held the screen door open, pressing herself
against the door frame. With a faint whisper of wings, the bird glided past
her.

"It must be time to feed the babies." Jo propped the door open so the mother bird could return.

Since moving in, the women had washed kerosene soot from the windows, whitewashed adobe walls, and scraped mud from the floor. They swept debris from the back stoop. Chased out a family of ducks, and sent them paddling away in the juie to another home.

From the doorway, Jo watched the swallow fly up and over the compound wall. It disappeared into a cloudless sky, and impulsively, she followed it out the door. She came down the concrete steps of the front stoop, into the heat and brightness of the compound.

A footpath meandered through an assortment of weeds growing tall and spindly in the dust, some of them shoulder-high. A small concrete slab covered the well, dug by hand to a depth of twelve meters. An electric pump had been placed at seven meters.

The two side compound walls were common walls between the Volunteers and their neighbors. A row of small buildings lined the back wall: an Afghan kitchen, a little room for Alex, and of course the tashnab—a pit, a hole in the ground, placed in the far corner.

Jo followed the path through the front yard, to a wooden door constructed flush with the front compound wall. A small alcove surrounded the door, making a convenient niche to store bicycles, coal, and wood. Jo entered the alcove and pushed the door open.

The footpath continued on the other side of the compound wall for perhaps twenty or thirty feet, until it ended at the bank of a small juie. A couple of wooden planks spanned the rivulet of water, and she stepped across, her footsteps bouncing lightly on the boards.

Immediately, she was in a dirt street. Compound walls and juies flanked her on both sides, the juies giving rise to parallel ribbons of grass, brush, and thickets of small trees; the stone walls interspersed with wooden doors much like their own.

She walked along the deserted road in the quiet and lazy stillness of mid-afternoon. A fly buzzed next to her ear, and was gone. A bird chirped unexpectedly. The faint sound of rushing water came from the juies, and through shimmering waves of heat, she could see the distant peaks of the Hindu Kush.

The top of her head became hot from the sun, and she turned back. Retracing her steps, she crossed the juie once again, surprised at how quickly she had become accustomed to living in a compound, the security she felt when closing the heavy wooden door. She went into the house, where her bucket sat exactly as she had left it.

Mary's whitewash also had been abandoned. Both of Jo's housemates were at the kitchen table, Nan taking a break, and Mary writing on a pad of paper.

"I'm done for the day," declared Nan. She kicked a chair out with her foot, not wanting to move. "Here, Jo. Sit down."

Mary looked over what she had written. "Well," she announced. "Here's what's left on the list: kitchen cupboards, window screens, get Mr. Arsala to fix the well pump, and plan a trip to Kabul for supplies."

Jo groaned. She crossed her arms on top of the table and put her head down. And yet, she understood Mary's impatience. How many times had her own mind gone off in a million directions at once? How many times had she been caught off guard, lost in her own thoughts, spinning daydreams while everyone else managed to stay focused on one idea?

Thankfully, she heard Nan suggest perhaps they should do one thing at a time. This sounded more hopeful. She raised her head.

"First," said Nan, "we fix the well pump. After that we can worry about cabinets. And … I assume we'll go back to our friend in Kunduz." It was more a statement than a question, and all three women smiled at the private joke.

The carpenter in Kunduz. Mary had picked him at random for their first piece of furniture: a chair for the tashnab.

"Really, he did a fabulous job," continued Nan. "There's probably not a chair like ours in all of Afghanistan."

Jo gave credit where credit was due. "That was a stroke of genius, Mary. Who would have thought to have a wooden box made?" She visualized their little chair, how it was made with a round opening at the top, a hinged lid, and no bottom. It worked perfectly, and was much better than squatting over a hole in the ground.

Nan started to laugh. "It should come with instructions, though. Remember the workers who came to repair the compound wall?"

Mary looked over at Nan with amusement. "So what will you do? Draw a picture?"

"Well, it's obvious they stood on the seat and squatted down. They left dusty footprints." Smiling at her own joke, Nan picked up the to-do list and wrote across the top: *Prepare visual aids for tashnab use.*

The to-do list. It seemed to get longer every day. They negotiated a price with Mr. Arsala to have the well pump repaired, and cheered when it started, thrilled to have water pumped to a fifty-gallon barrel on the roof of the house. A pipe ran from the barrel to a shower area off the kitchen, and a spigot released the water, which flowed down by gravity. They had lime delivered for the tashnab. It came in burlap bags and was dumped into a corner with a scoop on top.

They visited the carpenter in Kunduz once again, and watched him make cabinets without a single power tool, using pegs and glue. His blueprint was a picture from an old Sears catalog. They shopped the fabric bazaar, and settled on navy and white cotton muslin for the sitting room curtains, watching the tailor sew them on a foot-pedaled sewing machine. They stopped at the miscellaneous bazaar in Baghlan and found a used spring for the screen door.

Mary put on her straw hat and cleaned out the garden. Even though it was late June, she planted tomatoes, cucumbers, melons, and sunflowers, humming to herself as she worked the ground.

Finally, as Afghan law required, they registered with the police.

Jo went first.

She walked to the hospital and asked Dr. Ali to write the customary affidavit confirming that she was indeed a resident of Baghlan. It was standard procedure. As she expected, Dr. Ali took a drag from his cigarette and waved it above his head. "*Hêch moshkele!*" —No problem!

Jo took a seat, and Dr. Ali shuffled some papers on his desk. He worked in silence, becoming so absorbed in his task he seemed to forget she was present. Jo wondered if his behavior was meant to give her a message—the Americans were not as important as they liked to think they were. Confirming her suspicion, he suddenly jumped up, mumbled something about a meeting, and rushed from the room.

Jo looked around the office, thinking he would return soon. She listened for his footsteps coming down the hall. Nothing. She waited, becoming more annoyed by the minute. By the time an hour had passed, she was humiliated and angry. She thought about leaving, but what would that accomplish? She would have to come back another day and start all over again. When he returned almost two hours later, and presented the letter with a flourish, she was fuming.

Walking to the police station, she gripped the letter and her passport with clenched fingers, muttering the entire way: "Who does he think he is? He tells us how badly he wants us here, then acts like Mr. Oh-So-Important, with no time for us."

It was a relief to find the police official friendly and helpful. He returned her greeting effusively. He would be most happy to register her as a resident of Baghlan. "It will cost you only fifty afs," he said.

"Oh, there's a mistake," she said.

"No, it is correct," he said.

"But there's not a fee to register with the police."

"Oh, so sorry. Perhaps you are right after all. In that case, please hand over your passport."

As soon as it left her hands, Jo recognized her mistake. Her passport! What was the one thing drilled into them during training? *Keep your passport safe; you cannot get out of the country without it.*

She was angry with herself for blithely handing it over without even thinking. Outraged at the official for taking it. And yet, as she stood in the hot little box of an office, not knowing what to say or do next, a quiver of alarm passed through her body. She made a deliberate effort to keep her voice steady. "I want my passport back. You can't just take it away from me."

The official shrugged. He slid the document across the counter toward her as if it meant nothing to him.

Jo retrieved it, flooded with a sense of relief as soon as her fingers came in contact with the blue cover.

She glared at him. He smiled back innocently and waited. Now it was her turn.

The lines to this little play were already written, and he held the script in his hand. The ending never varied. Her choices were simple: pay the bribe, or become a displaced person.

Jo was seething by the time she got home. It had been a wasted morning—bad enough, but her fifty afs! Indignation rose in the back of her throat like bile every time she thought of it.

She let herself into the compound, hoping to be cheered by the sight of Mary's straw hat in the back garden, or perhaps some progress on the repairs to the house.

Ah, she could see the carpenter hanging their new door as she came up the path. He was replacing the old one, which had warped so badly it wouldn't close. She stopped at the bottom of the stoop. Hmmm. The door handle seemed a little high. And—wasn't it on the wrong side? She tilted her head and looked at it sideways. Unless she was mistaken, the door was upside down.

She peeked around to the back. No sign of Mary. Where was everybody? Nodding to the carpenter, she went inside and was about to call out, when she stopped at the doorway to the sitting room.

Huddled in blankets, Mary and Nan were curled up in the charpoy chairs, their faces pale and drawn.

"We'll be fine," said Mary. "You know how it is. Just give us a few hours."

Yes, Jo knew exactly how it was. Two or three days—sometimes even a week would go by without a hint of dysentery, then without warning, at any time of the day or night, the familiar symptoms returned.

She made tea for the two patients and sat with them awhile, contemplating her day so far. First she'd had to endure Dr. Ali's superior attitude, secondly the blatant corruption at the police station, thirdly a carpenter who couldn't hang a door, and now this. Would *nothing* go smoothly today?

Filled with restless energy, she wanted something to do—something physical to vent her irritation with everybody and everything in Afghanistan. She settled on the perfect activity. She would wash bedding.

It was a sweet release to scrub the sheets with furious energy in the tin bathtub. Lifting them from the water, heavy and dripping with suds, she twisted them, wringing out the water until her arms ached, then refilled the tub with clear water and repeated the process to rinse.

Pegged to the clothesline, the sheets billowed like white sails, releasing a clean laundered scent, cotton-like and sun-dried. Jo filled her lungs and returned to the back stoop in a better frame of mind. She braced her foot against the tub and tipped it over, allowing the water to spill onto the ground, making a large dark spot in the dust.

She was still bent over when the front bell rang. Her shoulders drooped. Now what? Would this day never end?

A young boy wearing a white tunic stood outside the alcove, on the strip of grass and weeds between the compound wall and the juie. With him were seven donkeys, loaded with bags of cement. The cement was from Mr. Arsala, he explained, sent over to finish the repairs to the compound wall. He led the animals to the backyard, and dropped the bags onto the ground, one by one. Each bag landed with a soft thud, shooting puffs of dust and dirt into the air. Jo watched helplessly as the dust billowed and settled on her clean sheets.

The washing had been enjoyable the first time. Not so much so the second time, she thought, lifting the heavy, dripping sheets once again. Her arms quivered when she raised them to peg the last pillowcase.

"We can't keep this up," said Nan that night. "Look at Jo. She's exhausted! And what will we do once we start working? It takes all day to clean and cook as it is. A simple trip to the bazaar can take hours."

Mary was the last holdout. "I don't know. I guess I never pictured myself with a servant." She tried to justify giving in to the idea. "But I guess if Kathleen and Rick have a *bacha* …"[43]

"So do Hans and Gunther," said Nan. "I'm sure they can recommend one for us."

"And he could watch the compound while we're at the hospital," offered Jo. "If anyone wants to get in, all they have to do is climb over the compound wall. Locking a wooden door doesn't mean a thing."

She didn't have to explain. Things left unattended were taken. Even though the Volunteers had little by American standards, their Peace Corps salary of 6,000 afs, or $70 a month, was more than most Afghans made in a year. If the Americans were foolish enough to leave their belongings unguarded, it was understood the items were free for the taking.

His name was Jaleal. Thin from recurring bouts of malaria, he was cheerful, hard working, and highly recommended by Hans and Gunther. He agreed to his pay of 1,000 afs a month and almost immediately became indispensable.

He washed dishes, cleaned, ironed, soaked vegetables in iodine water, cooked, did handy work, and shopped the bazaar. The women had not realized how much of their day had been taken up with domestic chores. How had they managed without him?

"My favorite part is when he lets himself in and makes breakfast every morning," said Nan. "It's almost like being at home and having your mom cook for you."

Yes, everything was finally going smoothly, thought Jo. Everything except the reason they were in Afghanistan in the first place. The activities of moving and setting up housekeeping were temporary diversions. It would all be inconsequential if they couldn't recruit enough young women to open a school. They had been working on it since Peggy Cannon left, contacting everyone they could think of, beginning with the governor of Baghlan. They had networked with the teachers at the Vo-Ag School, talked to the shopkeepers at the bazaar, and visited every elementary school for girls in the area.

Nan suggested they take a break. "Now that we're settled, I think we should entertain. Invite Mr. Muktar for tea and thank him for the picnic. It's the least we can do."

They gathered in the sitting room with their company a couple of days later. Mary served tea according to Afghan tradition, putting sugar in the cups first. The casual observer might easily think the women and Mr. Muktar had been friends and neighbors for years, judging from the amiable manner in which they chatted, comfortable and at ease with one another. They discussed the Vo-Ag School and the various teachers. They revisited the picnic, the food and music, and laughed a little at Jo and how she was so tired by the end of the night. They exclaimed over the good fortune at finding their house, the progress of Mary's garden.

Conversation turned to the nursing school, and Jo talked about the amount of work still to be done, especially with the curriculum. She described Tarshi, and how she had relied on him during training to help translate her lectures. "I still have so much left to do," she said. "And Tarshi's in Kabul, teaching the next group of Volunteers."

Mr. Muktar listened. He barely waited for Jo to finish before he spoke up. "I can help you. Help translate your lectures."

Jo was momentarily taken aback, and stared impolitely. She had postponed translating her lessons partly because she was discouraged by the lack of response from the community, and partly because without Tarshi it would be difficult at best. And now the solution to at least one of her problems had been delivered to her doorstep. Mr. Muktar would be a godsend.

"That would be wonderful! But there's one condition. If you help me with Farsi, I will teach you English."

Mr. Muktar's smile was reticent, even a little shy. "Yes," he said. "I would like that very much."

A week later, Mr. Hyatullah accepted his own invitation from the women. He sipped his first cup of tea and listened as they talked.

"It's nice to be settled in our own home," said Mary. "And it's all thanks to you. This is perfect."

"Even the compound wall has been repaired," said Nan. She didn't mention the bags of cement, or Jo's washing on the line. "Oh, and I can't forget the well! That's working too."

"Most of the time," added Jo. "If it's working, we see Mr. Arsala every day. But if it breaks, we can't find him." She smiled. "We do see his wives, though. They peek over the compound wall to watch what we're doing."

Mr. Hayatullah laughed. "You seem to have settled into the neighborhood pretty well." He set aside his teacup, rested his elbows on the arms of the chair and brought the tips of his fingers together, making a little tent under his chin. "And what about your school? How do you plan to attract young women to the program?" He asked in a casual, almost off-hand manner, but his question was direct and to the point.

Jo felt her face get hot. Exactly how *did* they plan to attract young women to the program? It was clear they really had no idea. "We gave the information to the Vo-Ag teachers," she said finally. "We visited the elementary schools, and even opened the classroom to give an entrance exam …" She stopped, ill at ease with her list of excuses, and quite honestly, irritated with the entire discussion. "We've done everything we can think of. I thought the young women in Baghlan would jump at this opportunity."

"Setting up a classroom won't get you any students." Mr. Hyatullah shook his head. "And talking to the girls themselves? No, that won't help you. It's the fathers you have to convince. Not a single girl will come to your school unless she has permission from her family." Mr. Hyatullah's voice softened. He offered a last bit of advice. "Get Dr. Ali to help you. He's got more influence than anyone."

Jo almost dropped her teacup. Dr. Ali! He'd never help them get a school started. All he wanted were nurses for his hospital. Although she thanked Mr. Hyatullah for his suggestion, she wondered if they could count on Dr. Ali for anything.

After their company had gone, the women boiled water to wash up. Jo sank into one of the kitchen chairs. "Well, now what?" She put her elbows on the table, holding her head in her hands, making little circles on her forehead with her fingertips. "I can't imagine Dr. Ali is the least bit interested in helping us."

"Maybe we just need the right approach." Nan came over and sat next to Jo. "Why not use his position to our advantage? Play up to his ego. Tell him we can't do it without him."

Jo thought about the morning Dr. Ali kept her waiting hours for a letter. It was his way of letting her know he was a busy man. Indispensable, and so very important. "Maybe you're right." She looked over at Nan with a thoughtful expression, the beginning of a smile tugging at the corners of her mouth. "If ever there was a man with a big ego, it's Dr. Ali. We might as well try it. We've tried everything else."

Once again the women sat in Dr. Ali's office, only this time they came prepared, each one with a rehearsed set of lines. They had elected Mary to speak first.

"I understand completely." Mary bowed her head in commiseration. "You are desperate for nurses, but ..."

Nan took her cue. "But what an opportunity you have! Think of it—a nursing school! You can be the person who makes it happen, Dr. Ali. You can be the one who takes credit for a wonderful new program."

Jo swallowed her pride. "The school will not open without your help. We need you to speak with the fathers of Baghlan."

Dr. Ali made a show of thinking it over, lighting another cigarette and leaning back in his chair. He rested an elbow on the chair arm and held the cigarette in the air, between his first two fingers. With his thumb and little finger, he meticulously removed a piece of loose tobacco from the tip of his tongue.

"*Mowâfeq*," he said finally. —Okay. "I will help you."

He immediately took charge, declaring he would contact a family on the very same street as the Volunteers, as a matter of fact, a family with three daughters, ages fourteen to seventeen. He would visit the home of Jamila, Paregul, and Anorgul, and he would speak with their father, man to man. Afghan to Afghan.

Before the meeting adjourned, they agreed to schedule another entrance exam for August 22. With the date set, the women finished the last of the to-do list, choosing to be optimistic, choosing to believe they needed to have everything in order, because after August 22 there would be no time for domestic affairs.

Jo spent hours with Mr. Muktar, revising and translating questions for the entrance exam. Mary put on her hat and weeded the garden. Nan surveyed their dwindling food supplies and offered to make a trip to Kabul.

She returned a few days later with mail, news from Peaches, and a bag filled with treasures, including canned goods that were unavailable at the bazaar. Mary brewed tea, and the women sat up to the table, ready for Nan's theatrical debut. She dramatically presented the items, one at a time.

A can of tuna and a bottle of ketchup. Applause.

A loaf of white bread. More applause.

A bag of cookies. A standing ovation.

And finally, a used portable record player, left behind by a Volunteer who was going home. Jo hopped up and hugged Nan out of sheer joy. Now they had music! Nan laughed so hard she began crying. "My God, we look like we're out of our minds!"

The three women shared a love of music. Jo grew up listening to the classics. Nan could sing the lyrics to almost every song from every Broadway show ever produced, and now she put on the first record, the soundtrack from "West Side Story."

"When you're a Jet, you're a Jet all the way," rocked through the little house, and Nan sang at the top of her lungs. Jo read her mail and was happy to note her dad had received his Karakul hat. She folded the letter so she could read it again in private, and opened a small packet.

"Guess what!?" She held up her gift and shouted above the music. "We have flea powder!"

"Oh—that reminds me." Nan stopped dancing. "I almost forgot. The Peace Corps doc. You know, Dr. Cole. Anyway, he wants to see you, Jo."

She resumed moving to the music and held her index finger to her temple. "The usual routine. He wants to make sure you're okay. Like we're not a little crazy to be here in the first place."

Jo started laughing. She almost hugged herself in delight. They had their own home at last, and in a sense, their own little family: Jo, Nan, Mary, Alex, and Jaleal.

Chapter 15

ROXANNE

*It was 113 degrees today, and yesterday it was 118. The carpenter came
with our new furniture.*

—July 6, 1968

Jo kept finding reasons to postpone her visit to Dr. Cole. It was a long taxi
ride across the Hindu Kush; she didn't know her way around Kabul; there
was work to be done at home, lessons that needed to be translated. Already,
Jo felt a sense of responsibility for the nursing school, and they hadn't even
started.

She finally left early on a July morning, while it was still cool. As the
taxi driver pulled out of the taxi bazaar, she couldn't help but reflect on her
adjustment to Baghlan in just a few short months. It had been strange and
unfamiliar when they unloaded the station wagons and Ken's truck. Now
it felt like home.

The quirks of everyday living had gradually become ordinary and
familiar, even bordering on normal. She couldn't imagine their street as
anything else but a dirt road. Their bacha Jaleal was part of the household.

Summer days were hot, dry and blistering, but the nights were cool, with temperatures dipping as low as sixty degrees. Neighbors brought little gifts: melons, cooked partridges, plants for the garden. Mr. Arsala had two wives. The neighborhood kids rang the front bell for entertainment.

The women stood in a row on the back stoop every morning to brush their teeth, their spit making a semi-permanent white circle on the ground. They boiled water and stored it in earthen-ware jugs, knowing that moisture seeps through the porous material, keeping the water cool even on the hottest days. Taxis were four-cylinder sedans, and they carried eight people. That's how it is, thought Jo. She moved to a more comfortable position. That's just Afghanistan.

But when the taxi arrived in Kabul, she was taken by surprise. The traffic! The noise and congestion! When did the city become so big? She could have sworn the American Embassy was a small, nondescript building the first time she saw it. Now it was official looking, even imposing, with the iron railing in front, and flags waving at the entrance. When did the Ashraf Hotel become so tall, so modern? What had happened while she was gone? She waited for yet another bus to pass before crossing the street, aware that she had adjusted to the slow pace of life in Baghlan. Kabul hadn't changed. She was the one who had changed.

Even the Peace Corps headquarters seemed bigger, the offices bustling with activity. In the midst of the commotion, Peaches appeared to be at home behind her desk, efficiently handling the myriad tasks involved with the entire Peace Corps operation in Afghanistan. When she saw Jo, she gave a cry of delight and came around to the front of her desk. The two women embraced. They had a million things to tell each other, but they would talk later. This was not the time or place. They quickly made plans for dinner that evening, followed by a party at the United States Information Agency (USIA) staff house.[44]

Then Jo went in to see Dr. Cole, wondering why she had delayed her appointment with him for so many weeks. Assigned to care for Peace Corps Volunteers in Afghanistan, Dr. Cole took a personal interest in his charges, and Jo thought he was the kindest person she had ever met. He put the ear buds of his stethoscope in his ears and looked at her over the top of his glasses. A series of questions indicated he was interested in more than her physical health.

"Sleeping okay?

"Good. Now take a deep breath.

"So how's life in Baghlan?

"Not too homesick?

"Uh, huh ...

"Okay, I'm going to listen to your heart."

He examined the healing scabs on her arms and ankles. "Have a run-in with a couple of fleas? I'll give you some ointment to stop the itching. And your supply of malaria medicine? Do you need a refill?"

He sat back after the exam and studied her face. "Anything else? Any questions? Okay, I'll see you in a couple of months. Take care."

From Dr. Cole's office Jo made her way to the basement of the Peace Corps building, where odds and ends were stored: discarded chairs, books, unused bookcases, and outdated magazines. They were all free for the taking, and she picked up a few back issues of *Time* and *Life*. They would be a treasure in Baghlan. In a corner of the basement, she noticed what seemed to be a stack of small, antiquated appliances. They were separated from the free items, and a closer inspection revealed they were half-size refrigerators. The mother lode! She scurried back up the stairs to the main office and appealed to the director.

"The Volunteers in Baghlan could certainly use one of them," she said, suddenly wishing she had Nan's panache, Nan's gift for dramatic flair. Regardless, she did the best she could. "We're storing food without refrigeration, for heaven's sake. Why, it's a wonder no one has died from food poisoning!"

"I understand." The director tried not to smile at Jo's impassioned plea. "I'll look into it. But I can't promise anything."

Jo spent the rest of the day running errands. She hired a truck, then picked up packages at the Cooperative for Assistance and Relief Everywhere (CARE) headquarters, and shopped for supplies. After everything was loaded, she made arrangements with the driver to pick her up early the next morning for the return trip to Baghlan. Finally, at the end of the day she sat down to dinner with Peaches in her apartment.

The two women talked nonstop as they ate. Peaches went first, reporting the news in Kabul, the unrest among the university students and the demonstrations. She brought Jo up to date on what everyone was doing. Charlotte Budum was teaching biology at a boy's high school in Jalalabad, and Carter was off somewhere in the countryside with the agriculture group. Harry was in Kabul, but she hadn't seen him in a while. Sooner or later they all came through the Peace Corps office, she said, admitting it was fun being at the center of all the activity.

In turn, Jo related the events of their moving day and the truck teetering on the edge of the juie bank. In retrospect, and especially after half a bottle of wine, it became hilariously funny.

"I wish I could have seen Nan's face," said Peaches, smiling at the picture Jo had painted. "And Mary! She never loses her cool."

Jo wiped her eyes, laughing all over again at the sight of Mary, walking in circles and waving her hat. "It seemed like a disaster at the time. But it's a memory that will link me to this place and these people for the rest of my life."

"Well, no time to get sentimental." Peaches stood, clearing the table. "It's time to party!"

Jo picked up her plate. "Geez, it's been a long time …"

Peaches smiled knowingly. "It's like riding a bike."

✦

It took a monumental effort to pry Jo away from an exaggerated sense of duty, but once she made the shift, she made it completely. As soon as she entered the USIA staff house, heard the music, and eyed a table filled with American food and hors d'oeuvres, she remembered what it was like to go out and have a good time.[45]

A couple of drinks, a plate of imported shrimp and appetizers, and Baghlan became a distant memory, the nursing school forgotten. She had another drink with Volunteers from Glasgow, Scotland and Yorkshire, England, entertained by their jokes and comments, captivated by their accents. She danced with several USIA personnel, vaguely aware that one of the American airmen was from Grant Park, Illinois, less than twenty miles from her hometown.

The staff house closed at midnight, and the party moved to PC 15—a Peace Corps house for American Volunteers and vaccinators. After that, it was on to Peaches' apartment for coffee and sandwiches. Jo laughed all the way there, and when she stumbled and fell, but kept on laughing, her friends knew it was time to get her to bed.

Peaches found a spot for Jo on the floor, among the other guests who had opted to stay for the night. She put Jo in a sleeping bag and zipped her up.

Jo couldn't stop giggling. She was in the softest bed she could imagine—and it was the funniest thing—she broke into another round of contagious laughter. She was on the floor!

She turned over, and the apartment quieted. Slipping into the sweet darkness of sleep, her last conscious thought was that she had to remember something, and that it was terribly important. Something about tomorrow. She struggled to think. Tomorrow ...

But tomorrow was already today.

Oh, yeah, that must be it.

Tomorrow was today.

Her eyes sprang open in the dark.

Today! The truck driver was picking her up today at five-thirty a.m.

She freed an arm to unzip her bag. She got up, stumbled to the window and checked her watch in the moonlight. Four-thirty. She couldn't fall asleep now.

Tiptoeing around the sleeping bodies, she gathered her things and opened the door. Already, birds chirped in the tree branches above her. She sat on the steps outside Peaches' apartment and put her head in her hands.

At five-thirty a truck pulled up and stopped. In the front seat was the driver, along with his wife and five children. The kids stared at Jo with big round eyes when she climbed into the cab, and for her part, Jo did her best, giving them a crooked smile in her hungover state. She even took one of the smaller ones onto her lap—after all, they were adorable—but when their father put the truck in gear and revved the engine, her head pounded and she saw stars.

Loaded on the truck were all the supplies going to Baghlan with her: fifty pounds of flour, ten pounds of powdered milk, canned goods, cocoa, coffee, custard powder, CARE packages, and one used Electrolux refrigerator. Made in Sweden, it could run on electricity or kerosene.

Alex bounded out to meet her when she returned, jumping up in his eagerness to have her back. He nuzzled against her, licking her face when she bent down to rub his ears. He ran back and forth as they unloaded the truck, barking once in excitement. Not until the driver left with his family and the house was quiet did he retreat to his usual spot on the back stoop.

The women put away supplies, astounded at their good fortune.

"A refrigerator!" Mary could hardly believe it. "Good work, Jo."

Nan opened and shut the door several times for the simple pleasure of doing so. "We have to name her, you know. What do you think?"

They talked about it over dinner, finally settling on Roxanne, as a nod to the Afghan princess bride of Alexander the Great. Jo's headache improved after the third cup of tea, and the voices of the women carried softly into the summer night.

Alex listened from the back stoop. He rested his head on his front paws, raising it occasionally at a particularly loud outburst of laughter. Each time he lowered his head again, waiting patiently.

It was dark when Jo finally left the house and made her way to the back corner of the compound. Without a sound, Alex got up and followed her, hiding in the shadows. The minute she set her flashlight on the ground, he sprang forward, snapped it up, and ran off.

Jo chased him into the house, shouting and swearing at him. She picked up one of their new magazines, but Alex nimbly dodged most of her swats. Regardless, it was a small price to pay. He had retaliated for his master's absence. After receiving Jo's final reprimand, he reclaimed his spot on the back stoop. And then, just as he did every night, he waited for the women to go to bed. When the last light was turned off, he got up and padded to his own bed at the back of the compound.

The next evening Jo sat at the kitchen table, the entrance exam questions spread out in front of her. She could hear Alex playing outside. Mary worked in the kitchen, filling the pressure cooker with meat and vegetables in preparation for dinner. Nan was engrossed in a book. Roxanne had been hooked up, and supplies put away. A cotton rug covered the floor in the sitting room.

The mother swallow and her babies had flown away.

"Little Women" Nan and Jo

Alex

Jo and Mr. Muktar

Mary and Wyhab

Jo with her girls

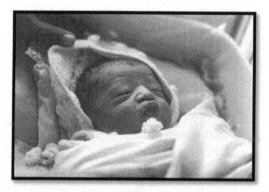

Newborn girl

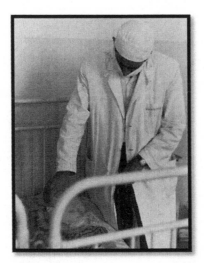

Afghan Physician, Kandahar Hospital

Kamila's brother and his uncle providing music

The camel owner in Lashkar Gar

Neighborhood kids playing in the juie

Nan washing clothes in the tin bathtub

Jo with Mr. Arsala and his family

Mr. Arsala's wives

Nan and her students

F Kamila pouring tea, with hair curlers hidden under her hijab

Jo riding a gaudie, on the wooden bench

Kamila working at the hospital

Anorgul with her youngest brother.

Waiting for the moving truck to be repaired. Mary in her dress and straw hat

Jo and Sedika

Chapter 16

CURRICULUM DEVELOPMENT

Finally thirteen students showed up for the entrance exam. It was bed-lam as far as cheating goes.

—August 22, 1968

Ostensibly, Mr. Hyatullah had come for tea, invited to admire the lat-est improvements to the house: the navy and white curtains in the sitting room, the new rug. Jo perched on the edge of her charpoy seat with a tea-cup in hand, making a conscious effort to follow the conversation around her. Instead, like a tongue playing with a loose tooth, her thoughts drifted to the same nagging worries: the entrance exam, and whether or not she would be a good teacher.

Mr. Hyatullah had been gracious and interested in everything the women had to show him, but Jo doubted he was there to see curtains and rugs. He was there because …

She looked up and met his direct gaze. In that unguarded moment she felt exposed and vulnerable, aware that he had been watching her. And yet, she was able to intuit his silent communication. *He's evaluating our odds* of success, she thought. He wants a better Afghanistan, and he's counting on us to help make it happen.

As if reading her thoughts, he spoke in a soft baritone. "Don't worry, Jo. I'm sure you'll make a fine teacher."

She allowed herself the barest hint of a smile. "We'll find out soon enough, I guess. The entrance exam is almost finished, thanks to Mr. Muktar. I couldn't have done it without him." She didn't elaborate. It would have taken all evening to describe the amount of work the two of them had done, the painstaking process of translating the questions and answers.

Most nights they had worked at the kitchen table, looking as if they could have been students themselves. Jo's feet barely touched the floor, and although Mr. Muktar was taller, it wasn't by much. Occasionally the electricity went out, and on those nights they put a kerosene lamp on the table between them, adjusted the wick, and continued, bending their heads toward each other as they worked, their faces illuminated by the circle of light—Jo frowning slightly in concentration, and Mr. Muktar's finely handsome features intent upon the task at hand, the scar above his eyebrow hardly noticeable in the steady flame.

It had been a long and arduous process from the beginning. Even before Jo wrote the first question, the women spent hours discussing the scope of the examination, debating how to most accurately assess the girls' education. How well could their prospective students read and write? Did they have basic math skills?

And the test itself—how would it be given? In Farsi, of course, but how? Certainly not written, the Volunteers didn't know the Arabic alphabet, and the Afghans couldn't read transliterated Farsi with its Roman letters. Someone would have to read the test out loud. Perhaps Dr. Ali should read the questions himself, so there would be no misunderstanding.

Each girl would be paid three dollars a month, the cost of the stipend shared jointly by the Peace Corps and the Afghan government. The two-year program would qualify the girls to attend midwifery school in Kabul.

It was an exciting concept, and Jo found it hard not to get carried away with her vision of educating professional nurses. Yes, it all sounded grand

and monumental—a siren call to the delusion that perhaps it was all possible. Jo had to remind herself that in the real world of Afghanistan, girls were discouraged from attending school, sometimes even grammar school, denied an education by controlling fathers, uncles, brothers, and husbands.

The majority of Afghan men refused to meddle with centuries of tradition. Why educate a young girl? It would fill her head with new ideas, and make it that much harder to keep her behind compound walls. Her very presence would undermine the established order of society.

Jo wondered if the Volunteers were wasting their time, if they would get even one student across the threshold and into the classroom. Still, she tried to remain optimistic. This was 1968, after all. Things were changing. Women's suffrage had passed in 1964, and women in Kabul were attending the university and wearing Western clothes. Although progress was tied to Afghanistan's dependence on the Soviet Union for economic and military assistance, it was progress, nonetheless.[46]

Changes were slow to reach the provinces, however. In the small, outlying villages of Afghanistan, women continued to linger in prisons of chador and compound, their incarceration self-imposed by the power of culture and society. It was in Baghlan that Jo first heard the accepted adage: *A woman should leave the seclusion of her compound walls only twice in her lifetime—on her wedding day, and the day she is carried out for her funeral.*

She was very much aware the men of Baghlan talked about the American women and their intrusive, new ideas. It was evident by the sidelong glances she received in public, the way conversations halted when she came within earshot. Other times she suspected the remarks were made purposefully. Shopping at the bazaar one day, she was certain the discussion was for her benefit.

"Of course, we welcome the Peace Corps," one of the men was saying. "But it is one thing to be a guest in our country and another thing to open a school."

One of the fathers countered with his own view. "They have come from the United States all the way to Afghanistan, just so they can educate our daughters."

A third man allowed his eyes to shift toward Jo. "*Bas.*" He spat out the word. —Enough. "So you want your daughters to become nurses? They will be forced to touch strange men!"

Jo completed her purchase. The message was clear. The Peace Corps Volunteers were welcome as long as they didn't tamper with tradition. Walking home with her eggs and tea, she thought about the fathers of Baghlan. It took a great deal of courage to stand up for change and risk being ostracized. And yet some of the men were willing to do exactly that, allowing their daughters to step into a new world, a world of literacy, a world they themselves would never enter.

On August 22, 1968, the three women gathered in the empty classroom on the second floor of Baghlan Hospital. Instead of her uniform, Jo wore a blouse and skirt, as did Nan. Mary wore a dress. It was a day Jo thought would never come, and now that it was here, she paced the floor.

Nan slipped into a student desk. "Relax, Jo. We've done everything humanly possible."

With an effort Mary folded her tall frame into a desk across the aisle. "What I wouldn't give for a cigarette." Catching the alarm on Jo's face, she hastily added, "Sorry—I guess I'm just nervous for you."

"Oh, that's a big help." Jo rolled her eyes.

The women laughed briefly.

Their laughter died away and the silence returned.

Mary fidgeted. Jo paced. Nan waited.

Footsteps came down the hall and stopped outside the door. Jo held her breath and did not exhale until Kathleen appeared in the doorway.

The fourth member of the group took a seat. "Sorry I'm late. But I see you guys have everything under control."

"Yeah, everything but the students." Jo resumed pacing, then stopped. Did she hear a group of young girls, chattering and laughing in Farsi? All four women looked toward the door. Jo stood with Nan and Kathleen, ready to greet their students. Mary struggled to extricate herself from her desk.

Months of preparation—the training in Estes Park, the hours of learning Farsi, the work on curriculum, and the adjustment to life in Baghlan—it all came down to this: roughly a dozen Afghan girls filing into the room.

They came dressed in trousers and tunics. Some were tall and full-figured, others not much more than little girls. Most had covered their heads with a hijab, the scarf crossed loosely in front and the ends draped over their shoulders.

The Volunteers greeted their students for the first time. *"Asalâmu alaykum."*

"Alaykum asalâm." Some greeted the teachers with bashful smiles, others with open curiosity. The room filled, and while there was no precedent for today's exam, nevertheless Jo had harbored a vague expectation of how the students would behave. They will take their seats more or less in silence, she thought. They will be shy and wait politely for the teachers to speak first. And so, she was caught off guard when there seemed to be one continuous conversation in Farsi. The girls chattered and laughed at their private jokes, glancing up occasionally for a cool assessment of the instructors at the front of the room. They spoke Farsi so rapidly Jo wondered if her worst nightmare was coming true—she would never understand them.

She had planned to start the exam with registration, and called Anorgul to the front of the room, the youngest sister to Jamila and Paregul. At least it was someone she recognized.

"My name means Pomegranate Flower," Anorgul informed them. "I am fourteen years old, and I graduated from eighth grade." She folded her arms, waiting for the next question.

"Do you have your eighth grade diploma?"

Anorgul shook her head. *"Nê, nê."*

"A birth certificate?"

Anorgul looked at Jo as if she had gone crazy. "Why do I need a piece of paper to prove I was born? Of course I was born." She held out her arms. "I'm right here. See?"

She turned and smirked to a couple of her friends, and the girls burst into laughter. Jo caught only a couple of Farsi words, but it was enough to get the general idea: *Don't the Americans know anything?*

Mr. Monier, one of the Vo-Ag teachers, came into the room to help, and the girls suddenly dropped their voices. When Dr. Ali walked in a few minutes later, they were silenced.

Dr. Ali made a few opening remarks about the test, explaining that he would read the questions, and the girls were to write down their answers. With paper and pencils distributed, and everyone ready, he began:

Write your name and today's date.
List the months of the year.
Name the king of Afghanistan.
Write the numbers from one to twenty.

He read a newspaper article and asked questions about what he had read: *Tell me what the story was about.* At that point, Anorgul could stand it no longer and leaned over to ask Paregul what she had written. Jamila turned around to make sure her answer was the same as that of her two sisters. Dr. Ali cautioned all three of them to be quiet.

Next, he gave them a math story problem: *If a woman goes to the bazaar with fifty afghanis and buys two watermelons for ten afghanis each, how much change will she get from the shopkeeper?*

The question set off a flurry of discussion. Led by a student named Kamila, the girls talked over the price of watermelons in general. They wondered how big the melons were, argued over which shopkeeper had the best ones, and debated whether or not it was a fair price. Once they were all in agreement, they worked out the calculation, compared answers, and made sure everyone wrote down the same amount.

Jo was stunned. Sure, the Volunteers had been forewarned about the communal society of Afghanistan. They had been told many times that while Americans prefer to work individually, Afghans are first and foremost part of a community that works together. But until this moment, she had understood it only on an intellectual level. To see the concept play out in front of her exceeded anything she had been taught in a classroom. Every activity, including taking a test, was done in cooperation. It wasn't cheating. It was a way of life.

After two hours of testing, Dr. Ali called a halt to the proceedings. He announced the school would open September 15. The girls were free to go.

They left as they had arrived, in groups and pairs, several of them arm in arm. Talking and laughing, they turned around for a last look at the Americans. Judging from their behavior, Jo was aware of being the foreigner, the one with the strange standoffish mannerisms, the one speaking Farsi with an odd accent.

The sound of their adolescent laughter faded as they went down the hall. Dr. Ali stayed for a few minutes to congratulate the Volunteers and then returned to his office. The Vo-Ag teacher went back to work. Once again the classroom was empty. Jo abruptly sat down in one of the student desks. She was drained, her knees trembling, her heart still pounding.

"Whew!" Nan ran her hands through her hair. "What a whirlwind. These girls are fabulous! I love them already."

Jo had not known what to expect. She wasn't quite ready to call the girls "fabulous," but entertaining? Yes, they certainly were that.

Mr. Muktar offered to help grade the exam, and came to the house as soon as he finished his day at the Vo-Ag School. They gathered around the kitchen table. Mr. Muktar translated the answers; the women tallied the results. A ninth grader—Habiba—had the best score, but even her paper had a number of mistakes. The sisters Jamila, Paregul, and Anorgul were about average, considering the average wasn't very high.

Malia was the oldest student at age twenty, and as Jo recorded her math and reading scores, she tried to remember something about the young woman. "Malia," she said, looking up at Nan for confirmation, "isn't she the one who's married with three children?"

"Umhmm." Nan agreed absently. "Yes, I think so." Nan was looking through the list, searching for an answer to her own question. "What about Kamila? You know—the one who started the watermelon discussion."

Jo smiled, remembering how easily Kamila had taken charge. A bit stocky, with somewhat of a matronly appearance, Kamila was a natural leader. "Take a look. Not the best score, but in the top half, at least."

Lastly, they graded Sedika's paper. Most of her questions were left blank.

Jo set down her pen. The girls may have attended elementary school, but it was evident from the test scores they were barely literate. The textbooks she brought with her were useless, and she would have to rework all her lessons. Even with Mr. Muktar's help, she wondered if she would be capable of pulling off the incredible balancing act that seemed to be unfolding: maintain an acceptable academic standard, yet present the material on a level the girls could understand.

Chapter 17

BAGHLAN SCHOOL OF NURSING

Made a discovery that all the students have an understanding much lower than the already low we knew about.
                                                      —September 16, 1968

Nan walked to Baghlan Hospital by herself. This was between her and Dr. Ali. She wondered what exactly she would say when she got there, if the lab would appear as antiquated on a second inspection as it had the first time she saw it.

Dr. Ali cordially received her into his office, almost as if he had been expecting her. Yes, he responded to her question. She was welcome to see the lab again. He stood, indicating they could go immediately if she wished.

The room was smaller than she remembered, the work counter narrow and inefficient, the equipment dated, supplies missing. Dust motes hung in a shaft of sunlight.

She turned to Dr. Ali. "I'll do my best to get this up and running. But I cannot work without a student."

To her astonishment, Dr. Ali agreed. *"Yaqinan."* —Certainly. "I will find a student for you." Without another word, he disappeared into the hallway.

Nan was left standing by herself wondering where he'd gone. What he was doing? She sat on one of the work stools. And how long was she supposed to wait?

Almost immediately, Dr. Ali reappeared in the doorway. "Here is your student," he said, and with a last look around, he turned on his heel and went back to his office. The problem was solved.

A bewildered auxiliary nurse came forward. The young man held out his hand. "I am Abdul Ahat. I took my training in Kabul." He glanced at the equipment and added quickly, "I've trained to be a nurse."

Nan was not prepared to have a student so soon, and scrambled to come up with a plan. She picked up a glass beaker covered with dust. "We'll clean the equipment," she announced. "And we'll start with this."

Abdul accepted his job without complaint. He went after soap and water, and followed Nan's lead for the rest of the day, ready to do whatever she asked.

Nan watched him as he worked. How could he be so cheerful, she wondered, so unconcerned at the arbitrary switch in career plans? He had gone from auxiliary nurse to lab student in a matter of minutes. Maybe there *was* something to the constant refrain, the mantra they heard over and over among the Afghans. *Insha'Allah.* If God willed it, he would be a lab tech instead of a nurse.

Because he was so agreeable, she overlooked a few irregularities in his technique. After all, one couldn't expect perfection from a nurse turned lab tech overnight. But a week later, he was still neglecting to sterilize the pipette between uses. He guessed at the hemoglobin and hematocrit in blood samples. And then one day she caught him recording the same result for every patient. She started to explain how lab results are used as a diagnostic tool, stopped at the confused expression on his face, changed her mind, and said instead that maybe it was time to quit and go home.

She related the incident that night at dinner, expecting at the very least some empathy from her friends. Instead, Jo laughed. Mary had a knowing smile on her face.

"Sorry," said Jo. "You might have caught Abdul making up numbers, but it doesn't matter. From what I've seen, most of the docs wouldn't know the difference anyway. As far as they're concerned, one value is the same as another."

Nan sat back from the table, absorbing this latest development. She had a primitive lab. A hand-cranked centrifuge. Docs who couldn't recognize fabricated test results, and now this: an auxiliary nurse who was not meant to be a lab tech, even if God was willing. Maybe it was time to face the facts. An auxiliary nurse was not a lab student, and frankly, the lab was unsalvageable.

The next day she relieved Abdul of his duties, took a final look at the useless equipment, closed the door, and left. She walked home deep in thought. If there was not a lab for her in Baghlan, what would she do? She had no choice but to notify the authorities in Kabul. Talk with Ken. Find out where the Peace Corps would send her next.

Worst of all, she would have to tell Jo and Mary.

~⌒⌒~

Jo was dumbfounded. "It just never occurred to me. I never thought of you leaving." She seemed to wilt, leaning back in her chair. After a moment she raised her head, her expression bright with an idea. "Maybe you could help us with the nursing program. Then you could stay here after all."

"I thought the same thing. But what about the higher-ups in Kabul? What will they have to say? And ..." Nan ran a hand through her hair. "And I'm still a lab tech. That's why I came to Afghanistan in the first place."

Nan had plenty of time to think about her predicament during the five-hour taxi ride to Kabul. She didn't know what to expect. What if the Peace Corps officials didn't give her a choice? What if they automatically transferred her somewhere else?

At the Peace Corps headquarters she took a seat in Ken's office and explained the situation. Normally very good at communicating, Nan found herself inexplicably starting in the middle, not making much sense at all. She loved Baghlan, she heard herself saying. And she was captivated by the girls in the nursing program, even though she had just met them. For reasons that escaped her, then and later, she leaned forward and described her favorite student, Kamila. "She has a great sense of humor. You should have heard how she solved a watermelon …"

Ken interrupted. "So what's the problem?"

"Oh. Um, well—there's not a working lab at the hospital."

"No?"

"No."

Nan bit the inside of her cheek. "And now I don't know what I'm supposed to do."

Ken leaned back in his chair and put his hands on top of his head. "Well, if you want a lab job, there are openings all over the country. Jalalabad, Bost, Kandahar—take your pick. And if you want a temporary job, I'm always looking for someone to fill spots when techs go on vacation."

Nan thought for a moment. "And if I want to stay in Baghlan?"

"You could teach English, of course. And with your expertise, you could teach germ theory. Help Jo with the nursing school."

Nan was quiet. When she didn't have a lab, she constantly thought about how badly she wanted one. Now that she had several at her disposal, it didn't seem all that important. Her home was in Baghlan with Jo and Mary. The women were three distinct individuals, with different interests, backgrounds, and character traits, yet they meshed perfectly, fitting together like the pieces of a puzzle. And after helping Jo prepare for the nursing program, Nan felt invested in its success. The more she thought about it, the more she wanted to try her hand at classroom teaching. The fledgling nursing school was off to a good start, and if anyone could make it work, it would be Jo, who continued to scrutinize every detail of preparation. Nan smiled to herself and shook her head. Jo was the most doggedly determined person she had ever met.

Ken waited for her answer.

"Yes," she said.

"Yes, what?" Ken teased her, already knowing what she meant. He needed lab techs all over the country, yet he understood more than Nan realized. Lab techs would come and go; there were few personality combinations like the women in Baghlan.

Nan returned home, and came into the house with a lopsided grin on her face. "Well, I hear there's an opening for a teacher," she said. "Germ theory and English."

With a squeal of delight Jo hopped up and hugged her. Nan would be more than another teacher. She was the friend, the spark that Jo knew she needed.

"I missed you!" said Jo. "And I know you'll be a great English teacher."

"Yep, that's me," laughed Nan. "*Mu'alim Inglisi*. And besides, who makes a better teacher of germ theory than a lab tech?"

Nan didn't waste any time looking back. Already, she had turned her attention to the first day of school.

⌐∩ἰ∩⌐

Were all first-year teachers this nervous? They can't be, thought Jo. How many teachers speak a different language from their students? How many come from a different culture? She eyed the rows of empty desks, anticipating the girls' arrival with a mixture of excitement and dread. The entrance exam had been nothing like she expected it would be, and now she wondered if the first day of school would be any better. She could not help herself from mentally reviewing their list of deficiencies. No textbooks. No library. No principal's office for discipline problems.

At that moment, the first student came into the classroom. It was Habiba, the ninth-grader who had excelled on the entrance exam. She breezed in wearing trousers and a tunic, and cheerfully offered the traditional greeting, "*Asalâmu alaykum.*"

A stream of young girls followed her, and Jo reviewed their names in her mind, half talking to herself.

Jamila, Paregul, and Anorgul … Okay, they're sisters, and they live down the street from us. Jamila is already a young lady and her dark eyes are beautiful. Anorgul—Pomegranate Flower—is the youngest sister, and the youngest in the class. She's wearing an exquisite embroidered top. I wonder if she wears it every day.

Kamila … well, how can I forget Kamila? There she is, solid as a house, surrounded by a group of friends.

Jo picked out a few more faces, and decided it was time to start class. She had the next two years to remember them all.[47]

She cleared her throat, feeling like an outsider, about to spoil a party to which she had not been invited. "*Khosh âmadêd!*" —Welcome!

Jo had practiced the Farsi words so many times she almost had them memorized. She gave a basic introduction to the art of nursing, telling the girls it was a profession to be proud of, and that the Volunteers were there to help them succeed. She followed her remarks with a review math lesson, relieved when the girls remained quiet and attentive. At the end of the review, she passed out work sheets.

It was like turning on a switch. The girls came to life, and snatched the assignment with enthusiasm. They resumed their conversations, giving Jo the distinct impression her lecture had been nothing more than a boring interruption. They called answers back and forth across the rows of desks, argued, erased what they had written, and copied from each other.

The Volunteers held an impromptu *loya jirga* —a meeting, an assembly of leaders, and quickly came to a consensus. They would grade the papers another day, they decided. Reviewing the answers in class would be mayhem: an open discussion with everyone talking at once.

Jo made the announcement. "We have finished with the assignment," she said. "Now you will learn something new. You will see how to make a hospital bed."

Jo and Kathleen gave a demonstration, tucking corners and placing draw sheets. Nan lined the girls up so they could give a return demonstration, one by one. Sedika offered to go first. Even though her performance on the entrance exam had been abysmal, her hands were quick and grace-ful. She would have no difficulty with the practical application of nursing.

The rest of the girls took their turns until Anorgul was the only student left. She had watched her classmates repeat the same task over and over, and was not about to make the same unimaginative movements. Instead, Anorgul approached the bed and danced around it as if she were dancing a ballet. Bolstered by her friends laughing and clapping, she executed a dramatic pirouette after each tuck, and raised her arms gracefully before gliding to the next corner.

Nan leaned over to Jo and whispered, "Welcome to the Baghlan School of Nursing."

Chapter 18

LESSON PLANS

Gave a test and gave Sedika a zero for cheating. Everyone is pretty shook up.

—*September 19, 1968*

"Yes, yes, the answer is true!" The girls could barely stay in their seats. They all talked at once, eager to convince Jo that she had most certainly been mistaken when she marked their test answers wrong.

"You said it yourself, *mu'alim*." Jamila spoke up. "You said that muscle groups work in pairs."

Anorgul all but gloated from the back of the room, sitting up straight and wiggling her shoulders. Weren't they such good students to remember all they had been taught?

Jo debated. Explain it again? Yes, muscle groups *do* work in pairs, she could tell them. Therefore, the statement that muscle groups do *not* work in pairs is a false statement.

No, she would let it go for now, she decided. Better yet, she would dismiss class for lunch a few minutes early. She walked home with Nan, still trying to figure out how to prove she was right, and yet, deep down she knew the true/false question had been poorly written.

"Forget the whole thing," said Nan when they sat down for their own lunch. "Start the afternoon with something new." She bit into her sandwich with gusto: her favorite, a thick scoop of Gouda cheese on nân, with mustard and onion.

Jo picked up her own sandwich, made without the pungent Afghan mustard. "Maybe the girls are giving us more information than we know. Maybe we need to revise our lesson plans. Teach the same way they learn. They don't use logic—"

"They memorize." Nan licked the mustard from her fingers. "If they don't understand the material, they compensate. They remember everything they hear."

Jo considered the classroom scene from that morning. It was true. The girls lived in a non-literate culture, in which fewer than two Afghans in ten could read. Consequently, her girls were exceptionally gifted at storing and retrieving facts, but they were nearly incapable of using reason or logic.

She was quiet on the way back to the hospital, the half-mile walk past the Arsala compound, along the familiar streets, and around the perimeter of a small park. Of course, she had always known of the illiteracy rate in Afghanistan—they all were aware of the fact. But now she couldn't get it out of her mind. The ability to read was a basic, human function. And yet, few Afghans would ever experience the pleasure of reading. They conducted the business of daily life by memorizing what they needed to know, everything from shopping lists for the bazaar and how to repair a truck, to family histories, dates, and recipes.

She tried to imagine what her life would be like if she couldn't read or write. *How long would I remember all the things I've learned and experienced over my lifetime* she wondered, *if it wasn't written down, if I couldn't look it up somewhere?*

Jo closed the page on anatomy and physiology. She moved on to the next unit: public health and sanitation. She wrote the test without any true/false questions or double negatives. On the day of the exam, she made sure everyone understood the material, and allowed time for last-minute questions.

Habiba raised her hand. "And well water, *mu'alim*?" She sounded skeptical. "Did you tell us we must boil it before we drink it?"

Jo hesitated. The Afghans didn't seem to have a problem with occasionally drinking well water. It was the Americans who suffered with dysentery. No wonder Habiba had questioned her. "Yes," Jo answered. "A rolling boil for at least one full minute."

With that settled, the conversation turned from well water to cleanliness, and from cleanliness it veered to a side discussion of laundry. It was an easy segue from laundry to clothes, and suddenly Anorgul was showing off her embroidered tunic.

Much as everyone was interested in Anorgul's wardrobe, Jo ended the review. She passed out the examination. To her surprise, the girls took their papers and started to work quietly. No whispered conversations. No peeking across the aisle to compare answers. She looked up and caught Nan's eye. Was it possible? Were they making headway? Even Anorgul was quiet, concentrating as she wrote. Sedika, too, was focused—unusually focused—with her head bent over her paper.

Jo sidled over to her young student and glanced down.

Sedika stealthily reached for the hem of her trousers. She slid the fabric over her calf, and bending her head even lower, inspected the rows of Farsi handwriting below her knee.

Jo quietly knelt in front of Sedika, meaning to get her attention and walk her out of the room without disturbing the rest of the class. She called her name softly.

Sedika's head jerked up. Her face turned white.

"*Nê!*" — "It means nothing!"

At once, the test was forgotten. The girls rushed out of their seats and crowded around Jo and Sedika. Everyone talked at once, each student trying to make her voice the one that was heard. *Oh, no, mu'alim sahib! Sedika was not cheating. See? It is in Farsi. It means nothing!*

Jo and Nan stepped to the front of the room and took a moment to confer, another *loya jirga*.

"Can you believe it? Sedika, of all people!" Jo turned to glare at the students, her mouth set in anger. Under her withering gaze, the girls began slinking back to their desks. "As far as I'm concerned, she gets a zero."

"Yes, of course. You're right." Nan looked away. The corners of her mouth twitched. Comic as it all appeared on the surface—Sedika's trousers and Jo's sputtering indignation—the issue of cheating was a serious matter. She put the images out of her mind. This was nothing to laugh about. Clearing her throat, she assumed a stern expression. "I agree. We nip this in the bud. Give her a zero."

The girls waited in silence. They had never seen their teachers quite like this. Even Nan, *mu'alim jân* —the dear teacher, the one who was always laughing and never angry, even she was no longer smiling.

Nan made it clear the teachers were united. "There will be no cheating," she said. "And no lying."

The room was quiet.

So quiet that Anorgul's voice could be heard distinctly from the back of the room. "*Parwâ na dâra.*" —It doesn't matter.

Nan was shocked. Appalled. For once, she was at a loss for words. Anorgul's comment was shameless—brazen, and so completely inappropriate Nan didn't know whether to laugh or raise her voice in anger.

"Yes!" she responded finally. "*Man parwâna!*" —Yes it *does* matter!

The class exploded in laughter.

What was going on? What was so funny? Nan folded her arms, waiting for an explanation.

It was Kamila who came forth with the answer—good-natured Kamila, who was a lot like Nan herself.

"You said, '*Man parwâna,*' *mu'alim*." Kamila held up her hands and made little fluttering movements.

"A butterfly?" asked Nan.

Now everyone wanted to help. "Yes, yes," they said. "A butterfly!"
This time it was Nan who was amused. "I am a butterfly."
"Yes," the girls echoed, laughing all over again. "You are a butterfly!"

—◡᪥◡—

Not too many days later, Nan had an announcement of her own. She would continue to teach them English, she said. But in return—could the girls help her with Farsi?

The simple request changed everything. It gave the students credibility. A feeling of importance. They had a job to do, and they embraced it. Nan had joked that she spoke "fractured Farsi," but—oh, *mu'alim jân*, said the students—that would no longer be the case. Not if they could help it.

It was an unorthodox teaching style, to say the least. But then, it was an unconventional group of students, in a less than traditional setting. The girls may not have known how to conduct themselves in a formal classroom, but they had two advantages: they were in their own country, and spoke their own language. In a sense they controlled the classroom dynamics. They had firmly established the tone on the first day, the day Anorgul disdainfully waived the need for a birth certificate.

And yet, who could argue with the girls' innocence, their naiveté, the transparent way they reacted to everything? Who could not help smiling at the bewildered looks, odd, nonsensical answers, and easy, open displays of affection?

The two groups met in the middle—the land between cultures, the place where Farsi meets English.

The venue was a concrete room with desks, a chalk board, and a bokhari for heat. A row of openings cut into the wall provided ventilation. There was no need for a discussion about raising or lowering the sash; construction on Baghlan Hospital seemed to have stopped before glass was installed. The classroom door was on the opposite side of the room, and the Volunteers generally left the door open on summer days, facilitating a breeze.

It was on a typical summer afternoon that Nan made her way through a unit on cholera. The door was open; a dusty breeze ruffled her lecture notes. She described the organism for cholera, explaining how the disease spreads through contaminated water. The nursing aspect, the importance of giving IV fluids to treat dehydration, would be left to Jo and Kathleen.

As usual, Nan stood at the front of the room, glancing down periodically at her transliterated Farsi notes—no point in repeating the "You Are a Butterfly" experience. The lecture seemed to be going well, and she was just congratulating herself when the girls jumped up in the middle of a sentence. They ran to the door, moving so quickly that someone tipped over a desk in her rush to get out. It fell with a crash, leaving papers fluttering to the floor.

Nan faced the rows of empty desks. The girls had done some bizarre things, but this … The floor moved beneath her, and she was forced to take a step sideways. She heard the rumble even as she scrambled out the door and down the stairs. Jumping the last three steps, she sprinted out of the front entrance and didn't stop running until she found the girls, gathered in a clear area near the park.

Only a small *zelzela*, they said. —A little earthquake. It happens.

"How did you know?" Nan's racing heart slowed down. "How did you know before it even started?"

Their young faces were puzzled. They didn't know how they knew. They just … knew. Didn't everyone?

Nan shook her head. How had they sensed the impending quake? It was intuition, she concluded. And we think we're the smart ones.

Now that it was over and declared a small *zelzela*, thanks to God, Nan feigned a hurt expression. "*Yaqinan.*" —Of course. "Run away and leave me behind."

She bowed her head and theatrically put the top of her wrist to her forehead.

"Oh, *mu'alim jân!*" The students clasped their faces, so profoundly sorry.

But the crease under Nan's eyes deepened, and she couldn't help smiling. "Aha," she said. "The joke is on you!"

The girls gasped at the cleverness of their teacher and her little *mazâq*, her joke. Soon they were all laughing, relieved to be safe.

〰◠◡◠〰

Jo regretted her words immediately. When she couldn't make herself heard unless she raised her voice, it was clear she had not adequately prepared the class for what was coming.

Nursing clinicals—the rotations through hospital wards—are a customary part of every nursing program, a way to give students the necessary experience working with patients. Before Jo could explain, however, the girls were formulating their own assumptions, based on gossip, conjecture, and misinformation—all rapidly becoming fact.

"The patients will be very sick," they told each other.

"We will be forced to look at terrible injuries."

"The men will call out to us with rude comments."

Jo held up her hand. "This will be easy. You will clear away teacups, fold blankets, and wipe off tables."

There was a stunned silence. Dangerous thrills and excitement had been snatched away, and the girls frowned in disappointment. This wasn't school. This was work! If they wanted to clear teacups, they could stay at home.

Complaints and protests faded at the doorway of the hospital ward. Brash, cocky attitudes disappeared. Faced with real patients—men wearing hospital gowns, revealing more anatomy than they had ever seen in their young lives—the girls were suddenly timid and shy.

Anorgul entered the room with her head down, her eyes focused on her feet. She approached a bedside table stacked with a couple of half-empty teacups and picked them up gingerly, as if she didn't want to touch them. Holding them away from her body, she tiptoed past the hospital bed and glanced sideways at the patient.

Back in the safety of the classroom, she recovered her bravado, talking from her usual spot in the back row. She turned to the student next to her and raised a shoulder dismissively. "*Hêch moshkele.*" —No problem.

Jo complimented them and upped the ante. "We will go again," she said. "But first I will teach you how to take vitals."

As they prepared for the next venture into the hospital wards, the girls' initial reticence was forgotten. They seemed excited, and if their assignment meant they would have to touch a man, well, they would do what they had to do. They were becoming nurses, were they not? They shrugged. No sacrifice was too great.

Not so intimidated this time, they took temperatures and counted pulses in a very professional manner, charting on each patient. Jo was immensely proud of them, even if the results were not always accurate. When she gently called their attention to the fact, they were quick to remind her. "*Parwâ na dâra, mu'alim sahib.*" —It doesn't matter. "We will do better next time."

Yes, all went well. That is, until one of the thermometers and the discipline book turned up missing at the end of the day.

Jo and Nan quizzed the girls in the downstairs hallway. No one came forward, but Anorgul's exaggerated claim of innocence was suspicious from the beginning. She denied any involvement, even declaring in surprise, "A discipline book? Why, I didn't even know you had one!"

The teachers reviewed the day's activities, and traced the thermometer's disappearance to the last user. Anorgul was trapped. Jo kept her behind and sent the rest of the girls up to the classroom.

Alone with her young student, she asked gently, "Well, Anorgul, can you tell me what happened to the thermometer?" Anorgul bowed her head, and as if speaking to the floor, said quietly. "I dropped it." She confessed everything—how she had cleaned up the shards of glass, and chased the beads of mercury until there was not a trace of anything left.

"The broken thermometer is okay," said Jo. She spoke kindly, wanting Anorgul to know she understood. "It was an accident, and accidents happen to everyone. It's much more important that you tell us about the discipline book. When you deliberately hide something, well, that's not acceptable."

Anorgul's posture—remorseful and penitent—changed so quickly Jo took a step backwards. Anorgul raised her head and squared her shoulders in rebellion. Defiant, she narrowed her eyes. "Why don't you go back to Kabul?"

The words came with a hurtful, cutting edge, as real as a slap delivered without warning. She might as well have said, "Go to hell." Jo's face turned red. She fought the urge to shake Anorgul until her teeth rattled.

If Anorgul regretted her remark, she didn't show it. Instead, she turned and climbed the stairs to the classroom.

Jo leaned against the wall. The excited chatter from the rest of the class, euphoric over their success at completing a real nurse's job, drifted down the stairway. It only made her feel worse. The joy and satisfaction of the first clinical rotation had been taken away. She followed Anorgul to the classroom, pulling herself up the stairs one tread at a time, steeling herself to conduct the group discussion that follows every clinical experience.

She reviewed the girls' work, congratulating them on what they had done well, and pointing out what needed improvement. She did not once look at Anorgul.

At the end of the day the girls left as always, arm in arm, talking and laughing. "*Bâmâni khodâ!*" a few called back. —Goodbye! Those in Baghlan would walk home. The girls from Fabrika—Sedika, Mastura, and Zakhara—would catch a ride with the hospital ambulance.

Anorgul hung back, waiting for everyone to leave. When the classroom emptied, she approached Jo. Her head was down, as it had been in the downstairs hallway, but this time she wiped a hand across her cheek, brushing away a couple of tears. If her contrition had been for show earlier, now it was genuine. She held out the discipline book. "*Mota' asefam.*"—I'm sorry. "Can *mu'alim jân* ever forgive me?"

Jo put her arms around Anorgul and let the young girl cry a little on her shoulder. She patted Anorgul's back. There had been a huge gap in their training in Estes Park, she thought; no one had warned them about teenagers.

Jo started class the next morning with a lighter heart, ready to put the incident with Anorgul behind her. She looked forward to the new lesson, showing the girls how to use a stethoscope. Mary closed her clinic for the day and offered to help, so each student could get individual attention.

They started with Habiba. Jo put the stethoscope earbuds in Habiba's ears, and placed the diaphragm over Anorgul's left chest. For once Anorgul stood perfectly still. Habiba's eyebrows flew up in surprise when she heard Anorgul's heartbeat.

Nan, Mary, and Kathleen each took a small group of students and demonstrated the blood pressure cuff, showing them how to inflate it, and how to coordinate listening with the stethoscope while slowly opening the stopcock. Once they had mastered the skill, the girls wanted to try again and again, so the women turned the equipment over to them, and gravitated to the front of the room.

It was a scene that repeated itself several times a day. The women frequently held an impromptu conference. They spoke in English, giving themselves a few minutes of privacy and the opportunity to say anything—an insight about the lesson, what they might have for lunch, what they needed from the bazaar.

But for the past week or so, Jo noticed that every time the women talked among themselves, the students stopped what they were doing and stared, their eyes fixed and mouths almost hanging open, taking in every movement and gesture the Americans made. She found it a bit unnerving, like having a camera aimed at her while she talked.

Today was no different. Nan made a little joke about Anorgul—how she had managed to stand still for once in her life—and the women laughed, aware they had twelve pairs of eyes upon them.

"What do you think they're doing?" asked Jo.

"I have no idea," said Nan. "They can't be listening. They barely understand what we're saying."

With that, she whirled around to the class and made a wild, crazy face. Stethoscopes forgotten, the students clapped and cheered.

This time everyone wanted to share the joke. They pointed to Mary. "*Muy safad,*" they declared. —White hair.

They made a diminutive gesture with their hands and indicated it was for Jo. "*Chucha.*" —Little.

And Nan?

The girls shouted with glee. "*Mezakie!*" —Joker!

By late autumn, life in Baghlan had settled into an ordinary, predictable routine. Every day the Volunteers walked the half mile to Baghlan Hospital, home for lunch, and back again for afternoon classes. Alex ran out of the compound gate to meet them every day after school. Neighbors left little gifts: a watermelon, a squash, a half dozen cucumbers. Mary harvested the last of the tomatoes from the garden.

They worked five and a half days a week. Friday, the Holy Day, was a free day. Thursday was a half day. Sometimes on a Thursday afternoon they took a gaudie to Fabrika and visited the families of Mastura, Zakhara, and Sedika. More often, though, Jo and Nan spent their free time with Kamila and her family in Baghlan, doing the ordinary things of family life: sharing meals, entertaining little brothers and sisters, and helping with household chores.

Habiba excelled in the classroom, Anorgul embraced the role of class clown, and Sedika continued to struggle. Malia, the oldest student, became a mentor to the younger girls. Kamila thrived, carrying her large frame with pride and self-confidence.

Jo gave an assignment one afternoon in October, gratified to see the girls quietly start to work. Their classroom behavior was much improved since the start of school, even if their academic progress still lagged far behind. One by one they finished the assignment and chatted. Several of the girls placed an arm on a friend's shoulder in a way that was familiar and endearing. An occasional cricket chirped from under the classroom window. Insects buzzed and whirred. The sky was a deep blue, and the air so clear it seemed to Jo that she could reach out and touch the Hindu Kush.

Chapter 19

SAINT ELSEWHERE

Gave my first solo ether anesthesia today and it was a rough one. The lady with a retained placenta fought and threw off the mask.

—July 17, 1968

"Keep the mask snug against her nose and mouth." Mary's instructions were direct, her manner calm and deliberate. She had done this many times before. But for Jo, it was a first—her first solo anesthesia—and she found that her hands were almost too small to hold the mask firmly in place and dispense ether at the same time.

No one had anticipated having to give anesthesia. Up to this point it had been a routine delivery. Dr. Wasel, the new *hâkem*, the new chief of staff, had encouraged the mother through a final contraction, then held up a healthy baby girl for her to admire. Mary clamped the cord with two hemostats and Dr. Wasel cut between them. Mary then handed the infant to Wyhab, the head nurse.

Everything had gone smoothly. The baby's newborn cries had escalated to tiny indignant screams when Wyhab washed her. The mother, who had been hunched forward for the last contraction, let her head fall back against the cart. Now that it was over she looked toward her new daughter, impatient to hold her. Mary gently massaged the mother's abdomen, encouraging the uterine contractions that would expel the placenta.

A thin trickle of blood ran onto the sheets, spreading out to a bright red circle. Mary applied more pressure, coaxing the muscles to contract, but still the patient's abdomen remained "boggy"—the perfect medical descriptor—soft and mushy, the uterus bleeding out where the placenta remained partially attached.

Minutes passed. The bleeding increased from a trickle to a steady flow, a normal delivery rapidly becoming an emergency. Dr. Wasel gave a nod to Jo, her cue to start anesthesia. He spoke a few words of reassurance to the mother, telling her that he would remove the placenta manually.

With her left hand, Jo positioned a basket-shaped mask over the patient's nose and mouth. The wire mesh had an indentation across the top to hold a piece of gauze, and she dispensed a few drops of ether onto the strands of fabric, hoping for a rapid induction. The first stage of anesthesia, the excitement phase, was always the most difficult, the phase during which the patient becomes disoriented and fights anything that restricts movement.

In an ether-induced delirium, the patient rolled her head back and forth, struggling to get out from under the mask. Jo spread the fingers of her left hand and grasped the patient's jaw more firmly, holding the mask with her index finger and thumb. Reaching again for the pipette, she dispensed another drop of ether onto the gauze. The patient's movements became slower. Another drop, and she became still.

Dr. Wasel inserted a gloved hand into the patient's vagina, gently manipulating the placenta away from the lining of the uterus. Jo barely noticed. She was absorbed in her own job, concentrating on the fine line between anesthesia and dangerous over-sedation. She had no monitors to gauge the level of medication. No pulse oximetry to determine oxygenation. No cardiac monitor, no gauges on a closed anesthesia delivery system, and no IV anesthesia agents that act so quickly the excitement phase is all but eliminated. She worked with drops from a vial of ether, judging their effectiveness by the patient's reaction, and a periodic blood pressure reading from Mary.

With one hand she maintained an open airway on the young woman, applying traction to her jaw, and with the other hand she lifted an eyelid. The pupils constricted immediately. Jo breathed a sigh of relief, unaware until then she had been holding her breath. She observed the patient's chest, reassured to see it rise and fall with even, easy respirations.

Dr. Wasel was almost finished. With a soft gush of blood, the placenta was expelled. Mary palpated the woman's abdomen and felt for the fundus, the top of the uterus. She massaged once again. Under her expert hands, it gradually became a hard knot as it contracted and clamped off the blood flow. The discharge from the patient's vagina slowed to a dark trickle. The crisis was over. Without intervention, most likely the woman would have bled to death.

Jo removed the mask. She was suddenly drained, her hands trembling. When the young mother emerged safely from anesthesia, Jo murmured into her ear, telling her the procedure was over.

"You are doing fine," she said. "And your daughter is healthy." Jo smiled down at the new mother. "Healthy and beautiful." Indeed, dressed by Wyhab and wrapped in a blanket, the baby was making little suckling noises.

Jo threw away the gauze, which still reeked of the sweet smell of ether. She experienced a few moments of exhilaration at her success. She had done a good job. The patient was safe and resting comfortably. But under Jo's elation was a nagging, uneasy worry. She was not licensed to give anesthesia. None of them were, yet since arriving in Afghanistan, they all did it, sooner or later.

From the beginning, Mary had forged ahead as the courageous heroine, taking charge of her obstetrical patients and refusing to accept the established practice of letting untrained auxiliary nurses give anesthesia.

Nan said they were crazy. Crazy to be in Afghanistan in the first place, and crazy to get caught between a rock and a hard place. "Whatever we do, we can't let the American Medical Association know about this," she said one day. "They'll send the little men in white coats after us!"

Joking was intrinsic to Nan's personality, and while it kept up everyone's spirits, it also kept the uncertainty of Afghan life at arm's length. No one had a clear explanation of what was accepted medical practice. Safe anesthesia was a necessity. Licensure seemed to be irrelevant.

Everything Jo had ever learned about the practice of safe medical care was irrelevant, it seemed. Syringes were boiled in a tin container over a kerosene stove and reused. Some days there was running water, and many days there was none. Patients had lice and fleas. Doctors were trained, or not. Oxygen was so scarce it was rationed for five minutes every hour. Flammable ether was dispensed in the presence of open flames, for God's sake, and intestinal surgery occasionally revealed the presence of roundworms. When Jo considered their circumstances, she thought perhaps Mary was right: they simply had to do what they could, the hell with protocol.

The Volunteers could adapt, or they could stand by and become judgmental, rendering them ineffective and useless. Neither was a satisfying solution, and over time, each woman worked within her personal capabilities, within the boundaries of what she was emotionally capable of accepting. As for the rest, well, there was always denial.

Whether she was consciously aware of it or not, Jo began to remove herself from what she saw every day. Consequently, her journal entries reflected an emotional detachment, variations on a recurring theme of withdrawal.

... We don't want any company today ... Locked the door on the outside ... Went to bed and escaped into sleep ...

Her medical entries in particular became flat, straightforward accounts of the day's events: contaminated surgeries, routine deliveries gone terribly wrong, and patients dying of treatable infections simply because there were not enough antibiotics. After yet another fetal demise, she recorded the ensuing Cesarean section for the expired infant:

Dr. Husini did a C-section on a lady who was in labor for four days and had a breech presentation. The dismembered body was removed with the placenta. No gloves were used, but all went fairly well. It's hotter than hell.

She glanced over the entry before closing her diary and was appalled at what she had written. *All went fairly well!?* What kind of person had she become? She held her pen, poised to add something—anything—that would somehow fit the events she had witnessed into the normal life she once knew. For a moment she came dangerously close to processing what she had seen, on the brink of tapping into the reservoir of emotion she kept tightly locked. Her hand trembled. She backed away. No, safer to keep everything at a distance. It was much easier that way. She would live with the delusion that she was unaffected—that maybe things were not so bad after all. She instinctively knew that if she acknowledged her grief, the unmitigated horror of what she had written, the events would become real. She could not allow that to happen. And so, she set down her pen and closed the journal, letting the entry stand as written.

Like other Volunteers in other parts of the world, Jo felt guilty for her lack of compassion. At the same time, she felt that she was not making much of a difference, and felt guilty for that, too.

~⌒⌒⌒~

Jo thought perhaps conditions would improve with the change in hospital administration. Surely things would be different when the new chief of staff came to Baghlan Hospital, sent to replace Dr. Ali.

No explanation had been given for Dr. Ali's unexpected dismissal, although of course there were rumors: whispers about a recent visit from the Minister of Public Health, and questions about the ongoing arguments between Dr. Ali and the staff physicians. But whatever the reason for his unexpected departure, Jo was surprised to find she missed her old nemesis.

He was crude, and yes, as Supreme Commander of the hospital, he spent the better part of the day in his office giving orders, cigarette in hand, surrounded by an entourage of people. Come to think of it, she never did see him actually work, but he was the person who had been instrumental in getting the nursing program off the ground. Ultimately, he had been the one who had obtained perhaps the most vital thing necessary to the success of the Peace Corps program: permission from the fathers of Baghlan, allowing their daughters access to an education.

Like most physicians in Afghanistan, Dr. Ali had been educated in Kabul and in Germany. In contrast, Dr. Wasel had been trained in the United States, and when he was introduced to the Volunteers, he responded in perfect English.

Jo had been encouraged. While she was indebted to Dr. Ali for all he had done, she also knew that he had surrounded himself with loyal staff members, and that his favoritism had allowed a few of the physicians and nurses to make their own rules.

Perhaps Dr. Wasel would change the power structure of the hospital—stand up to the male Afghan nurses and insist they follow the chain of command instead of working independently. Perhaps finally, the self-taught physicians would be held accountable for unsafe medical practices.

The hope was short lived.

Dr. Wasel soon made it clear he considered himself a cut above the rest of the staff, not willing to become embroiled in what he considered petty disagreements. He made very few substantive changes, and when he did make a decision, he rarely changed his mind. Above all, he did not want to appear weak, or admit he made a mistake.

So what if he's better educated and more sophisticated, thought Jo. It didn't matter. They had simply exchanged one *hâkem* for another.

Untrained doctors continued to perform surgery. Dressers—auxiliary nurses trained to apply bandages—continued to dispense anesthesia. The hospital staff continued to go home at four-thirty every afternoon. If there was an emergency during the night, well, there was always the *bâbâ*, the night watchman.

Jo considered Dr. Wasel's unenviable position. He supervised a medical team that ran the gamut from professional, competent physicians to doctors who had no training at all.[48] More dangerous, however, were the men who had a smattering of medical education—a couple of courses here and there—and considered themselves fit to practice medicine. It was this group of self-taught physicians who most often side-stepped the usual chain of command. They simply did what they wanted to do, and there was not a voice of authority to stop them, not even Dr. Wasel.

The Afghan nurses had their own problems: a long-standing personality conflict between Wyhab, the official head nurse, and a staff nurse named Ghulam.

Tall and almost painfully thin, Wyhab was attentive to his patients and sensitive to their needs, working with an empathy born perhaps from the struggle he had with his own demons. It was common knowledge Wyhab occasionally took morphine from the hospital pharmacy. His authority as head nurse was tenuous at best, and Ghulam was quick to take advantage of the situation.

Nosy and interfering, Ghulam roamed the halls in an oversized lab coat. He occasionally came unannounced into Jo's classroom, as if checking up on the Volunteers. It was Ghulam who spoke the best English, and Ghulam who knew the latest hospital gossip, often using it to his advantage.

For the most part, Dr. Wasel left things alone, choosing to work with the status quo rather than face dissention. The power struggle between Wyhab and Ghulam was left to play out without his interference. Self-taught physicians were allowed to continue without censure or restriction. Confronting either group was a battle Dr. Wasel was not willing to fight.

Not so for Mary. She had not left her family, endured training, and come all the way to Afghanistan just to struggle within a dysfunctional system. Confrontation? She didn't flinch. Older than anyone on staff, Mary had a Midwest work ethic combined with a determination to do what was right for her patients. She was perfectly capable of intimidating even the highest ranking physician.

To everyone's surprise, she developed a close relationship with Wyhab, teaching and mentoring the young man. The two were often seen deep in conversation, Wyhab's head inclined toward Mary, and the older woman's starched white cap moving up and down as she spoke. Whether they discussed medicine or his personal affairs, Jo never knew.

Mary could be gentle and understanding, and yet she bulldozed her way through the staff with a level of energy that left them staggering. She cleaned floors and washed walls. Refused to work in surgery unless the physicians wore gloves. Supervised the nurses and expected the same level of care that she gave herself. And finally one afternoon, she demanded the nursing staff stay past four-thirty to help deliver a baby. Eventually, she established an uneasy relationship of mutual respect with most of them. Perhaps she just wore them down.

It was Mary who admitted the young boy. He appeared to be about five or six years old, the age at which he might be in kindergarten or first grade—that is, if he went to school. Most likely he did not. His father laid him on the examining table, and Mary set out peroxide and bandages. She had already noted the abrasions on the boy's forehead.

The father explained while Mary set up the exam room. "We were in a gaudie," he said," and a car drove past us." He threw up his hands. "*Besyar zud!*" —Very fast! "The horse jerked and my son was thrown to the ground. *Didan!*" —Look! The father brushed the little boy's hair from his forehead so that Mary could see the swelling and bruising. "That was yesterday," the father added. "And now he is sick and vomiting. He stumbles around like he is learning to walk. He doesn't want to eat. Only sleep."

"Salâm." Dr. Husini's voice came from the doorway. Not much taller than Mary, he had a clean-shaven face, and like most physicians at Baghlan Hospital, trained or not, he wore a dark suit under his lab coat. Turning his attention to the patient, he spoke gently. "*Moshekel-e shomâ chist?*" — What's the trouble?

The little boy held his stomach and closed his eyes. His voice trembled. "*Oftâda'am*," he said. —I fell.

"That's all right." Dr. Husini carefully examined the bruised forehead. Felt the boy's scalp for swelling anywhere else.

Mary knew the visible bruising was the least of their concerns. It was what they couldn't see that was the greater worry—the possibility of bleeding into the brain, or swelling of the brain itself from trauma.

Anticipating Dr. Husini's next request, Mary dimmed the light in the room and closed the door. She handed him a flashlight. Obediently, the little boy looked up into the light. His eyes were brown, but even their dark pigment could not hide the uneven and sluggish response of his pupils, a sign of increased intracranial pressure.

Dr. Husini lowered the flashlight. "*Kho, kho,*" he said. —Well, well. He patted the boy gently on the cheek. Shook the father's hand and clasped him on the shoulder. "*Man mota'asefam.*" —I'm sorry.

Mary was stunned. Was the examination over?

"Wait …" Mary caught herself, aware that her distress was evident, judging from the movement of the father's eyes, shifting to her direction. She assumed a neutral expression and dropped her voice, falling into an experienced tone of professionalism. "Dr. Husini," she asked politely, "may I speak to you for a moment?"

As soon as they stepped into the hall and closed the door to the exam room, she practically hissed at him, keeping her voice low. "The boy needs to go to the hospital in Kabul! Either he's bleeding internally, or there's massive swelling. It might be too late already. And you're sending him home!?" Mary's fury was unmistakable, and it triggered a reaction of anger from Dr. Husini.

"And how do you think he will get to Kabul?" Not waiting for Mary's answer, he continued. "By taxi. And how long will that take? Five hours, at best. He will not survive the trip. Better to let the child die at home, in the arms of his parents."

Dr. Husini turned and went back into the exam room. Left standing in the hall, Mary heard his voice, deep and commanding, but not unkind. "Yes," he was saying. "Take your son home. *Insha'Allah.* It is in God's hands."

Mary watched them as they left, the father reaching down to hold the little boy's hand. They were almost to the end of the hall when the father picked up his son and carried him the rest of the way.

Mary was so distraught that night she left her dinner untouched. Jo and Nan were quiet. What could they say? Wee Willie Winkie, that's what they called Dr. Husini behind his back, a random, out-of-the-blue moniker that someone came up with one day, and the name stuck. He should not have been allowed to practice medicine. He botched surgeries and had almost no comprehension of sterile technique.

But in fairness, thought Jo, he worked against impossible odds. Patients tried every home remedy and begged the mullah for every prayer in the prayer book before they came to the hospital. Usually it was too late, forcing the physicians to become reckless—desperate to do anything to save their patients, and accepting the inevitable when they could not.

Regardless of how it appeared to the outside observer, a large percentage of the physicians were talented, well-trained and capable. Almost all of them had their patients' best interests at heart, including Dr. Husini. He could be unexpectedly kind, an advocate for those who could not speak for themselves. Jo had been present in the exam room the day he cajoled, even bullied, a husband into giving consent for his wife's treatment.

Only a small percentage of the self-taught doctors allowed conceit and self-importance to cloud their judgment. Ignorance and pride are a lethal combination, and as far as Jo was concerned, the resulting behavior was unforgivable. The day she witnessed one such physician's arrogance was the day she was pulled from her protective shell of detachment.

~⌒ᴥ⌒~

The young woman was exhausted. Jo could see it in the way her eyes closed between contractions. It was her first pregnancy, and she had been in labor for almost twenty-four hours—past the point of endurance—when her husband relented and brought her to the hospital.

Jo and Mary admitted her and immediately assembled the supplies for an emergency Cesarean delivery. As soon as the admitting physician arrived, they could start. The sooner, the better.

Expecting Dr. Husini, Jo stepped back in surprise at the self-taught physician coming into the room: a notoriously backward staff member. He examined the woman and pronounced her perfectly capable of delivery.

"Jo?" Mary kept her tone light, conversational. "I wonder if you'd like to go and see Dr. Wasel. Maybe let him know about our young lady." Although Mary's comment was directed at Jo, her piercing blue eyes were fixed on the staff physician like a laser, daring him to object. Jo didn't wait to hear what he had to say. She flew down the hall and into Dr. Wasel's office, breathlessly explaining the situation. Then half-walking, half-running, she returned with Dr. Wasel close behind her. They came into the exam room just as Mary finished taping an IV in place. Dr. Wasel introduced himself to the patient and took a few minutes to perform his own exam.

The baby's head was engaged, but the patient's hips and pelvis were too narrow for delivery, a common obstetrical complication for young girls having children. Dr. Wasel nodded toward Mary. He didn't have to explain to the experienced OB nurse. This was a clear indication for an emergency C-section.

"I think she can deliver." The attending physician reiterated his position, refusing to give up his authority over the patient he had admitted. He ordered Mary to start IV pitocin.

Dr. Wasel took a breath as if to speak, then closed his mouth and was silent. It was clear he wanted to avoid a disagreement with his subordinate in front of everyone.

Mary's experience told her pitocin was a bad idea, and she knew Dr. Wasel was in agreement. The patient didn't need pitocin to strengthen her contractions. It was the bony structure of her hips that was the problem.

The attending physician pushed on her abdomen. He attempted a high forceps delivery and the patient moaned, convulsed with yet another contraction. Mary was almost in tears. She checked fetal heart tones. The baby's heart sounds were diminished, the rate slowing dramatically. At that point Dr. Wasel exercised his authority over his colleague. He instructed the staff to prepare the patient for surgery.

Mary continued to monitor fetal heart tones while the nurses frantically prepped the woman's abdomen with iodine. They started anesthesia. Jo concentrated on surgical packs, fumbling in her haste to get them open. She didn't notice Mary reposition the diaphragm of her stethoscope low on the patient's abdomen, searching for a heartbeat, nor did she see Mary reach up and remove both earbuds, fold the stethoscope, and quietly set it down.

It took only minutes to make the incision, but from Jo's perspective everything was moving in slow motion. Dr. Wasel delivered a little boy, beautiful and perfectly formed. The room was quiet. No wailing cry pierced the stillness; no movement came from the flaccid, blue-tinged arms and legs.

Jo thought she might be sick. She gagged and swallowed. Her own heart thudded, feeling as if it might explode from her chest. Not knowing what else to do, she started mouth-to-mouth resuscitation on the lifeless form, choking on her sobs, her tears falling across the infant's face.

Chapter 20

BIBI DEEBA

Assisted a mother in delivering a beautiful baby girl with no complications.

—August 12, 1968

The life expectancy of a child born in Afghanistan in 1968 was thirty-four years.[49] While malnutrition and contaminated water were not direct causes of death, they were contributing factors. For women of child-bearing age, fifty percent of all deaths were directly related to pregnancy and childbirth. And of course, there was tuberculosis.

Her name was Deeba. Derived from Persian, the name loosely translates as "silk." It seemed well suited for the young woman with a soft, melodious voice. Her hands moved in a fluid, graceful way when she spoke. Deeba was in her twenties when Jo saw her for the first time, but already, Deeba's appearance had been ravaged by her illness, the skin beneath her cheekbones shrunken and concave, her movements slow and deliberate.

It began like it always does for the women in Afghanistan: a general feeling of tiredness, a little cough. Nothing to worry about, they would tell themselves. Who isn't tired, taking care of children, up during the night with babies? The cough? A bit of dust in one's throat, nothing more. The night sweats? From the heat, surely. And then, inevitably, comes the otherwise ordinary day, the day one first sees the blood-tinged sputum.

A sense of foreboding took up residence within the folds of Deeba's chador. She did not expect nor did she ask for medical care, knowing her husband would not allow her to be examined by a male physician. And so, her illness had progressed. Tuberculosis disseminated from her lungs to her entire body, wearing her down, sapping her strength, until there came a point when she could no longer care for herself. It was then that the family admitted her to Baghlan Hospital and left her there.

The admitting doctors had seen disseminated tuberculosis before, typically manifested by tubercular cysts, but Deeba's case was far advanced, even by their standards. Dr. Husini started her on the antibiotic streptomycin and performed surgery to remove a tumor from her abdomen, a tumor so invasive he was forced to create a colostomy.

After the surgery, Jo and Nan lifted her from the operating cart to a hospital bed. It was like lifting a child, the dressing on her abdomen too big somehow, as if it covered an incision no one wanted to think about. A small breath of air left her body with an involuntary sigh as they positioned her in the bed, her tiny frame barely making a dent in the mattress.

The doctors were surprised that Deeba had survived the surgery at all. Jo and Mary gently bathed her every day, softly calling her *bibi* as they worked—a term of respect and endearment. The nursing students were permitted to observe, a few at a time, and for once they were quiet as they watched, even Anorgul.

Deeba never recovered. The massive surgery, the antibiotics—they were all too late. A week after the surgery, Deeba no longer had the strength to eat, or even sip tea. Toward the end, during the last few days, she withdrew into herself. She covered her face with her veil and turned toward the wall. And then one afternoon she slipped away without a sound.

The physicians at Baghlan Hospital wrote in their reports that Deeba died of tuberculosis. If asked, Jo would have given a different answer: Deeba's true cause of death was her gender.

Deeba's husband and his family wrapped her remains in a white cloth and removed them to a waiting gaudie for burial. After they left, Jo and Nan stood quietly by the empty bed. A cleaning lady came in, and without knowing why, Jo put out her hand. "No," she said. "We will do this ourselves."

The two women removed Deeba's blanket and washed the bed frame. They put on clean linens. Out of respect, they wheeled the bed toward the OB department and left it along the hallway to the delivery room. It would be out of the way there, most likely not used again for a very long time.

They walked home without talking, past the familiar landmarks: the park, compounds, and open fields. They passed Mr. Arsala's house and crossed the juie to their own compound.

Jo tossed her books over the compound wall. Then, standing on one foot, she slid the toes of her other foot into a little niche, a worn crevice hidden in the stone and concrete. She pushed off and grasped the top of the wall, hoisting herself up and over, landing with a little jump on the other side.

How many times had they climbed this wall? How many times had they left the gate locked on the outside, trying to fool the neighbors into thinking they were not home? They did it all the time: after late parties, on free days when they wanted to sleep in, or simply when they wanted some private time to themselves. But never like this, Jo thought. Never had she so desperately wanted to be left alone.

She picked up her books from the dust and stepped out of the way for Nan, who landed beside her. Together, they walked up the path and into the house. Nan made tea and they sat quietly for a while, then Jo went into her bedroom, closed the door, and escaped into sleep.

For a while after Deeba's death, the physicians at Baghlan Hospital were a bit more attentive to their patients, the teachers more considerate, the students slightly better behaved. Wyhab left the morphine alone. It seemed as if no one wanted Deeba's death to be for nothing.

Mary, too, re-evaluated her role in Afghanistan. She felt an increased sense of urgency regarding her work in the clinic. It was impossible to see more patients in a day, but if she could teach as she worked—show the women how to care for themselves and their babies—she could be far more effective. And if she could involve the husbands, so much the better.

Such were her thoughts the day a young couple came to see her. Mary recognized them immediately. This was their second visit in less than four months. Once again, the wife presented with the familiar signs and symptoms: two missed periods, then cramping, a backache, and several days of heavy bleeding. The woman's face had an unnatural waxen pallor. Her fingertips were almost white.

A brief examination revealed there were no fetal heart tones. Mary confirmed what they both already knew. The patient had suffered a complete miscarriage.

She called the husband into the room. "I'm sorry," she said. "Your wife has lost the baby. But you must understand …" She hesitated. It was always a dilemma. How to get the message across, yet not speak openly of birth control?

She chose her words carefully. "Your wife will not give birth to a healthy baby unless she has time to recover. She must not get pregnant again right away. It will mean another miscarriage. And it is dangerous. Do you want to lose your wife, too?"

Mary tried to read the husband's reaction, but his face was impassive, and she repeated her point, drawing herself up to her full height. "Your wife must not get pregnant again for at least three months. Do you understand what I am saying?"

The husband nodded—like they all did, as if in perfect agreement—but what they did at home was another matter. When they were gone, Mary leaned against the doorway and rubbed her temples. After a few minutes she sighed and raised her head. She still had a waiting room filled with patients.

Among them was a young girl with both hands pressed into her stomach. Her eyes were closed, and she rocked back and forth slightly. Her husband nervously fingered the hem of his tunic, periodically glancing over at his wife with an expression of concern and bewilderment.

Mary assessed the couple, her practiced eye taking in the situation. The girl's tunic did not hide the thickening bulge in her abdomen. Coming to a swift decision, she called them in ahead of the others.

The stomach pains were getting worse, the husband explained. They didn't know what to do. His eyebrows drew together in distress. What was wrong with his wife?

Mary knew exactly what was wrong, even before she completed the examination. Not only was the wife pregnant, she was also in premature labor. Mary broke the news to them gently, and urged them to have the baby in the hospital, not at home. She appealed to the husband. "This is your wife's first pregnancy, and the baby is early. Let us take care of them both."

The young husband nodded, his dark face ashen. Under the circumstances, thought Mary, suppressing a smile, he would have probably agreed to almost anything.

She took them to the OB department and told the Afghan nurses she would come back as soon as she finished her clinic. She was halfway down the hall when she called over her shoulder, "Oh—and get a message up to Jo and Nan, will you? Ask them to come down as soon as they can."

The girls buzzed with excitement when the news traveled up to the classroom. A new baby! From the back of the room, Anorgul spoke up. "You should go right away, *mu'alim*." She closed her book as if that settled it. "Our lessons can wait. This is much more important."

Jo made a last few remarks and dismissed class. They would finish tomorrow. The Baghlan girls left to walk home. The girls from Fabrika went looking for the ambulance driver. Perhaps he would take them a few minutes early.

Jo and Nan hurried down the stairs, turned a corner, and entered the OB hallway. A window at the end of the hall provided the only light, and

Jo squinted into the dim corridor. Was someone peering out at them? The light was behind the figure, and all she could see was an outline. They went further into the hallway and the silhouette materialized into a young girl, hunkered down on the floor. Surely it wasn't Mary's patient having her baby already! Where was everyone!? Had the patient been admitted, then left unattended?

The girl had her gown pulled up around her knees. She gripped it with both hands and bent forward, groaning with a contraction. Jo quickly introduced herself as the *qâbela*, the nurse, and knelt on the floor beside her. She spoke a few words of reassurance, and gently lifted the gown to assess how far labor had progressed. She was shocked to see a bulging perineum, and the top of a tiny head. "Nan," she called out, suddenly a little frightened. "Get a blanket—the head's crowning!"

Jo cradled the infant's head with the next contraction, then a miniature torso, wet and slippery. It was a girl, and she greeted the world with a shrill, healthy cry. The new mother burst into tears of relief. Jo and Nan gently transitioned her to her feet, and awkwardly shuffled with her and her new daughter to the nearest bed—the bed they had washed and covered with linens, the bed that had been pushed to the OB hallway and left there, so that it would not be used again for a long time.

Footsteps and voices came down the hall as they settled the patient and covered the baby. Mary arrived first, out of breath and surprised that her patient had delivered so soon. "Well, you could have fooled me. I surely didn't think it would go this fast." The physician came right behind her, and now that it was over, Jo and Nan were surrounded by help.

Nan found the husband and brought him into the room. He stood at the bedside, dazed when his wife received their new daughter.

"Well, do you have a name for this little girl?" Mary stood with her arms folded. It had been an unorthodox hospital delivery, but thankfully, mother and baby were doing well.

The husband shook his head. He didn't know. Everything had happened much too fast.

It was then that Mary made the suggestion. "What about Deeba?"

The young couple looked at each other. The wife nodded her approval. Little Deeba it was.

~✿~

Mr. Muktar came for a lesson as usual that evening, but Jo wasn't interested in working. How could she concentrate? It had been such a happy day, and a strangely sad day at the same time, a reminder of how unfair life was for Afghan women. Would little Deeba learn to read and write? Would she have a husband who looked out for her welfare?

Mr. Muktar reached over and pulled Jo's books toward his side of the table. "Put these away for tonight. It's a beautiful evening, and too nice to study." He turned to include Mary and Nan. "We should go for a walk before the sun goes down. A long walk, far into the countryside."

He took them in a direction Jo had not gone before, not the usual route past the hospital, but toward the opposite side of the village. They walked until the streets of Baghlan disappeared, then along a path until they came to a high bluff and could go no further.

Already the mountains to the west were cast in shadow. A translucent sliver of the moon appeared to be hanging from an invisible thread like a precious jewel, sheer and transparent.

Jo listened as Mr. Muktar chatted with Mary and Nan. It was the end of the old moon, he was saying. In a couple of days, a new moon would signal the start of Ramadan.[50]

Jo stood on the edge of the bluff. The valley extended for miles below her, the folds and contours marked by tree lines. Guarded by the Hindu Kush, the vast landscape appeared the same as it had for centuries, untouched and pristine, and she felt surrounded by something pure and true.

A flock of swallows glided past her on the updraft, gathering in readiness for their migration south toward Africa and Madagascar for the winter. As if given a silent command, they banked in formation, becoming nearly invisible as each bird crested on a wing's edge. They turned again, suddenly appearing in full view, not unlike the unfurling of silk, rippling across the sky.

The eastern mountains caught the last rays from the setting sun and burst into vivid colors of red, green, and brown. Jo imagined bibi Deeba beyond the highest peaks, free from suffering; embraced by Allah, the Sacred, the God of every name, and the nameless God of all, loved unconditionally at long last.

Chapter 21

AUTUMN LEAVES

Nan and I started vaccinating in the rain and mud.
—*November 20, 1968*

Jo and Mary discussed politics with increasing intensity as the presidential campaigns of Richard Nixon and Hubert Humphrey began to heat up in the fall of 1968. The two women had much in common, despite their age difference. Both came from the Midwest, and both were nurses. They could spend hours discussing Jo's students and the young mothers Mary saw in her clinic, always coming to the same conclusion: education and health care were basic rights. They were dedicated to their work, and equally committed to the Peace Corps.

On other issues, however, their differences were irreconcilable. Mary supported the Vietnam War and took Jo's dissent as an affront to the military and to the United States government. Jo argued that if Nixon got elected, the Peace Corps Volunteers would be sent home.

"Ridiculous." Mary dismissed the idea with a little huff.[51]

Jo let the matter drop. Her friendship with Mary was more important than fostering an ongoing argument, and when her absentee ballot arrived with the next packet of mail, she retrieved it quietly and without comment. She filled it out in the privacy of her room and carried it to the taxi bazaar in Baghlan, where she hired a driver for the fifty-mile trip to Kunduz. From there one of the Volunteers would take it to the post office in Kabul. One vote cast among millions, but her vote nonetheless, and she was strangely moved by her participation in the process so far from home.

It was a close race, and although Election Day was Tuesday, November 5, the television networks were not able to declare the winner until the following morning. The news reached Baghlan the evening of November 6, via Jo's shortwave radio. Nixon won by a margin of 500,000 votes. Jo pressed her lips together in disappointment. Mary did not say a word. For that, at least, Jo was grateful.

In the meantime there had been other news. On October 11, NASA launched the Apollo 7 engineering test flight. The United States and South Vietnamese forces launched a new offensive in the Mekong Delta. Detroit won the World Series.

In the village of Baghlan, the women prepared for winter. They nailed sheets of plastic over the ill-fitting window frames, made apricot preserves, and pickled tomatoes. Nan mixed a batch of Afghan mustard, combining aromatic mustard powder from the bazaar with vinegar so concentrated and acidic it brought tears to her eyes. Her mouth watered as she mixed it.

They bought dried mulberry wood and coal dust at the bazaar. The wood was delivered to the alcove; the coal dust was brought into the compound in a wheelbarrow and dumped into the back yard. Workers came to mix the dust with a sticky by-product from the sugar refinery, and they looked like little boys making mud pies, sitting cross-legged in the yard. They formed the dust into hard, baseball-size coal balls. After the balls had dried in the sun, the women stored them in the alcove along with the stacks of wood.

Jaleal cleaned out the bokhari—a metal drum that stood on end, resting on a couple of bricks. A slender pipe came up through the top cover and was vented to an outside wall. A curved, hinged door toward the bottom of the barrel provided an opening for fuel—just the right size for coal balls and wood.

Jo and Mary discussed the shower and how they would manage in January, when the water temperature would be close to freezing. They finally decided to send Jaleal to the bazaar in Puli-Khumri. He returned with a workman who installed a wood burner amid a tangle of pipes and tanks that forced hot water to the top of the shower. When he had finished, Jo thought the shower room looked like the inside of an old German submarine, with pressure gauges and stopcocks to release the steam. The thought crossed her mind that she could very well end her time in Afghanistan with an explosion.

Mr. Arsala wrapped the outside pipes with rags, and when he finished, came in for tea. "The pipes are an easy job," he said, "but the roof!" He shook his head. "That's another matter. When the rains come, it will leak." He took a sip of tea. "I will fix it for you. And it will cost you almost nothing! Only one thousand afghanis." He sat back and folded his arms. "I have hired the workers already. They will be here next week."

Jo glanced up at the ceiling. Did the roof leak? They had no way of knowing. It had been a typical Afghan summer, with not one cloud, not one drop of rain since their days in the Sugar Hotel. She looked again at the logs and branches above them. The swallow's nest was still there, empty and abandoned. The mother swallow and her family had flown away months ago.

Not too many days after their conversation with Mr. Arsala, the women were awakened by the sound of mats and branches being ripped from the roof above them. They jumped out of bed, hurriedly got ready for work, and left for the hospital, closing the compound gate behind them. No point in locking it. The workmen would be coming and going all day. In her rush to leave, Jo didn't think to tie up Alex.

He waited until the women were safely gone before nosing along the ground, jumping out of the way as debris fell from the roof. When the workers came down and started to dig a shallow pit in the backyard, he got right up with them, sniffing at the turned-over dust and dirt.

One of the men jabbed a shovel toward him. "*Boro!*" —Go! Who needed a tame juie dog? It was nothing more than a nuisance.

Alex moved away, but within minutes he was back, not willing to give up his spot at the center of activity. The man turned to his co-worker. "*Hâ! Yaqin dâshtan.*" —Yes, certainly. "The American women have strange habits. Why keep a dog if it's not useful?" He took another look at Alex. "They probably feed him, too."

Alex barked once and panted, his tongue hanging out with pleasure.

"*Mowâfeq,*" the man said finally. —Okay. "Stay if you want. It's all the same to me." He sprinkled a layer of straw over the crumbling soil, and poured water over the straw. The men stepped into the mixture. With bare feet, they marched in circles, working the straw into the soil.

Alex danced around the edge of the mud. He pranced. He stepped gingerly into the clay mixture and backed away, only to come trotting up again. Each time he advanced further, coating his legs and underbelly with sticky, wet adobe.

By the time the women came home, the workers were gone. The roof was finished, the yard a mess, and Alex caked with mud. Jo was furious. "Bad dog!" She got out the tin bathtub. Alex whimpered and licked her face while she filled it. He stood obediently while she scrubbed, if perhaps a bit more vigorously than necessary, and didn't move until she had rinsed the soap from his coat. Then he shook himself and pressed his nose up under her hand. Sooner or later she would rub his ears and talk to him affectionately. She always did.

⌐∩∙∩⌐

In mid-October, autumn winds began rushing into Baghlan Valley, swirling through dusty streets and shrouding compounds in a yellow-brown haze of dirt and sand. The mud roof changed from dark brown to a light-colored adobe that dried hard as concrete.

The mud pit disappeared. A few spindly tomato plants hung limp in a parched and sere garden. Leaves turned brown and brittle. Summer didn't really end; it turned to dust.

The Soviet-built hydroelectric plant in Puli-Khumri was forced to shut down in the windstorms, and the entire Baghlan Valley lost power. Jo's shortwave remained silent. The water pump was useless.

Sand gritted on everything Jo touched. The women swept every day, yet within hours, dusty footprints crisscrossed the floor. When Rick and Kathleen offered to have a Halloween party on Thursday, October 31, Jo was happy to accept. It would be a chance to forget the everlasting wind and dust for a few hours.

She craved a reckless and extravagant shower as she got ready. Instead, mindful of the limited amount of water in the barrels on the roof, she opened and closed the spigot in the shower room quickly, allowing a miserly amount of water to run out, barely enough to lift the sand and dust from her scalp. Wrapped in towels, she padded into Nan's room for help selecting an outfit. They needed costumes, they had decided, and settled on dressing in each other's clothes. Jo laughed as she modeled Nan's blouse. She anticipated a good time.

Like almost all the parties in Afghanistan, the gathering at Rick and Kathleen's house gave Jo a chance to feel normal for awhile, to have the reassurance that she still had a place in mainstream American culture, that she was still part of the times, the free spirit of the 1960s. The Volunteers didn't have to censor what they said, mindful they might offend someone. They didn't have to apologize for the loud rock and roll music, the wild dancing, the booze, the games, or the inside jokes.

The customs were familiar, the conversations in English. And while Jo had real potato chips from a cellophane bag—compliments of a guest with UN commissary privileges—while she played games with the Volunteers from Puli-Khumri, while she tucked in Nan's blouse after a dance with one of the Kunduz Volunteers and was reminded that … oh, yeah, this was her Halloween costume; while she had another glass of Rick's mystery punch, something was happening in the skies over Baghlan Province. The weather pattern was about to shift.

Just before midnight a current of air shivered across the countryside and was gone, leaving in its wake an expectation, a sense of something to come. Moments later, the rain slipped in quietly, unobtrusively, as if entering through a back door. The first drops fell softly, shattered in the dust, and beaded into tiny droplets.

The residents of Baghlan slept; children turned over in their beds, and adults dreamed their dreams. The party guests had another drink, while the ground outside became pockmarked with miniature craters. The drops increased to a steady rain that fell in the darkness, gently washing dust from leaves and brush.

Jo, Mary, and Nan emerged from the party to a downpour. Singing and laughing, they slipped and slid home, clinging to each other as they made their way through slick, oily mud. For the first time, Jo understood why people sometimes fell into the juie. Still laughing and soaking wet, wearing a pair of Rick's old shoes, she tightened her grip on Nan and Mary.

～∩⁀∩～

Jo woke the next morning with thoughts of school and the day's lesson. And then she remembered. It was Friday, November 1. Juma. There would be no school today. She rolled over with pleasure and stretched luxuriously, pointing and flexing her toes. The rain lingered, the clouds and drizzle a novelty after five months of blistering sun.

She heard Mary and Nan in the kitchen, talking softly while they started coffee, and she inhaled, savoring the aroma. Times like this were her favorite, the peaceful mornings with just the three of them. She looked forward to a lazy breakfast, sitting around the table and discussing the previous night's party. She was about to get up and join them when she was stopped by the sound of the front bell, sharp and insistent. She sagged back into the mattress, her quiet morning spoiled. Who was it this time? Kamila? Habiba with a couple of little brothers and sisters?

No, it was the distinct voice of Mr. Arsala that carried into her bedroom. Jo groaned softly and put the pillow over her head. What did he want now? Everything was working just fine, thank-you-very-much, and here he was, uninvited, no doubt looking for some tea and conversation.

He was still talking when she entered the kitchen, explaining something about his kids, or maybe one of his wives. She got her coffee, not paying much attention, until Nan got up from the table and stood behind his chair. Out of Mr. Arsala's line of vision, Nan mouthed something over the top of his head. Her lips moved with exaggerated syllables.

Jo held her cup in mid-air. Trying not to be obvious, she moved her eyes from Nan to Mr. Arsala, suddenly very interested in what he had to say.

"Yes, they are the first in the neighborhood." He waved a hand indifferently. "It will pass. *Insha'Allah*, they will get better."

Mary interrupted. "The kids need to be examined. And your wives. Both of them."

Mr. Arsala shrugged. The women could please themselves. He knew smallpox when he saw it. Why were they so worried? If the Volunteers wanted to come, they could come. It was all the same to him. He finished his tea and led the way.

Coffee forgotten, Jo followed him across the compound. Smallpox!? It was something out of a history book. The Middle Ages. Colonial America.

The kids were playing outside, their faces covered with translucent water-filled blisters. Jo had a pang of guilt for the times she had yelled at them for ringing the bell and running away.

Inside, the younger Mrs. Arsala turned from the Americans, self-conscious of the blisters that covered her face and neck. Like the children, she had developed sores in her mouth and on her tongue in the beginning. A few days later the rash appeared on her face, spreading to her arms and legs, even to her hands and feet. Typical of smallpox, the blisters were initially filled with a watery substance. Now they were filled with pus. In another couple of days the pustules would scab over. If she was lucky and didn't scratch as they healed, the permanent scars would not be noticeable.

With no treatment for smallpox—only prevention by vaccination—there was not much the Volunteers could do. They gave the Arsala family aspirin, and left a series of instructions. Drink plenty of fluids. Keep the kids indoors. Watch for secondary bacterial infections from scratching.

Rest, certainly. The last instruction was added as a matter of protocol, but who were they fooling? Who was going to prepare meals and care for the kids? Mr. Arsala?

The Volunteers returned home and sat around the table. How many residents of Baghlan had been vaccinated for smallpox? Probably none. A few cases today meant they could have an epidemic tomorrow. The mortality rate? Approximately 30 percent.[52]

"First thing tomorrow morning," said Nan. "I'll go to Kabul. Notify the authorities. I can't imagine there's enough vaccine here—if they have any at all."

"I'll go with you," said Jo. "We'll talk to Ken. Or better yet, Dr. Cole. He'll know what to do."

Mary got up to light a cigarette. "The kids are contagious. Especially now, before the rash dries up and scabs over."

She came back and sat down. "We can't get started soon enough."

⌐∩ᴗ∩⌐

Ken and the Peace Corps officials worked through the bureaucracy of the Afghan government as quickly as possible. And yet, nearly three weeks passed before he finally arrived in Baghlan with enough vaccine and WHO vaccinators to set up a full-scale inoculation program.

On November 20, 1968, in the mist and dampness of early morning, a small entourage of Jeeps left Baghlan Hospital. It had rained during the night, and the skies remained overcast, the air cold and raw. The vehicles bounced across dirt and stone roads, tires splashing through water and mud. Gusts of wind penetrated the two wool sweaters under Jo's coat. The mist and rain seeped through Nan's long underwear.

The routine was the same in every village. The mullah and his elders greeted the Volunteers in the town square, sometimes in the open, sometimes on a little platform under a thatched roof. The vaccinators explained how the medicine would keep everyone from getting sick, from getting *chechak* —smallpox.

Each mullah invariably offered himself as a test case, ceremoniously lifting the long sleeves of his robe to get the first injection. Then everyone had tea and waited. If the mullah suffered no ill effects after a period of time, the Volunteers had his permission to vaccinate the rest of the village.

Working from small makeshift tables, the Volunteers set out supplies while the men and children queued up. The Afghans endured the rain and mist while they waited; Jo and Nan wore rubber boots, often standing in cold water and mud up to their ankles.

When the Volunteers had finished with the men and children at each location, the female vaccinators then went from house to house, immunizing the women who were not allowed out, coaxing those who were hiding not to be afraid of the *pechkari* —the syringe. After the last person was inoculated, the Volunteers boiled the syringes in a little tin container over a Bunsen burner and went on to the next village to start the process all over again.

At the end of the day Jo and Nan opened the compound door and dragged themselves up the muddy path. Jo's right boot had developed a crack along the seam and her foot was soaking wet. She limped and squished into the house, wondering where she would get another pair. Good boots were hard to find at the used clothing bazaar.

Mary met them at the door and brought them in. She started a fire under the water tank so they could take a hot shower, and when they sat down to eat, warm and in dry clothes, they were like two little girls, basking in her attention.

They talked about the day and about Baghlan Hospital while they ate. "There were so many people," said Jo. "I thought the lines would never end. We must have given hundreds of injections."

"Thank God we did." Nan took another spoonful of Mary's vegetable soup. "How would we cope out here—in the middle of nowhere? Baghlan Hospital barely has the staff or supplies to manage as it is. A smallpox outbreak ..."

Jo nodded. There was no need to say it. A smallpox epidemic would have been a nightmare.

Chapter 22

HAPPY HOLIDAYS

Had a wonderful meal of turkey, mashed potatoes, dressing, cranberries, rolls, pumpkin pie, bourbon and homemade wine. We sang, talked, danced, and had a hell of a good time.
—*November 28, 1968*

The turkeys strutted through the backyard, heads turning with little jerking movements every time they took a step. The women had started with three birds, but Alex had eliminated one of them, and now there were two. Although he had whined and cowered when Jo called him "bad dog," nevertheless, he continued to take immense pleasure in chasing the birds in a circle around the house.

Buying the turkeys had been Nan's idea. "Forget the tough, scrawny birds at the bazaar," she had argued. "We'll get a couple of young ones and fatten them up."

And now, two days before Thanksgiving, the women were in the backyard of the compound, watching them from a distance. Alex had been safely tied up, and the birds wandered about in crooked circles, meandering aimlessly through the weeds, occasionally stopping to peck at something in the dust. Jo wondered if she could go through with it. She tried to remember how the Afghan farmer had done it, how he had simply reached out and scooped them up, making it look easy.

The women advanced. They singled out one of the turkeys and backed it into a corner. Half-afraid of the bird—its beak, glassy eyes, and weird little thing hanging down from its neck—Jo lunged and latched onto it awkwardly. She gasped at the strength of its wings as it struggled to get free, at the sharpness of the claws against her chest.

Mary approached her from the side.

"No—no! Wait!" Jo shouted breathlessly. She tightened her hold, taking a few steps to keep her balance. "Okay! Yes—quick, quick. Do it quick!" She turned her head and closed her eyes, crying to herself in distress, her voice high-pitched and wailing. Her arms jerked involuntarily at the sound of Mary snapping the bird's neck, and her knees went weak as Mary took the limp bird from her. She sat on the back stoop and closed her eyes while Nan caught the second bird, then bent her head and held her hands over her ears when Mary beheaded each turkey with one quick motion of a sharp knife.

Next, the women filled the tin bathtub with hot water and lowered the carcasses into the tub, pulling off wet, hot feathers. Steam rose from the scalding water. Jo's eyes watered—the stench was overpowering.

Nan pushed her hair out of her eyes with a forearm. "Ugh, this smells to high heaven." She wiped her nose on her sleeve. "If my mom could see me now! I feel like a pickle-packing chicken plucker!"

The newer, softer feathers sloughed off easily, leaving heavy, coarse feathers and quills that were hard to pull out. By the time they were done, Jo's fingers were stinging.

The women had boiled gallons of water the previous day and allowed it to cool. Now they used it to rinse the birds again and again, until the turkeys were clean and glistening. Mary ceremoniously placed them on a platter and put them in the fridge. The women stood in front of Roxanne with the door open to admire their work. It had taken all afternoon.

"What happened to the days when we just went to the grocery store?" asked Nan. "When we bought a frozen turkey wrapped in plastic?"

"And our moms cooked them," added Jo.

~⌒⌣⌒~

Peaches had not forgotten her promise to visit Baghlan. She arrived the day before Thanksgiving, ready to help cook. But first, she wanted a tour of the compound. The women were delighted to accommodate her request, calling her attention to the sitting room windows, trimmed with navy and white curtains. They opened Roxanne and admired the turkeys, then went outside, where Mary showed off her garden. Jo pointed out the repairs to the compound wall, telling Peaches about her sheets on the line and the donkeys loaded with bags of cement. The women came back inside, washed their hands under the spigot in the shower room, and went to work.

They soaked vegetables in iodine water and talked about the nursing school, Anorgul's comments, and the abysmal literacy rate in Afghanistan. They peeled potatoes and discussed Mary's clinic; they pared apples and told Peaches about life in Baghlan, the mother swallow and her nest on the kitchen ceiling, and Mr. Arsala's wives peeking over the wall. They mixed the stuffing—or as Nan corrected her non–East Coast friends, the "filling"—and asked Peaches about the rest of Group Thirteen, especially Charlotte Budum and Harry.

"Oh, Budum's fine," said Peaches. "She's been in Jalalabad for awhile now."

"What about Harry?" Jo reached for a mixing bowl.

"Peaches shook her head. "Not much news, sorry to say. Still teaching, but we don't see him very often."

When the stuffing was finished, they boiled water to wash dishes, then started on the pies, substituting squash in place of pumpkin and sweetening it with molasses. Their oven was a little tin box over a hot plate, and the pies baked one at a time. Between batches they exchanged news from home, the letters they had received, and what their families were doing for

Thanksgiving. Tarshi arrived with his companion Siede late that afternoon, and they all played cards until the last pie was taken out of the oven.

Early Thanksgiving morning, Mary supervised the final few hours of cooking, choreographing a pressure cooker and three hot-plate burners. The house filled with guests. Ken and his family came from Kabul, as did Dr. Cole and his family, and another Peace Corps administrator, Al Perrin and his wife Patty. The Puli-Khumri group was there, a few vaccinators, the German Peace Corps boys, Mr. Muktar, and of course, Rick and Kathleen. Eighteen in all.

They set everything out buffet style, an honest-to-God Thanksgiving feast. They ate until they were stuffed, drank bourbon, Drambuie, and homemade wine. Finished off a gin-injected watermelon, compliments of the vaccinators. They danced to music on the radio, then made their own music with two guitars, a banjo, a harmonica, and Tarshi's upright dhol. They sang and played every song they could think of, and when they ran out of songs, they started on Christmas carols.

They made "The Twelve Days of Christmas," into a little production, assigning lords, swans, and milking maids to various singers. Nan shouted instructions above the increasing din and laughter, and the German boys added a few more. "Ja, and you must stand up when it's your turn," said Hans, grinning.

Peaches and Nan jumped up as the French hen and turtle dove, respectively. Jo missed her turn as the calling bird and had to be prompted. Dr. Cole bobbed up and down; Mr. Muktar was lost, not knowing the song at all, and as the final rounds went faster and faster, Mary fell further and further behind, standing up long past her cue.

The women had agreed from the beginning—tonight was Mary's turn to be the "spectacle of the evening," and it would seem she was well on her way. It was a term they came up with partly as a joke, and mostly as a safety precaution. They all took turns at being the person who could drink and not worry, knowing the other two would look out for her.

The song ended as a garbled mishmash of swans leaping and maids swimming, an exaggerated "five gold-en rings," then a quick tumble through calling birds, French hens, and turtle doves to a safe landing on "a par-tri-idge in a pear tree!"

The muscles of Jo's face ached from laughing. She had a vague sense of how easily and completely they seemed to forget the hardships and heartache of Afghanistan, just as they did at so many other parties. What appeared as mindless fun in the midst of disease, poverty, and the inhumane treatment of women, was in fact a necessity. It kept the Volunteers from becoming so homesick they quit.

⌁⌁⌁

I went to the telephone office and called home and talked for six minutes. I could hear them all so well I almost felt like crying. But I was able to wish them a Merry Christmas and a Happy New Year.

—December 11, 1968

"But *mu'alim*, what's a reindeer?" The girls had long since left their seats, crowding around the Americans. They laughed at the surprise Christmas party, the novelty of pastries and tea in the classroom. Every Christmas carol the Americans sang brought a new round of questions.

"What's a manger?"

"Is a sleigh like a gaudie?"

Anorgul wanted to know every last detail about her teachers. She looked at Nan first. "And *mu'alim jân*—what is it *exactly* that you do for Christmas?"

Nan described her family customs, the food her mother prepared, the visits from Santa when she was a child, the candlelight church service on Christmas Eve. The familiar Bible story, the foundation of the Christian religion, played out in response to the girls' questions.

Anorgul frowned slightly, her expression one of skepticism, even as she continued to press Nan for more details. "A stable, *mu'alim*? A *setâra*?"—a star?

Jo took a step back. She folded her arms and became the observer, entertained by Nan's animated rendition of what Christmas was all about. And yet, Jo had a distinct feeling there was more to this little vignette than Nan's storytelling. She scanned the upturned faces of her girls. They listened with rapt attention, but it was Anorgul's curiosity in particular—so ingenuous and open—that revealed a deeper truth. The girls perceive the story from their point of view, she realized. How strange it must seem to them—a virgin birth, a god-man. As Jo watched her students absorb the story, her paradigm shifted. Our tradition is one of many, she thought. There have been prophets in every age and in every culture.

Nan finished her narrative. The school day was almost over, and with a little flurry of activity the students helped clear pastry dishes and teacups. Anorgul whisked away the last few crumbs. Her eyes were bright with the excitement of a classroom party and she went up to Jo, who seemed to have become her confidant since the incident with the discipline book.

"Yes," she said in the most grown-up fourteen-year-old tone she could manage. "We should do this again, don't you think?"

Jo smiled. "Maybe next semester, when we come back. I don't have to remind you there's no school for three weeks, do I?"

"Oh, no," said Anorgul. "We will all be on vacation. Even you, *mu'alim jân!*"

Jo laughed. Yes, she thought, even me.

After eight months in Afghanistan, the women had been granted a three-week leave by the Peace Corps. They were free to travel as far as time and money would allow, and although Jo was thrilled at the prospect of a break—some time off and the chance to travel outside Afghanistan—she found it odd to be thinking about vacation when she was already seven thousand miles from home.

Home. It was never far from Jo's mind. Like everyone else, she missed her family and everything familiar. Homesickness was a dull ache that never went away, and the impending holidays only made it worse. She remembered the Midnight Masses she had attended, first as a little girl, then as a young adult, the candles and incense, the feeling of warmth and security from sitting next to Jackie and their parents.

The women made the best of their situation, keeping the traditions they could, and finding replacements for what they didn't have. They shopped the bazaar, and bought pens for the students, postcards and scarves for each other. They baked cookies in the tin oven. Jo found Christmas music on her shortwave radio. They put up a few branches and greenery as decoration, but it was a poor substitute for a Christmas tree. Jo resigned herself to the inevitable. They would simply do without.

And then, Mr. Hyatullah showed up at their door one evening unannounced, bringing an unexpected gift. He had taken his Jeep to the tree line that marks the foothills of the Hindu Kush and cut a small pine tree for them. Strangely enough, it was a Muslim who gave them the best Christmas gift of all.

The women put it in the sitting room and decorated it with the few ornaments Nan's mother had sent them, just in case. The stark simplicity was lovely, the scent of pine heady and familiar.

"Perfect," said Nan.

"Except for one more thing." Without explanation, Mary went into the kitchen. Humming under her breath, she opened Roxanne and retrieved an egg. She drew a face on it, inserted a needle into each end, and blew out the contents. Next she glued a few strands of white cotton on each side of the oval face for hair. Finally she made the ultimate sacrifice, a couple of her Winston cigarettes, peeling away the paper from the tobacco so the newly created angel could have a pair of wings. Nestled on a high branch, she looked out with an expression that was ... "Well, sort of angelic," said Nan, cocking her head sideways and laughing.

Their tree was not the only thing out of the ordinary. *Eid-al-Fitr*—the Festival of Fast Breaking that follows the holy month of Ramadan—fell the same week as Christmas in 1968, something that happens once every thirty years.[53] Consequently, the women celebrated both holidays, beginning with a dinner invitation from Mr. Hyatullah.

~⌒◊⌒~

Like the Volunteers, Mr. Hyatullah and his family lived in a traditional adobe home, the yard enclosed by a compound wall. Inside, there was little furniture. The dining room had neither table nor chairs; rather, an array of cushions had been scattered around the perimeter of an exquisite Persian carpet.

A moderate and progressive Muslim, Mr. Hyatullah had one wife. She joined her husband as an equal for the meal, sitting next to him on a cushion. Their children sat with them—two boys and a girl.

Jo wore trousers under her skirt, just as they had done at the picnic, only this time she wore a full skirt that covered her knees, so she could sit cross-legged on the floor.

The two sons, ages eight and seven, came in with the *dastarkhan,* a cloth they spread over the carpet. They looked like little gentlemen, thought Jo, with their tiny Western sports jackets from the used clothing bazaar.

After the traditional hand-washing ceremony, Mrs. Hyatullah set out pilau—rice that had been parboiled, drained, and baked in an oven with oil, butter, and salt. With it she served *qorma,* a stew made with sautéed onions. She had caramelized the onions, then added meat, fruit, vegetables, saffron, coriander, and cardamom. Accompanying the main dishes were homemade chutneys, pickles, and condiments. Like the Afghans, the Volunteers ate qorma with the light and fluffy pilau, scooping it up from a communal serving platter with pieces of nân.

The Volunteers opened their front door to receive the Vo-Ag principal, Mr. Areff, and his family several days later. The women had been guests at Mr. Areff's home a number of times since Jo played checkers with him at Mr. Muktar's picnic. Now they were happy to return the favor.

The children stopped at the doorway to the sitting room and stared at the Christmas tree. The tinsel shimmered, and the angel looked out from the top branch with a seemingly benevolent smile at the festivities. Mr. Areff's three-year-old daughter stood transfixed. She pointed to the ornaments, one by one. *"An chi-st?"* she asked. —What's this? She pointed to the next one, repeating herself as young children often do, looking back at the adults. *"An chi-st?"*

Nan pulled out several packages from under the tree, items she had purchased at the bazaar earlier in the day. The boys opened toy trucks, and the little girl opened a doll. She clutched it for the rest of the evening, and when it was time to leave, she refused to let her father put it back in the box, insisting she would hold it all the way home.

And then it was December 24. The women had planned long ago that although they would celebrate at midnight with Rick and Kathleen, first they would have a quiet dinner by themselves. They splurged with a can of oyster soup as a starter, and for the main course, Mary served chicken with potatoes, carrots, parsnips, and onions, all purchased at the bazaar. They talked about Mr. Areff's little girl and how cute she was, about Anorgul and the classroom party.

"It's been a lot of fun," said Nan, spearing a carrot with her fork. "And just think—Christmas will be here and gone before we know it. After that we'll be in Kabul for the New Year's Eve party, and after *that* ..." she waved her carrot dramatically. "Vacation!"

Jo was encouraged. Yes, thankfully Christmas would pass. Life would go on. And the travel plans for vacation were already completed. She had submitted the itinerary to the Peace Corps office herself.

"Do you know what Ken and Dr. Cole said when I told them we were all going to the same place?" Jo set down her fork. "They couldn't believe it. I guess they assumed since we live together twenty-four hours a day, seven days a week, we would want separate vacations. When I said we were traveling together, Ken laughed and shook his head. He called us the 'Little Women of Baghlan!'"

After dinner the women cleared the table and set out clothes for the trek to Rick and Kathleen's house. With a shiver of anticipation, partly for the Christmas Eve celebration, mostly for the cold walk getting there, Jo pulled out sweaters, leggings, a winter jacket, and gloves. Regardless, by the time they crossed the juie and turned down their street, her fingers were stinging. When they reached the end of the block and started across the countryside, her breath was frozen on the inside of her muffler. Once in the open, they faced into the wind: three figures walking abreast, heads bent against the cold. And while they made their way across the fields and juies of Baghlan, their footsteps crunching on the frosty ground, another trio of Americans traveled that same night.

Three astronauts—Frank Borman, James Lovell, and Bill Anders—had escaped Earth's gravity and traveled 240,000 miles into space. On December 24, 1968, the men fired their spacecraft's main engine, thrusting them into lunar orbit. While the Peace Corps Volunteers walked under the sliver of a new moon, the astronauts were on its far side, and witnessed the extraordinary sight of Earth rising above the lunar horizon.[54] From the spacecraft window, they saw planet Earth as a blue luminescent sphere with swirls of white; a planet teeming with people speaking different languages and observing different customs; a planet where some lived in wealth and others lived in poverty; a planet marked by violence and yet a place where most people yearned for peace.

The Christmas Eve message the astronauts transmitted that night was heard around the world. Frank Borman spoke last:

And from the crew of Apollo 8, we close with goodnight, good luck, a Merry Christmas—and God bless all of you, all of you on the good Earth.

Chapter 23

PESHAWAR

Went to the air base. All the guys are protective towards us, but they appreciate looking at us. They are so lonesome and they hate Pakistan.
—*January 18, 1969*

Charlotte Budum met them in Kabul, and from there the women went as far from Baghlan as they could get on a Peace Corps budget—fifteen hundred miles to Madras, India.

For Jo, the weeks of vacation passed in a blur, a manic panorama of places and events interspersed with still moments that came into focus for a brief second before dissolving again into a vortex of spinning colors and sounds—moments frozen in time, so clear she could almost hear the shutter click in her mind, the memories burned into the synapses of her brain: getting off the train in Pakistan and walking across the border to board the same train again in India, crawling to the top of a plank that served as a luggage rack to share a sleeping bag with Budum, and falling asleep to the ceaseless clack of metal on metal as the rails passed beneath them.

She walked the streets of New Delhi with Mary, Nan, and Budum, startled to realize there were no juies. She reveled in the lush, tropical scenery, and tried not to stare at the women in brightly colored saris. Lined up with her friends, she stood in awe before the white marble Taj Mahal before they pressed on to the Coromandel Coast on the southeastern tip of India, finally arriving at Madras and the Indian Ocean. With a sharp tang in her nostrils, she dug her toes into hot sand and played in white, frothy surf, the salty, piquant sting of the ocean waves bracing and pleasurable against her skin.

Lastly, on the return trip to Kabul, the women made a little detour and stopped to visit the United States Air Force base in Peshawar, Pakistan.

"What's not to like about this?" Nan accepted another soft drink. The Volunteers were surrounded by servicemen eager for attention. The men vied for spots to sit by the women, entertaining them with jokes and stories, bringing sodas and snacks—anything they wanted. Potato chips? A Coke? All they had to do was ask.

Jo almost giggled when the phrase "Your wish is my command" popped into her mind. But it was true. If she took even a sip from her glass, someone rushed to refill it. If Nan ate one potato chip, three airmen came to replenish the bowl to overflowing.

Overhead the Peshawar radio station played the latest hits. Jo sat on a couch with an enlisted man on each side of her. A staff sergeant named Jake was telling her about Peshawar, how it was really not an airfield at all, but a communications center. After months of female company, the very masculinity of his voice enthralled her. His speech had no trace of the guttural sounds of Farsi that surrounded them in Baghlan. On the contrary, it was smooth, the vowels softened and slightly drawn out. Texas? she wondered. Oklahoma? He seemed almost boyish in his eagerness to tell her about the base, but under his enthusiasm was a demeanor of competence and self-assurance. She was fascinated.[55]

When he asked about her work with the Peace Corps, she hesitated. Baghlan seemed out of place in the military setting, and really, she didn't know where to start. Jake waited patiently, his gaze never wavering, indicating he was very interested in what she had to say.

She tried to come up with an opening line and looked around at the rec room. "Well it's a lot different from this. Even our house is different. Our school is a classroom at the hospital. And the girls, well, they wear tunics and hijabs. We walk to school every day ..."

Laughing, Jake interrupted her monologue. "Okay, okay. Start at the beginning. So what is it about your house?

"It's adobe."

"Really? And the school? Are you saying your students are all girls?"

Sparked by his interest, Jo found herself talking freely, grateful for an appreciative audience. It was the first time since arriving in Afghanistan that she had the opportunity to actually tell anyone about her experiences. She saw Nan and Mary every day; they all shared the same inside jokes, frustrations, and living conditions. This was different. She had to explain herself, and she processed her thoughts even as she spoke, telling Jake about everything: the move to their house and the truck in the juie. The hospital. Bibi Deeba. Her girls and their blatant cheating.

She stopped when a sudden and unexpected roar from the men interrupted her story. The airmen jumped to their feet, singing to something on the radio. Jo automatically stood because everyone else was standing.

Jake explained, leaning over to shout in her ear. "It's sort of a ritual. We do this at least once a day."

Turning from Jo, he half-sang, half-shouted with the rest of the men, "We gotta get out of this place. . ."

Jo laughed. "I know," she shouted back, even though no one could hear. Many days she too, wanted out—if it was the last thing she ever did.

The song ended, and after a final cheer, everyone sat down. Conversations resumed. A couple of men playing pool at the far end of the hall continued their game, and Jo found herself once again sitting next to Jake. She was aware of his closeness as he put his arm over the back of the couch and leaned in toward her.

"Sorry," he said with a grin. "We can't help ourselves. It's crazy, I know."

Jo didn't think it was crazy at all. There were times when she thought she would never get home either. Before she could respond, however, Jake picked up the conversation where they had left off.

"So I want to hear the rest. What happened? Did Sedika really have the answers written on her knee?"

Jo laughed at the memory. "We never did find out for sure. It was written in Farsi!"

She looked up. His attention was focused on her every word, her every gesture, and with his face turned toward her, she couldn't help but notice a sprinkling of freckles across the bridge of his nose.

"So what did you do?"

"Oh, umm." Mesmerized by his features, Jo looked away, afraid she might stutter. "Well, there wasn't much we could do. We gave her a zero."

Jake's laughter was deep and easy. Conscious of his arm behind her, Jo felt secure, smart, and funny, all at the same time. It was a pleasant sensation, and she felt as if she could talk all night.

She wanted to give her experiences a deeper meaning, and under Jake's questioning it seemed she needed to come to a conclusion, not only for the sake of conversation, but for herself as well. All their work—did it amount to anything at all? There had been changes, certainly. But it seemed most of the changes had taken place within herself. She had been so naive when she stepped off the plane in Kabul. "Everything seemed new and full of promise," she told him. "But that was a long time ago. I barely recognize that girl anymore." She felt she had not explained herself very well, yet Jake didn't seem confused at all.

"It's not so different for us," Jake said. "We sit at our radios with our headsets on, intercepting messages eight hours a day. What I hear has certainly changed me." He stopped. "And I can't tell you a thing about it. We're not permitted to talk, even among ourselves, unless we're in a secure location."[56]

Jo thought about the endless conversations she had with Nan and Mary. She could not imagine working in solitude, and was about to say something to that effect when an announcement came over the speakers. The evening was over. The rec hall was about to close for the night.

It seemed her conversation with Jake had just started. She had so much more to say, but already they were crowding into someone's car for a ride back to the hotel. Mary and Charlotte Budum sat in the front. Nan sat on someone's lap in the back seat. Jake squeezed in next to Jo and pulled the door closed.

"We'll pick you up again tomorrow," one of the men offered. "We can watch a movie, go bowling—whatever you want."

Nan was laughing as they bounced over the road, her head bent so it wouldn't hit the roof of the car. "Too bad," she said from her crouched position. "We leave for Kabul tomorrow."

"You can't," said one of the men. "There's a dance at the club tomorrow night!"

Jake whispered to Jo. "You can stay one more night, can't you?"

The driver settled it by calling out from behind the wheel. "We'll pick you up bright and early tomorrow, and breakfast is on us!"

~✦~

The base in broad daylight was like a piece of the United States transplanted to Pakistan, a little community, complete with lawns, sidewalks, and trees. There were bowling alleys, tennis courts, a swimming pool, movie theaters, and even a grade school.

The women were treated to a full breakfast of eggs, ham, and pancakes in the mess hall, then given a tour of the base. They played a pickup game of basketball, watched a movie, and went bowling. It was like spending a day back home. After dinner, they wandered into the dance hall where a drum set and microphones were center stage.

"What's this?" Jo asked. "First you tell me you have your own radio station—"

"107 FM, Peshawar," Jake interrupted.

"Yeah, yeah," said Jo, laughing. "But now what? Are you going to tell me you have your own band?"

Jake shrugged. "Well, there was a group here that played a little bit for fun, and when they transferred out, they left the sound equipment behind. A couple of the guys got together and decided to continue the tradition. They have a crazy name, though. 'Six Below Zero.'"

Airmen started to drift into the hall, some by themselves, most with a couple of buddies, along with smaller groups of women who worked as clerks, secretaries, nurses, and teachers. The officers with dependents on base came with their wives. Tables and chairs filled up quickly. Latecomers were left standing.

The anticipatory buzz of conversation filled the air, and when the band members took their place on stage, the crowd broke into spontaneous applause. A few minutes to warm up, an adjustment to one of the speakers, and the musicians were in full swing.

Jake did not let Jo out of his sight the entire evening. He entertained her with stories, introduced her to his friends, and sat with her when they took a break between dances. Across the room, Nan and Budum changed partners with every new song. As usual, Mary entertained a variety of personnel at her table.

Sometime during the last set Jake suggested they get some air, and led her through the crowd to an open doorway. Jo faced out for a few minutes, grateful for a breeze. She turned toward him. "I had a good time tonight. It was a lot of fun."

Jake didn't answer. Instead, he bent his head and kissed her, gently at first, then with more urgency as he pulled her close.

Jo responded without reservation. The last thing she expected was to feel him abruptly pull back. Surprised, she quickly withdrew as well, the music expanding to fill an uncomfortable void.

"The last dance." Jake took her hand and led her back to the dance floor, threading his way among the couples. A small space opened up, and he slid his arm around her waist, drawing her almost possessively into a close embrace, so close she could feel his heart beating.

Even as her body fit snugly into the contours of his frame, Jo was puzzled. The past two days have been almost perfect, she thought. When

I'm with Jake the world is bright, funny, and wonderful. So why did he pull away when we kissed? She mentally sifted through possible scenarios. *He's going to say he's going home soon. Or that he's being deployed somewhere else.*

Jake repositioned his arm slightly, pulling her even closer, until he was holding her with a fierceness that left her breathless. He kept her close as he began to talk, as if he didn't want to see her face. He spoke into her ear.

"Jo, I have to tell you. I'm married."

The synapses in Jo's brain momentarily shut down. Then spontaneously, they fired. Air. She needed air. The fun, the excitement, and magic were gone, replaced by air-sucking claustrophobia. She had been a stupid, stupid fool. Other couples bumped into her while she struggled for breath, trapped on the crowded dance floor.

Jake's arms held her as she tried to back away, and suddenly deflated, perhaps hoping she had misunderstood, Jo stopped resisting. They moved to the music automatically, their outward appearance giving little indication of the words they exchanged.

"What did you think!?" Jo could barely speak. "That it wouldn't matter?"

"Of course it matters. But when I saw you, everything else faded away."

"You deliberately …" Jo's heart was pounding too, and she struggled for breath. "You let me think everything was fine."

"I didn't mean to." Jake pulled back slightly, so that he could look directly at Jo. "You're smart, and beautiful, and … well, I guess I didn't want it to end."

Jo wanted to slap him. Right in his contrite, sorry face. She was furious, not only with Jake, but with herself—with Peshawar, the stupid dance—everything. It wasn't fair. Even now, they moved together in unison, as one to the music. They laughed at the same things, found each other interesting, and talked for hours. But with a few words it had all been spoiled.

The dance ended, and they faced each other awkwardly. Jo found her voice. "Please don't come back with us to the hotel."

Jake nodded once, a clipped, short movement. "I understand. Good luck, Jo. Good luck with your school in Baghlan."

Jo looked at him for the last time, every detail springing into sharp relief: his khaki shirt, the fabric so close she could almost feel the nubby texture, the scent of his aftershave mixed with sweat, the pressed khaki pants, boyish crew cut, and freckles across the bridge of his nose. Without a reply, she turned and left.

She squeezed into the back seat of the car for the ride to the hotel. Everyone was talking and laughing, but she had only one thought on her mind: to get the hell out of Peshawar.

They left for Kabul the next morning, taking a bus for the last 150 miles of their trip. Jo hunched down in her seat. Chilled in spite of her recent sunburn, she pulled at her coat and leaned her head against the window. She barely noticed when they passed through the stone arch near Peshawar and entered the Khyber Pass—the link between Pakistan and Afghanistan—a dangerously narrow thirty-mile crossing over the Hindu Kush.[57]

Instead, the soundtrack in her mind was stuck, repeating the same refrain. "We Gotta Get Out of This Place" played over and over, until she became aware that Nan was humming beside her.

Jo didn't move from her position. She turned her head slightly, and gave Nan a look of annoyance from under hooded eyes.

Nan burst into laughter. "Okay, okay. But you have to admit we all got out in the nick of time. I thought there was going to be an out-and-out brawl!"

"Well, no wonder. You had three airmen fighting over you. And I had my own problems."

Nan stopped laughing. "Jo—I'm so sorry. But just think. You never have to see him again."

"Thank God." Jo rose slightly from her slouched position. "What a jerk." She sighed. "Was I really attracted to him? Or flattered by his attention?"

"I'll tell you what it was," said Nan. "It was the simple fact he wore a uniform, was American, not so bad looking, I guess, and spoke English!"

Jo laughed for the first time since leaving the air base. "Look at us. We're pathetic. We'll fall for anyone in a pair of pants as long as they don't speak Farsi!" She settled into a more comfortable position. "I know one thing. I can't wait to get home to Baghlan." She put her head on Nan's shoulder. Then she closed her eyes and did not open them until the bus reached the little town of Torkham, on the border of Afghanistan.

The four women disembarked with their luggage and pulled out passports and visas for the last time, standing in line at the entrance station to Afghanistan. They were back in the world of Farsi, and it was worse than Jo remembered. No one seemed to understand anything. What was the problem? Here was her passport. She returned it to the official. See? And here was her visa.

The agent explained it for the second time, jabbing his finger at an empty page. When the women left Afghanistan, their visas had not been entered into their passports. It was a mistake, an oversight. They would have to go back to the Pakistani exit station.

The exit station!? Would they *never* get out of Pakistan? Jo picked up her bags and walked with Nan and Mary across the road, where they stood in line again. The Pakistani agent shook his head. He couldn't allow them to stay in Pakistan, he said, because according to the documentation, they never left Afghanistan. It was the Afghans' mistake and the Afghans' problem. He sent them back to the Afghan entry checkpoint.

The entry agent was exasperated to see them again. "*Nê, nê,*" he said. "*Man mota'asefam!*" —I'm sorry! He could not let them back into the country because, officially, they had never left.

Jo had a moment of real fear. The safety of Baghlan was so close, the border only steps away, and they couldn't get in because of a stupid, clerical mistake. The Afghan entry agent conferred with the head official, and the women sat on their suitcases to wait. How long would they be stuck on the border? And what if the bus driver and passengers got tired of waiting? What if the bus went on without them? My God! What if they never got back to Afghanistan?

The entry official returned. The women would be allowed to reenter Afghanistan, he said, but they were to continue as if they had never left the country. He practically waved his finger in their faces. "Do not register with the police when you return." He shook his head and waved his arms for emphasis. "No police!"

He didn't care if it was a government requirement; the women were to disregard the law and simply return home. If they didn't follow his instructions, it would be bad—very bad—for everyone concerned. In other words, their little jaunt to India and Peshawar had never happened.

That was just fine with Jo.

Chapter 24

THE LONG WINTER

Went to the hospital alone and eight bodies of men caught in an avalanche in the Salang were all frozen and in grotesque positions. All the girls were crying. Jamila was worried about her father.
—February 3, 1969

The taxi dipped and bucked across the frozen mud streets of Baghlan. Tires slipped in and out of icy grooves, making the steering wheel jerk back and forth as if possessed. The driver held it loosely, allowing it to play through his hands. He braked in front of the compound; it was like stopping on a slick washboard. He shimmied to a standstill and honked the horn.

Jaleal's voice could be heard from behind the compound wall, shouting all the way down the path. "*Salâm! Khosh âmadêd!*" —Welcome! The gate opened and Alex scampered out, barking and turning in circles, his breath hanging in little clouds in the frigid air.

Jaleal made no attempt to hide his delight at having the women back home. He took an armload of supplies from Mary and made his way up the path, almost staggering under the weight. He would make some tea, he jabbered, and would put more fuel in the bokhari right away.

He must have cleaned the house from top to bottom, thought Jo. Everything was in order—the floor swept and dishes washed. Their Christmas tree stood in the sitting room exactly as they had left it. She found herself gazing at the homemade angel, the oval painted face slightly accusatory, as if asking, "Where have you been?" Jo blinked and looked again. The angel stared unseeing, impassive as ever.

The women put away sundresses and bathing suits. Gone were the days when they played in the surf of the Indian Ocean, and dug their toes into warm sand. Now they hopped on a cold concrete floor every morning to get dressed. They watched their spit freeze almost before it hit the ground when they brushed their teeth over the back stoop. They taught in ski jackets and long underwear, shopped the outdoor stalls of the bazaar with mufflers wrapped around their faces, and ended most days gathered close to the bokhari in the sitting room, huddled in quilts, coats, and sleeping bags.

They put three stones on top of the little stove every night, then transferred the stones to the foot of their beds before going to sleep. The anticipation of a warm bed was sort of a reward, thought Jo, picking hers up with a towel one night—something that made the last excruciating run to the tashnab bearable. She could feel the heat as she tucked it between the sheets. Then with a shiver she ran outside, careful not to turn her ankle on the frozen ground. Coming back into the house red-faced and breathless, she dove straight under the quilts and gingerly slid her feet down to touch the hot stone, thinking the only time she was truly warm was in bed, wearing sweaters, socks, and sometimes her coat.

The neat stacks of wood and mounds of coal balls had seemed enormous in October, the alcove so full there was barely enough room for a little passageway. But now, with the wind whistling through gaps in the window openings, and currents of cold air flowing across the floor, the stacks of fuel didn't seem quite so big. By end of January the voracious appetite of the bokhari had eaten through half their supply.

It appeared that everything was depleting rapidly, including the food supplies they had picked up on the way home from vacation. Nan took an inventory and volunteered for the long ride to Kabul. "Give me a list," she said. "I'll go in a couple of days."

～⌒⌒⌒～

Jo saw her off at the taxi bazaar on a gray, overcast morning. The peaks of the Hindu Kush had disappeared under a layer of clouds, and a soft mist was settling into the snowy folds and crevices of the mountainsides. She waited until Nan's taxi was safely on its way, then walked across town to Baghlan Hospital and started class as usual.

She reminded the girls why Nan wasn't there, and took a few minutes to review her notes. Hmmm ... She flipped through the pages. This had to be the most boring, mind-numbing lesson of the entire curriculum—a litany of medications, dosages, contraindications, and side effects. No wonder Nan had picked today of all days to be gone.

From acetaminophen and aspirin, Jo relentlessly worked her way through the alphabet to Quinine, the drug of choice for malaria. Without an occasional wisecrack from Nan to break the monotony, the lesson seemed interminable, incredibly boring, even to herself.

She droned on. Turned the page and peeked at her watch. Mid-morning. Nan was probably halfway to Kabul by now, and in the meantime, Anorgul had one elbow on top of her desk, propping up her head.

The sound of tires crunching on gravel and snow came from beneath the windows. It was an everyday occurrence, with the classroom situated over the main entrance of the hospital. No one took notice.

Jo continued. "Common side effects of Quinine: dizziness, flushing, headache, and nausea. Next: Streptomycin."

A car door opened and closed. Anorgul lifted her head.

Muffled voices drifted into the room and then it became quiet again. Anorgul resumed her position, her cheek resting on her knuckles.

"Tigan: Antiemetic. Used for post-operative nausea and vomiting."

The voices emerged from inside the building, voices with a hard and desperate edge. *"Barf kuch!"* —Avalanche! "There's been an avalanche in the Salang!"

Jamila's anguished voice pierced the air. *"Nê! Nê! Na Padar!"*—No! Not father!

Paregul jumped up, her face drained of color. Anorgul stood and turned to the open window in confusion, then all three girls rushed toward the open door of the classroom.

Her own heart pounding from the shouting, and the unexpected reaction from her girls, Jo lunged forward, stopping them at the doorway, wanting to protect them from … what? She didn't know.

Jamila pulled away. "But our father is on a bus to Kabul." Her voice was high-pitched with fear. "He is making his *hajj* —his trip to Mecca."[58] She broke away from Jo's grasp, and the three sisters were gone.

Jo ran after them, nearly tripping on the stairs in her rush to stop them before they got to the hospital entrance. She was too late. She could not turn them around before they saw the taxi and its cargo. Already Jamila was screaming. Paregul sobbed openly. Anorgul had her hands over her mouth. Jo herself took an involuntary step back. The girls are too young to see this, she thought. She wished she had not seen it herself, knowing she would remember it forever. All four taxi doors were open, the trunk lid raised up. The driver and hospital personnel were pulling bodies out of the car: bodies that were stiff and frozen like mannequins—arms and legs bent, heads turned grotesquely, crushed by the avalanche.

The girls' father was not identified among the bodies, and Jamila collapsed on the floor in relief. Jo knelt to help her up and into the waiting arms of her sisters.

"Go home," she told them. "Tell your mother. Let her know your father's safe, and not among the victims. If she hears about this, she will be frantic."

"Yes, *mu'alim*." Jo was surprised to meet Anorgul's gaze, steady and calm.

The driver had other news. A truck was half buried at the bottom of a ravine, he said. And a taxi had gone over the side of the road. There was no need to elaborate. The passengers had plunged over the steep abyss to certain death. Jo involuntarily took in a breath. *Surely Nan was all right.*

Left unattended, the rest of the class had begun creeping down the stairs in curiosity. Some of the students were crying at the glimpse of chaos they witnessed; others cried because everyone else was crying. Jo herded them back into the classroom and explained the absence of Jamila and her sisters. Putting aside her own worry about Nan, she calmed the girls to the best of her ability, considering her own emotional state, until they dismissed for lunch.

Then she bolted to the Baghlan phone office as fast as she could run, arriving out of breath and barely able to state her request, suddenly desperate for the reassurance that Nan had arrived safely. When the connection to the Peace Corps office was finally made and the phone handed to Jo, it was Peaches who answered.

"Oh, sure." Peaches seemed to indicate there was nothing to worry about. "Nan's here, safe and sound. As a matter of fact, she's in a meeting with Ken right now."

Jo leaned against the wall, limp with gratitude. She would have slid down and collapsed on the floor much like Jamila, if not for the watchful eyes of the operator. Thank God. Nan was safe. As soon as Jo heard those words, she stopped listening. The rest didn't matter. The question simply didn't occur to her. *Why would Nan be in a meeting with Ken?*

～◠ຯ◠～

It was two days before the Salang was re-opened and Nan could return home. Jo was at the table writing out lesson plans when the front bell rang three times. Three short rings. Their code! She flew out the door and ran down the path, not stopping to get her coat. She opened the heavy compound door. There was Nan, big as life, the taxi driver waiting with supplies.

Jo hugged her quickly, then grabbed armloads of powdered milk, sugar and flour. Jaleal picked up a box of canned goods. Mary snatched the packet of mail and a package. With a draft of cold air, they burst into the house, everyone talking at once. Bags of sugar and flour were carelessly set aside, boxes of canned goods left on the floor. Mary tossed the mail bag into a corner, letters from home momentarily forgotten.

They settled Nan at the kitchen table, pulling their chairs right up next to her. Jaleal put a cup of tea in front of her, and absently picked up a cooking spoon. Heedless of dinner bubbling on the bokhari, he held his utensil in the air, waiting for Nan's story.

She wrapped her hands around the tea mug and began.

"I knew we were in trouble from the beginning. It started to snow as soon as we left Baghlan, and with every mile it got worse. I don't remember seeing Kunduz at all—it had disappeared completely in the blowing snow. By the time we got to Puli-Khumri we couldn't see a thing. Everything was white. The mountains, the road—gone." Nan looked at the ring of faces surrounding her. "We crawled along in first gear, hoping we were still on the road. The driver finally opened the window and stuck out his head, but it was no use. We were driving blind. How we didn't drive straight off a cliff I'll never know." She stopped to take a sip of tea. Her audience didn't move.

"It took us eleven hours to get to Kabul. When I got out of the taxi, my knees almost buckled. My hands were shaking from the cold—or maybe it was nerves, I don't know. I went straight to the staff house to get a beer and something to eat. I didn't think to call the phone office in Baghlan. I just wanted to get to Peaches' apartment and collapse."

"We heard a truck went over the side," interrupted Jo. She finished with a catch in her voice. "And a taxi."

Jaleal busied himself with final preparations for dinner, his head bent over the bokhari.

"Anyway, you're home now," said Mary. She cleared her throat. "All's well that ends well."

Nan took a deep breath and blew it out through pursed lips. "What a trip! All for a little coffee, flour, and powdered milk." She set aside her teacup and turned to Mary. "But you're right. I'm home, safe and sound."

Jo gave a little nod of agreement, not trusting herself to speak. In any case, there was nothing more to say. The house was quiet except for Jaleal's bulani, sizzling in the pan.

After a few minutes Nan roused herself. Ready to put the trip behind her, she got up from the table and retrieved her bags. "Don't forget," she said. "We also have mail!" She came back with a stack of letters and a package wrapped in brown paper. It landed on the table with a thud.

It was always a dilemma. Rip the letters open immediately? Wait and open them in private? Open some, and save the rest? Nan took the letters with a Philadelphia postmark, and Mary retrieved hers. Jo had a thick one from her parents, several from Jackie, and a small envelope addressed to her with unfamiliar handwriting. She picked it up to read the return address. Peshawar. With an oblique glance around the table to make sure no one had noticed, she slipped it into her pocket. Then she turned over the package. "Well, what do you know? It's from my mom. A late Christmas package from home."

She ripped the sturdy brown paper, and the box exploded with candy, pretzels, nuts, and games. There were gifts for everyone, including a package for Jaleal—a blue shirt with an oxford collar and long sleeves. Jaleal held it for a long time, turning it over, looking at it, crisp and new, still in the plastic bag. It was the first time in his life he had received a brand new article of clothing.

Jo got into bed that night and slid her feet to the hot stone. When she stopped shivering, she curled into a round ball and pulled the blankets up to her chin. She listened to the wind, a constant rushing sound that seemed to sweep the events of the past few days into the past: Nan's eleven-hour trip across the Hindu Kush, the tragedy of the avalanche victims, the arbitrary safety of others. Falling asleep, she dreamed of her mother, envisioning how she must have looked as she assembled the package, what she was wearing, the expression on her face. It was so real Jo felt she was there, watching from a corner in the kitchen. In the dream her mother stood at the table, her blouse tucked into a pair of slacks that accentuated her tiny frame, her dark hair peppered with gray, neatly coiffed as always, her eyes snapping with delight as she tied the ribbons. *Thank you*, Jo wanted to say. *Thank you for thinking of Jaleal.*

It took a few minutes to remember where she was. Jo's dream and the vision of her mother vanished—ripped apart by the gritty, scraping sound of something being dragged across the roof. She slid her feet from the warm cocoon of her blankets and gingerly stepped into her slippers. Shivering, tiptoeing across the icy floor, she went to the window and looked out. An expanse of unbroken white sparkled in the morning sun. She heard footsteps above her head, another scrape, then a cascade of clumpy snow fell in front of the window. Mr. Arsala was shoveling their flat, recently mudded adobe roof.

He finished and threw his shovel to the ground. He climbed down after it, then cleared a path to the tashnab. He gathered an armload of wood and coal from the alcove and brought it into the house. There would be no school and no Jaleal, he said, wiping his frozen mustache and accepting tea. They were snowed in.

A snow day! Like we used to have at home when we were kids, thought Jo. An unexpected holiday. After Mr. Arsala returned to his own house, she made coffee, and the women gathered around the table. Wrapped in blankets, they played a new Scrabble game and ate their way through the rest of the Christmas package, cutting away the moldy edges from a block of fudge. It snowed again while they played, the wind shrieking through the compound, making the plastic on the windows billow and flatten in turn, until the flimsy covering adhered to the glass, frozen in place by a crust of ice.

That afternoon, Mary assembled mixing bowls, yeast, and flour, deciding it was the perfect day to bake bread. Nan settled herself in the sitting room with a book.

Trailing her blanket behind her, Jo came out with her own book. She read for a while, then marked the page, giving her full attention to the pleasurable snowed-in sounds of the house: the rhythmic tap of Mary's spoon against the side of a bowl, the sleety rustle of snow driven into the plastic by the wind, and the anticipatory hiss of burning wood in the bokhari, followed by an explosive snap of resin.

She glanced over at Nan, expecting that as usual, Nan would be oblivious to everything except the printed page in front of her nose. Instead, Nan's book had fallen to her lap, and she was staring into space, her eyebrows drawn together.

Jo leaned in toward her.

"Hey," she said softly. "You okay?"

Caught in the pretense of reading, Nan closed her book. "Well, I …"

The tin oven rattled in the kitchen.

Nan ran her hands through her hair. "I met with Ken while I was in Kabul."

"Oh?" Jo didn't know what else to say. In the recess of her mind, she already knew. But how? The phone conversation with Peaches? She couldn't remember.

"He's having a hard time filling lab openings and teaching jobs," Nan was saying. "He asked me if I would go to the lab in Jalalabad for a few weeks, then teach in Kabul."

"Oh."

Jo's mind had become slow and thick. Could she think of nothing else to say?

Oh.

"I'd like to help him out with the lab job, at least," said Nan. "But working in Kabul … I'm not sure if that's what I want."

Jo nodded. She tried to make her voice convincing when she said, "It's your decision, Nan," because even as she spoke, she could not imagine life in Baghlan without her friend.

A piece of crockery chinked in the kitchen. Nan shifted in her chair, turning so that she faced Jo. "And you?"

"And me what?"

"The letter from Peshawar? Come on, Jo. Did you think I wouldn't notice?"

Now it was Jo's turn to be pensive, and she traced the quilt pattern with her index finger. "Jake wants me to meet him in Kabul."

The little crease under Nan's eyes disappeared, replaced by an expression of concern. "What will you do?"

Jo stood and rearranged her quilt, pulling it up over her shoulders, gathering the edges in her hands. Wrapping it snugly around her, she sat down again. "I don't know."

They ate Mary's bread with dinner that evening, warm from the tin oven. All had ended well for almost everyone, Jo thought as she spread butter over a thick slice. Nan was home safely and would finally get her lab job, after all. Jamila, Paregul, and Anorgul's father had been spared. Yes, all's well that ends well—just not for me.[59]

⌁⌒ʘⵣʘ⌒⌁

Jo said goodbye to Nan on February 21, 1969, a bitterly cold day in Baghlan. The women hired a gaudie for the trip to the taxi bazaar, and sat huddled together, trying to keep warm. Nan talked about her new assignment, and how excited she was to be working in a lab again.

"I'm happy for you," said Jo, and indeed, she was truly happy for her friend. But riding in the gaudie, swaying as the wheels dipped into ruts and rose up over chunks of ice, she couldn't help but wonder: what if Nan likes her job so well she forgets about Baghlan? What if she never comes back?

She gave Nan a long hug at the taxi bazaar and waved good-bye as the taxi pulled away. Then she hired a gaudie for the trip home, feeling very lonely as she sat all by herself on the wooden seat.

Jo tried to pretend that not much changed, but really, after Nan left, nothing was the same. The house was quiet. If possible, the weather turned colder than ever. The rags Mr. Arsala had wrapped around the pipes were not nearly enough insulation for sub-zero temperatures, and the pipes froze, leaving Jo and Mary without water. They were forced to fill pans with snow and melt it over the bokhari.

And when the weather warmed enough for the pipes to thaw and they had water again, the roof began to leak.

Even shopping at the bazaar lost its charm. When Jo found another pair of boots at the used clothing bazaar, Mary was pleased for her. And yet,

Jo couldn't help but imagine what Nan's reaction would have been. Nan would have held them up and admired them, would have exclaimed over them. *Made in Russia!? And only two dollars? These are fabulous. And what a bargain!* Jo would have loved her boots from that moment on.

The classroom, too, was subdued. And although Jo should have been happy with the girls' behavior—no discipline problems, no outbursts, no animated disputes over a lesson—she felt instead that something was missing. Oh, the girls were polite, but Jo missed the give and take, the arguments, the laughter. She was very much aware she didn't joke with the girls in the same manner as Nan, but it wasn't because she loved them any less. Her teaching style simply reflected her more serious nature. From the beginning she had the girls' best interests at heart, and when she was strict, expecting them to work hard, it was because she wanted them to succeed. Even with Nan gone, Jo was determined to get through the material in her curriculum. One less teacher was no excuse to lower her standards.

It was Habiba who first responded to Jo's relentless determination, raising her hand one day to ask a question. The young student seemed to understand. Yes, they were working hard. But it meant only one thing. *Mu'alim* believed in them.

And then Anorgul began making fewer remarks from the last row. Perhaps she was following Habiba's lead. Perhaps she had seen a softer side to Jo when she returned the discipline book. They all began to see Jo for what she was: someone who loved them, someone who was working hard for them. Over the next several weeks they made a greater effort to pay attention, wanting to please *mu'alim jân*, the dear teacher.

But the dear teacher had problems of her own, and it wasn't teaching without Nan, and it wasn't even the leaking roof, although that was bad enough. Mary had pulled out every pan and container they owned, setting them all over the house. No, inconvenient as it was, a leaking roof was the least of her worries. She thought constantly about her answer to Jake's letter.

Nights were the worst. No matter how tired she was, no matter how late she listened to VOA—the volume set low enough so it would not disturb Mary—it was always the same. Eventually, Jo turned it off, and in the silence she could hear the blips of dripping water. They seemed to answer each other: low, resonant, two-syllable kerplunks into large buckets, and little, high-pitched pings into small containers. Back and forth, they tormented her with two answers to Jake's letter. She could choose only one.

She was angry that he had contacted her at all. He only wanted to see her again, he had written, nothing more. Likely story, thought Jo. She turned over and pulled at the blanket in irritation. She might be naive, but she wasn't completely stupid. She knew damn well what he wanted, and it was hers for the taking. She could have an affair with him in Kabul, and no one would ever know.

She cursed herself in the darkness, unable to answer her own question: *And what happens after that?*

The spring wind howled around the corners of the house, but there was nothing in the lonesome sound that could help her. She finally settled on her back and stared into the darkness, as if the answer might be hiding right in front of her. When she fell asleep, she dreamed that Nan and Jackie were calling out to her in the wind.

Chapter 25

LITTLE WOMEN

Our roof is leaking badly. Stayed up until one o'clock in the morning doing "homework."

—*March 2, 1969*

Jo entered the Khyber Restaurant in Kabul and saw him first, before he knew she was there. He was seated at a table along the wall, and had momentarily turned his head away from the door. He leaned back and stretched his legs out to the side, crossing his ankles. With a casual, self-assured movement he draped an arm over the empty chair back next to him. Jo caught his profile, his expression of cool detachment as he surveyed the people and activity around him.

In that instant she knew. She was not the first, and would not be the last. Perhaps she would leave right now, slip away unnoticed before he saw her, but already he had turned toward the door.

"Jo!" He quickly came toward her. In spite of everything, she was still attracted to him, and she took a little step back as he approached, overwhelmed by his nearness, his scent, his voice.

If it was not the welcome he had hoped for, he covered his disappointment smoothly, taking her arm and leading her back to his table. "Now I get to see you on your own turf," he said, pulling up his chair. "And you're right. This is certainly different from Peshawar." He leaned in slightly across the table and smiled, teasing her, drawing her in. "So tell me—any tips for a poor traveler in Kabul? Like how to survive the traffic, for instance?" He ran his hand across the top of his head, ruffling his buzz haircut. "I don't think the taxis stop for anything. Drivers plow through the intersections without even slowing down!"

Jo had to laugh. "Yeah, I'd say that's an accurate description. I guess we're used to it."

"And the food?" Jake picked up a menu, written in Farsi. "I'm at your mercy, Jo. You'll have to help me. And after that, I want to hear everything. All about your school, what you're doing—everything—starting with your trip back to Afghanistan."

"Well, we didn't get home without a story." Jo reached for the menu. "We were stopped at the border because of a snafu with our visas. The officials didn't know what to do with us. They shuffled us from the entry station to the exit station and back again. For awhile I wondered if we would get back at all."

Jake smiled. "Imagine—spending the rest of your life on the border. A Volunteer without a country."

"Pretty much. It's funny now, but at the time I was scared to death our bus driver would just drive away and leave us there."

The amused smile lingered on Jake's features, but all the same, his eyes were probing, questioning. Jo was keenly aware of the excitement and sexual tension between them, the unspoken question that hung in the air, but … she flushed and dropped her eyes. *But if I sleep with him, it will be that much harder to break it off. Why get involved just to have my heart broken?*

She looked up and saw that he too had stopped talking. Had she been that obvious, that transparent? There was a clatter of dishes and snatches of Farsi conversation around them. He stood abruptly. "Come on, Jo. Let's get out of here."

She allowed him to take her hand as they left, and when they stepped outside, she was aware of how good it felt: his palm up against her own, his grip secure. Her knees trembled.

"I'm sorry, Jake. "I can't … I can't do this. I'm sorry."

Jake held her hand a moment longer. "Not even a few hours? Show me around Kabul?"

Jo shook her head. She stood on tiptoes and kissed his cheek, feeling the slight bristle of his closely shaved beard, the bony leanness of his cheek. Then she turned and walked away.

She put one foot in front of the other, unaware of people, traffic, or even where she was going. She only knew that every step increased the distance between them. Would he call out to her? Or was it too late? Had he already turned to walk in the opposite direction?

She felt shaky, so unsteady on her feet she wondered if she might trip and fall. Yet she kept going because she didn't know what else to do, her steps propelled by a surge of emotions—the euphoria of relief, the bitter sting of regret.

~⌒ẏ⌒~

Jo returned to Baghlan in a downpour. Clutching an armload of supplies, she ran from the taxi and up the dirt path to the house, trying to keep the custard powder and coffee dry, and at the same time, not slip in the mud. Mary held the door open for her, and she ducked inside.

The electricity had gone out with the storm, and Mary placed a kerosene lamp on the kitchen table. Jo changed into dry clothes, and as soon as supplies were put away, the two women sat down with tea. The soft yellow flame from the wick flickered on their faces, and the circle of light seemed to draw them toward each other as they talked. Jo told Mary everything: the dance in Peshawar, Jake's letter, and the plans to meet in Kabul.

She came to the end of the story, explaining how Jake had expected her to stay with him for a couple of days, and how she had turned down his offer. She allowed herself a wry smile and ran her fingers over the rim of her tea mug. "Oh, not that I didn't want to…"

Mary laughed softly. "I had my suspicions all along, Jo. When you told me you were going to Kabul to see Peaches, you didn't fool me one bit. I wasn't born yesterday—and I do remember what it was like to be young, believe it or not." She put her hand on Jo's arm. "But I was worried about you. This wasn't the usual, casual affair—and we both know there are plenty of those. And it wasn't about any of the other things that go on around here." She smiled at Jo's surprised expression. "Yes, I know about it all. I'd have to be deaf and blind not to know about the drugs—the parties, the hashish. But this was different. It was about you getting hurt, and I didn't want to see that happen." Mary finished her monologue with a little sniff. "Well anyway—"

Laughing, Jo finished her sentence. "All's well that ends well."

From somewhere in the darkness of the house, a drop of water was swallowed into a bucket with a plunk.

～✦～

The rain washed away the last of the snow. The frozen streets of Baghlan once again turned to rivers of mud, and the drips from the ceiling increased to little waterfalls. The fleas resurfaced. Young Afghan boys appeared with short haircuts—the easiest and most practical way of eliminating lice. Frogs croaked, the juies swelled with runoff from the Hindu Kush, and everything turned green almost overnight. The long winter was over.

Jo renewed her efforts in the classroom, often working on lesson plans late into the night, as if she had momentarily forgotten why she had come to Afghanistan, and felt it was imperative to make up for lost time.

And then, just as in the previous year, the rains ended. Jo and Mary no longer held books and papers above their heads as they walked to work, their legs and white uniforms spattered with mud. Now they arrived at the hospital hot and sweaty, their arms and faces sunburned, spots dancing before their eyes.

The summer Afghan wind snatched the calendar pages and blew them along the dusty street until the flimsy pieces of paper for May, June, July, and August tumbled end-over-end and disappeared.

In May, Jo registered with the police, prepared with her bribe of fifty afs this time. She completed the transaction with smiles and nods all around. The Afghan officials thanked her cordially—effusively—as if sending her a message: "See how easy life can be if one follows the rules?"

In June, a group of dignitaries with WHO came to see the hospital. After they left, Anorgul approached Jo. "The men that came here," she wanted to know, "were they Americans, or were they *khareji*?" —foreigners?[60] Jo was about to answer absently they were from all over the world— France, Holland, and England, when the subtext of Anorgul's question registered. We're no longer considered different, she realized. Anorgul had asked in innocence. It was simply a matter of differentiating between "us" and "them," but her question revealed a deeper truth. As far as the girls were concerned, "us" now included the American Peace Corps Volunteers.

In July, Apollo 11 blasted off from the Kennedy Space Center in Orlando, Florida. Jo wrote in her diary: *July 21, 1969: Well, the 'Eagle has landed.' I heard it on VOA at twelve minutes to one a.m. Afghan time. Two men walked on the moon. God help them get back safely.*

In August, when they least expected it, Nan came back. Jo opened the gate one afternoon after school and there she was, waiting for them on the front stoop, bag and baggage, clutching a container of strawberries she'd brought from Kabul.

Jo ran up the path, swatting at the weeds in her way. Nan was back! She hadn't forgotten Baghlan after all. Jo suddenly realized she had been marking time, waiting for her friend to return, waiting to hear Nan's ready laughter, her familiar, distinctive east coast accent once again.

The story came out over dinner. Nan took her usual spot at the table, as if she had never left. "Well, you know I was at the lab in Jalalabad," she started. "And from there I went to a lab in Bost. After that I ended up in Kabul teaching kindergarten."

"Kindergarten!?" Jo smiled, visualizing Nan with a class of small children. "You were probably rolling on the floor playing with the kids!"

"Not quite. I had a lot of the American diplomats' kids, and even a few of the King's grandchildren."

Jo stared, her smile gone. "King Zahir?"

"The one and only."

Even Mary was impressed, her jaw slack with astonishment. She looked at Nan closely. "So what made you decide to come back?"

"Ken and I talked it over. I really missed Baghlan—the school, and the girls, especially Kamila …" She let her voice trail off and casually reached for the salt. "Oh yeah. Maybe I missed you guys a little bit."

Mary tossed a radish at Nan's head. Jaleal didn't understand everything, but he understood this much: Nan was back—the *mezaki*, the joker, and with her, the house in Baghlan seemed to come alive.

After the dishes were done, Jo and Nan took the last of the strawberries and sat on the back stoop. Alex was plainly visible in the moonlight, resting in his usual spot, watching the women as they talked.

"So what's been happening in Baghlan since I've been gone?" Nan set the container of berries between them. "How are the girls?"

"Well, some days I think they're making great progress. They can start IV drips and help Mary with deliveries. Other times, they don't get the simplest little thing. Try explaining how to give oxygen at three liters per minute when they can barely tell time. Oh—and we have a new visitor at night. Mary's giving English lessons to a kid named Jon Momad."

"Mary? Giving English lessons? Boy, things have really changed around here."

"He's a student at the Vo-Ag School," said Jo. "The skinniest thing I've ever seen. Can't be more than fifteen years old, and very bright."

She bit into a strawberry and threw the stem into the dust. "And I might as well warn you about our latest development. We have entertainment now. Mr. Hyatullah comes almost every night. He plays the harmonica, Jon Momad sings, and Alex howls."

At the mention of his name, Alex raised his head. His ears perked forward. Nan leveled a look at Jo, the crease under her eyes deepening. "Maybe I should go back to Kabul while I still can. How bad is it?"

Jo laughed. "Pretty bad."

Nan's smile turned half-serious. "I'll stay under one condition. I find out the rest of the story."

"The rest of the story?"

"Uh-huh. Did you ever meet Jake in Kabul? What happened?"

Jo made a pretense of choosing the biggest and ripest strawberry in the box. "Hmmm," she said, cocking her wrist as she looked over the luscious fruit. "To answer your question, yes, I did go to Kabul." She plucked a berry from the top. "Let's just say it's too bad. Jake wasted a perfectly good leave and made the long trip to Kabul for nothing."

Nan laughed. Jo smiled, savoring the sweet, tangy strawberry taste on her tongue.

By September, it was as if Nan had never left. The quiet, empty spaces of the house were filled once again. Even Jo's lessons with Mr. Muktar took on new life, with Nan making remarks to them as they worked.

"We are all together again," said Mr. Muktar one night. "We need to celebrate. I have been thinking about it, and I have a plan—something I would like to do for you."

"You don't have to do a thing," said Jo. "This is celebration enough. Or wait—" She closed her book as the thought occurred to her. Turning in her chair, she called out to Nan and Mary. "Hey guys! What do you think? What about next week, when Ken comes for his visit? Should we have a little party?"

"*Âli!*" —Perfect! Mr. Muktar closed his book as well. "I will arrange the most wonderful thing for you when he comes. It will be a surprise."

"Wait a minute," said Nan, coming over to the table. "You can't tell us you have a surprise and then not tell us what it is. Come on. Spill the beans."

"Spill beans?" Mr. Muktar looked confused. "Why would I want to spill beans?"

"Oh, never mind! Just tell us." Nan put her elbows on the table and leaned forward, hunching her shoulders, looking Mr. Muktar in the eye.

"*Mowâfeq!*" he said, laughing. —Okay!

He moved his chair slightly, away from the table and away from Nan. "I would like to show you Afghanistan," he said. "Not just Baghlan, but the countryside. How beautiful it is."

"A walk through the country?" Nan took her elbows off the table.

"Oh, no! This will not be an ordinary trip. It will be very special. I have already asked my friends, and they are going to help me."

Nan resumed her position.

Mr. Muktar continued. "Some of the teachers at the Vo-Ag have their own horses and saddles. They are going to do me a favor and let me borrow them. I will have a horse for everyone, and we can ride far into the countryside."

Nan jumped up from her chair. "What a great idea!"

Jo didn't move. She couldn't remember the last time she had been on a horse.

～⌒∩⋆∩⌒～

Dust rose in front of the compound. The horses circled each other, bits and stirrups jingling. Leather saddles emitted that distinctive tut-tut-tut stretching sound as riders mounted. Jo selected one of the smaller black mares. Nan decided on a chestnut stallion, and Ken rode a black gelding. Rick had his own horse, a *Buzkashi* stallion he had purchased for himself months ago.[61]

They rode two and three abreast through the street until it petered out to a faintly visible pathway: two parallel lines in the dust, meandering through brush and rock. They left the village behind, riding through gorges, up hills, and across windswept plains. They followed the Kunduz River for miles, passed through a herd of camels, and finally paused at the top of a rise.

Nan sat upright in her saddle. She surveyed a vast, open landscape that extended to the mountain peaks rising majestically on the horizon. Her mount broke into a little sideways dance, fighting for the bit. He had been straining for the lead since leaving Baghlan. Now, with a plateau stretching for miles, and a magnificent animal coiled beneath her, Nan impulsively touched her heels to his flanks, barely making contact with the sensitive underside of his ribs.

The explosion of power nearly toppled her backward, stripping the reins from her hands. She pressed her knees together and forced her body forward, fighting to stay in the saddle even as the stallion galloped at full speed, streaking across the plateau.

He approached the edge of a ravine and crossed the narrow, stony ledge with thundering strides. Nan hugged his neck, wrapping her fingers in his mane. She wouldn't fight him now. Not with a forty-foot drop-off just inches from his flashing hooves. Her life depended on his instinct and sure-footed balance.

Once they had crossed the ravine, the horse slowed enough for Nan to reach forward and finally grasp the dangling reins. Pulling with all the strength she had, she brought him to a stop and caught her breath. Then she turned him around and headed back toward the group.

She kept the reins short, not giving him even the slightest opportunity to stretch his head forward and take the lead again. When they came to an open, flat area, however, she had an overwhelming urge to ride free and unrestrained, if for no other reason than to prove to herself she could do it. She relaxed her hold. He broke into a gallop, but this time she moved with every stride. When she came back to the group, she was exhilarated, her face flushed and her eyes open wide, the pupils pinpoint from adrenalin.

Jo had not been completely surprised when Nan took off in a cloud of dust. Granted, it was an abrupt departure, but that was just like Nan, always ready for an adventure. Sooner or later she would come galloping back.

And then Jo saw the silhouette of a runaway horse and rider at the top of the ravine. My God! What had Nan done this time? If the horse stumbled, Nan would be killed. And when horse and rider turned from the ridge and disappeared, Jo was terrified. She fixed her gaze on the horizon, frantically willing Nan to appear, wondering how long to wait before going out in search of her friend.

The top of Nan's head came into view, and Jo wanted to sob with relief. She wanted to hug Nan long and fiercely, but most of all she wanted to shout and swear at her for being so damn reckless and scaring them all to death. She wanted to scream "What the hell were you thinking?" Instead, she burst into laughter.

Nan looked like a wild woman, covered in dust. Her thick, black hair, tangled by the wind, made a corona around her head, and she ran a shaking hand through it. "I sure was blindsided." She smiled crookedly. Her teeth were white in a black, dirt-smudged face.

The two women rode together as they headed back toward Baghlan. "Geez, Nan," said Jo quietly. "I didn't think you were going to stop until you got to Pakistan. What would I have told your parents?"

Nan's heart rate slowly returned to normal. Her knees stopped shaking, and her arms no longer quivered from the effort of pulling on the reins. The steepest, most difficult ski run in the world could never compare to this. Everything about it had been wild and untamed—the speed and power of the stallion, and the wind in her face, whipping her hair as they thundered across the steppes of Afghanistan.

The riders entered the flat valley floor at a walk, and although Nan kept control of the bit, all the while she yearned for one more ride. She turned in the saddle. "I'm going to let him go again, Jo. I won't be caught off guard this time, and I won't give everyone such a scare. Just once more." She leaned forward and lightly touched his flank. When he bolted, she was ready.

She didn't anticipate that her right foot would slip from the stirrup. Wriggling her toes back and forth, she tried to fit her instep into the metal bar, but with every stride it slipped farther away. Once again, she pressed her knees together as they galloped toward the village of Baghlan. The dust roads came into view. A juie loomed ahead. Nan glanced down and frantically tried to get her foot secured before the horse jumped. It was the last thing she remembered.

Someone was holding her. Was it Mr. Muktar? She could hear his voice murmuring above her. It seemed they were swaying to the motion of a gaudie. Her eyes were packed shut with something. Dirt? She couldn't see, or move her eyelids to blink. Mr. Muktar's soothing voice penetrated the darkness. Resting in his arms, she heard his gentle words, "You've fallen from a horse." She nodded automatically, as if she understood.

She had no memory of any such thing.

"You're going to be okay," he said.

She nodded again.

"We're taking you to the hospital," he told her.

The hospital? She struggled to get up. Not the hospital! She knew too much, had seen too much. She would take her chances without medical care, and had a swift moment of empathy for the Afghans who resisted coming to Baghlan Hospital. She was now one of them.

Over her protests, Mr. Muktar lifted her from the gaudie, carried her into Mary's office, and put her on a couch. He had been horrified when he saw her hit the ground, and was filled with terror when she didn't move. He had ridden his horse like a man possessed to get to her, then picked her up and carried her to the bazaar. Usually quiet and reserved, he had screamed for a gaudie. Now he paced the floor in Mary's office, wringing his hands, taking full blame for Nan's accident.

Nan called out from the couch. "Jo! Mary! Where are you?"

"Right here." Jo's voice was next to her ear.

Nan turned her face toward Jo and whispered, "Don't let them touch me."

Jo put a hand on Nan's shoulder and whispered back. "Do you think I'm crazy?"

Nan allowed her head to rest against the cushion and listened as Jo raised her voice and took charge.

"Yes, I want the water boiled before we rinse her eyes.

"No, we don't need to admit her. We're taking her home with us.

"Yes, she's going to Kabul first thing in the morning.

Nan's eyes were on fire, and her head was in a vise. She tried to smile at Jo's bossiness, but the muscles of her face wouldn't work. She wanted to say something … something that was clever and funny, but the words were lodged in her brain, and she had lost the ability to get them past her lips. Finally, she mumbled into the darkness, "Jo, you're like a football tackle, running interference for me."

News of the teacher's fall spread through the village quickly. By the time Nan came out of the front entrance of the hospital, putting one unsteady foot in front of the other, supported by Dr. Husini and Ken, a small group of people had gathered. They stood expectantly, waiting for word that *mu'alim* would be all right.

Dr. Husini drove them home. He helped get Nan into the house, then left. There was nothing more that could be done until morning. The entrance to the Salang Road had closed hours ago.

Jo and Mary spent the night at her bedside. They packed her suitcase around 4 a.m., just before dawn. Moments later, Ken was coming up the path. He went straight to Nan's bedroom, his features pale and drawn beneath his tan. As their supervisor he was responsible for their well-being, but he was also their friend. He carried Nan to his Jeep and laid her in the back seat. Mary went with them and also rode in the back, holding Nan's head in her lap.

Jo got ready for work after they left, wondering how she would face the students. Much as she dreaded going to school, however, anything was better than staying in the house by herself. The rooms were quiet—eerie and vacant. Mary's suitcase stood upright next to the door, left behind in the rush to leave.

"*Mu'alim!*" The students surrounded Jo, clamoring for news like so many tiny birds in a nest, beaks open, looking for food. Anorgul put her hands to her cheeks. "I cried all night, I was so worried."

Jo nodded in a perfunctory, distracted manner. "Yes, Anorgul. We're all worried." It was like a bad dream, everything surreal and far away. When she began teaching, it was in an automatic, mechanical manner, and she heard her voice give the lecture in a suspended, muted blur.

She dismissed the class for lunch, and the day became real again, sounds intruding, jarring. Worry and anxiety gripped at her core. Once again she found herself running to the phone office in Baghlan, chanting to herself breathlessly. *Zud zud shodan* —hurry, hurry. *Zud zud shodan* —hurry, hurry, the words a cadence and refrain as she sprinted through the streets.

The men put her call through in six minutes: a record. The connection was clear and the report as good as Jo could have hoped for, considering the extent of Nan's injuries. She had a slight concussion, multiple bruises, and a trachoma infection in her right eye from the dust and dirt. There were no broken bones.[62]

Nan returned with a black eye that was almost swollen shut. Although she was impatient to get back to work, she had strict orders to rest for at least a week. Eventually, the swelling in her eye subsided and the bruising faded. Her massive headaches came less and less frequently. When she started teaching again, Jo and Mary released their vigilance and no longer treated her like a patient. Life in Baghlan returned to normal.

Mr. Muktar finally stopped apologizing.

Anorgul resumed talking in class.

Chapter 26

JO'S GIRLS

Nan and I went to Habiba's wedding which lasted until 3 a.m.
—September 15, 1969

As always, Kamila chose her spot at the hub of activity in the middle of the room. Sedika's desk was off to the side. Anorgul had long ago claimed exclusive ownership of her seat in the back of the classroom—the better to direct her ongoing commentary—while Habiba liked to sit right up front. The dress code was simple: trousers and a tunic, layered with a sweater on cold days. Hijabs were optional.

Jo glanced through the day's lecture. She was about to start class when Habiba raised her hand. Absorbed in her notes, Jo looked up absently. "Yes, Habiba. What is it?"

Habiba stood beside her desk. "*Man mâyelom ...*" —I should like to ... She faltered, started again. "I should like to make an announcement."

The settling-in noises of the classroom—the shuffling, scraping, creaking sounds of desks and papers, the murmur of voices—all vanished. The atmosphere in the room changed so quickly that Jo was startled. A warning bell went off somewhere in the back of her mind.

Habiba arranged her lips in a tremulous smile. "I am very happy," she said. "I am so happy because I am engaged to be married!"

Jo felt a prickly rush of apprehension. She had known of this possibility from the beginning. The odds were very good that several of her girls would have husbands picked out for them before the two-year program was finished. So why was she so surprised, so unprepared for the news? And why did it have to be Habiba? Starting with the entrance exam, Habiba had been her best student—the first one with a greeting in the morning and the last to say goodbye at the end of the day.

The girls left their seats and congratulated their classmate. They embraced Habiba, and kissed her on each cheek. Jo stepped back and let the classroom scene play out without interference, giving herself a few minutes to absorb the news.

Habiba received the good wishes from her friends, and returned each embrace. She seemed to be happy, but something was missing. Habiba's smile did not reach her eyes.

Jo was distraught, but what could she do? And why look for trouble? Habiba's marriage didn't necessarily mean the end of her education. After all, Malia was permitted to attend school as a married woman, so why not Habiba? Indeed, when Habiba continued to take her usual spot in the front row, Jo was encouraged. Perhaps Habiba's future husband would allow her to continue with her studies.

And then one morning it all changed. Habiba appeared in the doorway wearing a floor length black chador. She passed up her seat in the front, and slipped into an empty desk in the back row, next to Anorgul.

Jo could not think of a single thing to say. Congratulate Habiba? Reveal her disappointment? She felt that neither response was appropriate, and took another look at her gifted student. Habiba sat upright, almost as if she wore the chador proudly. Jo was the one who was ill at ease, not knowing whether to acknowledge the situation, or pretend there was nothing out of the ordinary. She would start class, she finally decided, and not call further attention to Habiba. Surely that would be the kindest thing to do. Making an effort to keep her voice steady, she launched into a discussion of pediatrics and childhood immunizations as if they were the most important topics in the world.

Habiba made a show of paying attention, but over the next several days her distracted answers indicated that although she was physically present in the classroom, in a sense, she was no longer with them. Once the class leader, her attitude slipped to a studied indifference. She stared into space during lectures. In the hospital ward she refused to touch a man in order to take his pulse.

But in the end, her small attempts at rebellion amounted to nothing. A month later she had another announcement to make. In a voice that held a strange combination of defiance and defeat, she simply said, "Tomorrow will be my last day."

Nan came through the rows of desks and put an arm around Habiba's shoulders. "We wish you happiness. And we will visit you, even when you are *Mêrman* Habiba." Seeing the barest shadow of a smile, Nan continued. "And would you serve us tea in your new house?"

Yes, Habiba promised that she would.

"And are we invited to your wedding?"

Habiba became incrementally animated. "Yes," she said. "Yes, of course. You are all invited."

The bride price offered by the prospective bridegroom had been exceptionally large. So substantial in fact, it caused Habiba's father to turn a deaf ear to his daughter's pleading. She would become the second wife to a man forty-five years old, a man who already had six children. No matter that Habiba was still a teenager and sexually innocent, she would spend her wedding night with a man more than twice her age. Not yet fully grown, she would be expected to bear children immediately.

Shortly after Habiba's announcement, Mr. Arsala tried to explain his worldview to the American Volunteers. He had come to collect the rent, and as usual, stayed for tea. Upon hearing the news about Habiba, he was quick to point out that in his opinion it is the Americans who have no respect for women.

"American men allow their wives and daughters out in public," he said. "And the women wear revealing clothes for everyone to see. We protect our wives and daughters. They are safe behind the chador. We keep them from being stared at by strange men—or worse."

He warmed up to his subject. "And you think we are so bad for having more than one wife? A man in the West wants a new wife so he divorces his old wife when he is tired of her. And then what? She is out on the street! In Afghanistan a man keeps his first wife. He takes care of her and allows her to stay with her children."

Tell that to Habiba, thought Jo. Ask her what she thinks. I can't imagine what it must be like to have an education snatched away, to be sixteen and forced into marriage.

Mr. Arsala finished his diatribe, tipped his cup for the last few drops of tea, and left.

There was no announcement for Malia: no cries of delight, no kisses on each cheek. The news filtered in quietly, without fanfare. Somehow, by the end of the day, everyone just knew. Malia's husband was taking a second wife.

Once loved exclusively, Malia would share her household and her husband with a new bride. To add further insult, custom dictated that she attend the wedding. But if Malia felt the sting and humiliation of the second marriage, no one would guess as much from her behavior. After the ceremony she took her seat as usual, her chin raised, her eyes directed at *mu'alim*.

The women were somber at dinner that evening.

"Honestly, I don't know how she did it." Jo pulled her chair up to the table. "I've never seen Malia so pale."

Nan eyed her plate, not much interested in eating. "I thought I knew her pretty well. You know—hard worker, role model. But I never expected this. She must have felt awful, but she was back in school like nothing happened."

Jo shook her head as if she still couldn't believe it. "She came in spite of everything—even though women are told they don't matter so many times they start to believe it."

"But not Malia," said Nan.

No, thought Jo. Not Malia. Under a quiet and unassuming demeanor there was a spark of self-esteem that could not be extinguished.

Sedika had been quiet and shy from the first day of school, observing everything from her desk in the corner of the classroom, seldom raising her hand to volunteer an answer. If possible, she had become even more timid in the months following the cheating incident. There were days it seemed she would make herself invisible if possible, and on this particular day she was even more reticent than usual.

Jo didn't notice. Her attention was focused on the lecture, explaining IV therapy—flow rates, drops per minute, milliliters of medication per hour. It was a difficult lesson, and by the end of the day she was exhausted. She was about to give the assignment when someone asked a question.

Jo backtracked. She clarified the point, looking up and down the rows of young faces turned toward her, wanting to make sure everyone understood. Sedika dropped her head. The movement was quick, but not quick enough. Jo caught a glimpse of her forehead.

Jo and Nan kept her after school, but Sedika was clearly uncomfortable with their line of questioning. She edged her way to the door, even as she explained. "I was too slow," she said. "My brother asked for tea, and I didn't serve him right away. Of course my father would punish me. I don't understand. Why is everyone so upset?"

Jo took another look at the purple bruise on Sedika's forehead, one edge scabbed over, as if cut by something sharp. "What was it?" Jo asked. "What did he hit you with?"

"Only a brick." Sedika shrugged. "*Parwâ na dâra.*" —It doesn't matter.

A shout came up the stairwell. "Sedika! *Byâ!*" —Come! The ambulance driver was about to leave for Fabrika.

Sedika took another step toward the door. "*Mowâfeq!*"—Okay! "I'm coming!" She darted to freedom.

Jo felt slightly ill, and leaned against the wall. "Getting hit with a brick is bad enough, but you know what's even worse?"

"Sure I do," said Nan. "Sedika thinks she deserved it."

Jo wanted to kick one of the empty desks. Hard. Really hard, smashing it into a thousand splinters of wood. "Over a stupid cup of tea."

"There's one thing I can't figure out," said Nan as they closed up the classroom and started for home. "When we visit the families in Fabrika, who's the one person who insists we stay for a meal? Who walks us to the road every time, and puts us in a gaudie for the ride to Baghlan?"

"I know, I know." Jo sighed. "Sedika's father. He goes out of his way for us, always friendly and hospitable."

The two women came out of the hospital entrance and walked through the street, side-by-side. Nan shifted some books in her arms. "One day the women are petted and praised, and the next day they're hit on the head with a brick. Talk about mixed messages."

"That's not the only thing that doesn't make sense." Jo turned to Nan, squinting slightly against the late afternoon sun. "Remember when Habiba came to school in her chador? Didn't it strike you as odd? I mean, even though she sat in the back, there was something different about her. She was grown up, all of a sudden. And when she announced she was quitting—well, she acted like school didn't matter anymore. That it was just for little kids."

"She was wearing a status symbol." Nan shrugged. "The burqa, the chador—they're symbols of womanhood."

Jo considered Nan's remark. She thought of the times they visited Mastura and Zakhara, and how their little sisters played house, dressing up in their mother's burqa—not that much different than little girls at home dressing up in their mother's high heels. "To us it's awful," she said finally. "To them it's a way of life."

"Even the arranged marriages," said Nan. They're accepted as a matter of course. The girls have no choice. They follow the rules and hope for the best."

"Hope their parents will do the right thing and choose a good husband, you mean."

A gust of wind came up behind them, and Nan brushed a strand of hair away from her face. "But on the other hand, how many times have the girls told us? 'Our parents know us better than we know ourselves. Who better to choose a husband?'"

Jo frowned at the convoluted logic. Habiba notwithstanding, it was true. Many arranged marriages had a very satisfactory outcome. Parents often picked out suitable matches for their children—that is, if they had the best interests of their daughters and sons at heart. Still, it was a logic that was based on the premise that women had a lesser value than men, and she chafed under the oppressive lack of freedom for her girls, at the irrefutable fact they were pawns in an elaborate bargaining system.

Jamila blushed, stammered, and gave a shy smile before announcing her own engagement. Anorgul was quick to supply the details. "Oh, yes, *mu'alim*. He is very nice." She threw her sister a knowing smile. "And very handsome!"

When Jo met Jamila's prospective bridegroom at the *shimee khoree* — the engagement party, she had to agree. He was very handsome indeed: tall and thin, with the classic sharp and angular Pashtun features. He was dressed in a white shirt and black suit, and he wore his Karakul hat at a slightly jaunty angle. Following the Afghan custom, he had provided everything for the party, and had been particularly generous with the food and gifts for the bride and her family members, showering them with dishes, household items, jewelry, and clothing.

At his insistence Jo took another cookie, made with butter, rice flour, sugar, and pistachios, flavored with cardamom. It melted in her mouth. Nor could she pass up *halwa*, a dish made with grated carrots, milk, cream, butter, honey, and rosewater, all simmered to perfection and topped with toasted almonds.

Jamila wore a silk tunic and long flowing trousers, with a pair of floral patterned slippers on her feet. The couple exchanged glances all evening, becoming bold enough for a few words when they thought no one was watching, their faces flushed, their eyes bright.

Anorgul and Paregul were in a corner talking like two conspirators, already making plans for their sister's *takht e khina*—the henna party, hosted at the bride's home the night before the wedding. They blushed and giggled, talking about what to buy for her trousseau. A bevy of aunts and older cousins discussed food, deciding what they would prepare for the day of the wedding, and how much they would need.

It happened only days after the engagement party. Jamila's father had dug a trench to divert juie water to his fields for irrigation, and what started as a simple disagreement over a small ditch quickly escalated to a full-blown dispute over land ownership. Questions were raised about property boundaries and water rights. Accusations were made and denied. Voices became loud, escalating to shouts and threats. Someone gave the first push. A fist shot out in retaliation, followed by swinging shovel, the full strength and weight of a man behind it, and Jamila's father lay dead in the field, murdered by a massive blow to his head.

Jo heard the sounds even before the Volunteers came into the girls' compound: piercing, high-pitched screeching that sent shivers up her arms. So this was keening, a word she had read somewhere, but a word she would not have used at any other time in her life until now.

The Afghan women rocked back and forth in anguish. They pulled at their hair; they pounded fists into their thighs. Sobs and moans escalated to screams then subsided, only to start again. The Americans sat quietly with their Afghan sisters, and respectfully accepted tea when it was offered, but gripped her teacup, her nerves on edge. She couldn't wait to leave, and hoped she would never witness anything like this, ever again.

Like most Afghans, the girls' father had been unfailingly polite. He loved his daughters, and when they wanted to emulate the American Volunteers, he had indulged them, giving them as much freedom as possible within the rigid norms of culture and society.

The three sisters were subdued when they came back to school. Anorgul made her way to the back of the room with slow, hesitant steps, as if she had lost her way. Their mother would stay in the house, she told the teachers. Uncles—their father's brothers—would take care of her. Perhaps one day an uncle would take her as a second wife. Their grandfather would help. Jamila's fiancé was almost part of the family, and he too, would see to her welfare.

Life would continue.

The marriage would go on as planned.

Jamila bent her knees slightly and leaned forward. Her mother slipped the wedding dress over her head. The dress was unfitted, and when Jamila straightened, layers of gauzy white fabric fell from her shoulders, cascading to the floor. Her mother fastened a necklace of red stones at the nape of her neck. Jamila turned and lowered her head once again to receive a strand of white artificial flowers.

Jamila's sisters applied her makeup, and their mother painted a red henna dot between her eyebrows. Her wedding veil was a swatch of white pleated material. The deeply hemmed edges fanned across her forehead, leaving her face exposed. She put on her lipstick. She was ready. Now she prepared to wait, cloistered in her room. From the open doorway Jamila could hear the arrival of aunts and female cousins, each new addition to the group bringing the squeals of laughter and conversation to a higher pitch.

Anorgul and Paregul came in to check on her periodically, usually with one or more cousins. Aunties came for a sneak preview, and her mother came with tea. The Volunteers helped entertain toddlers and small children in another room.

It was dusk before the procession of men from Jamila's family came singing and dancing up the street, escorting the groom and his brothers, uncles, and male cousins. Some of the men held platters of food above their heads, others carried candles and flowers. One man held a small table aloft as he danced. Upon entering the house, he positioned the table in front of a sofa. The rest of the men handed their platters of food to Jamila's aunts. A male cousin ushered the groom to another part of the house, out of sight. When the flowers and candles had been arranged on the table, everything was complete.

The guests became quiet. After a few minutes the men began to sing *Ahesta Boro* —"Walk Slowly," the signal for the respective families to escort the bride and groom into the room. Jamila blushed as she came in, adding color to her already rouged cheeks.

The young couple took their places next to each other in front of the sofa, but they did not take a seat immediately. Instead, Jamila and her fiancé stood several minutes for dramatic effect. According to tradition, whoever sits first will always be dominated by the other, and so, like many young couples, they had agreed before the ceremony to sit at the same time.

They recited passages from the Quran to each other, returned the holy book to the mullah, and bowed their heads.[63] A witness draped a large shawl over both of them; another witness handed them a mirror wrapped in cloth. Jamila and her new husband looked at their reflection as a married couple for the first time in privacy, and when the shawl was lifted, applause filled the room. Simultaneously it seemed, everyone started talking, food appeared, and the musicians began to play.

The newlyweds received the good wishes from both families, and as Jo waited her turn to congratulate them, she hoped Jamila would always be as happy as she was at this moment; that she would always be cherished as the only wife, and never have to bear the title 'First Wife.' Although Jamila was radiant, and her husband attentive, Jo was aware the odds were not in Jamila's favor. According to law, Jamila's husband was permitted to take as many as four wives if he could afford it. And although the law was being challenged by progressive Muslims, Jo knew from first-hand experience it was still an accepted practice in Baghlan Province.

Indeed, almost every student in her class came from a household with more than one wife. It was an established convention of society, and after living in Afghanistan for over a year, after countless visits to the students' compounds, the Volunteers had become accustomed to the arrangement.

Over the past months, they had participated in almost every activity of ordinary family life. They held babies, played with toddlers, weeded gardens, and picked mulberries. They went to the park on Juma and holidays. Had endless cups of tea. Shared so many meals they lost count.

They felt especially comfortable and at ease with Kamila's family. Her little brothers and sisters squealed with delight every time the Americans appeared. Her father treated the Volunteers like members of the family, and Kamila herself behaved like any other adolescent, sometimes hiding the lumpy, tell-tale bulges of hair curlers under her hijab.

Kamila's mother welcomed the Americans like her own daughters, serving them tea and special pastries, pampering them and laughing at their teasing and banter. But when she turned serious, she spoke with a voice of authority. Everyone listened, including her husband.[64]

When Nan met Kamila's older brother, she was struck not just by his affable personality—it seemed to be a family trait—but also by his remarkably handsome features, especially when he began to wear a white shirt and narrow black tie every time the Americans came to visit. And how could she not be captivated by the one persistent lock of curly hair that fell over his forehead, or the way his broad shoulders strained at the fabric of his shirt?

The flirting began in earnest at an extended family gathering. Interspersed among an assortment of aunts, uncles, and cousins, Nan looked up to find him seated across from her, whether by chance or by design, she didn't know. With amusement in his knowing, dark eyes, he leaned against a toshak and folded his arms, regarding her with an open, familiar manner, a half-smile on his lips. He raised his eyebrows in a way that made her laugh.

She leaned back, folded her arms and mimicked his expression and posture exactly, issuing a non-verbal challenge of her own. In reply, he picked up a saucer and balanced it on his thumb, holding it toward her as if to say, "Match this if you can." Conversations around the carpet died away as family members and guests watched the exchange. They clapped when Nan balanced her own saucer, then all eyes were back to Kamila's brother.

Before he could think of the next little trick, two younger male cousins came up to him with a pitcher of water and a basin for the hand-washing ceremony. He did not take his eyes from Nan as he held out his hands and allowed water to be poured over them, nor did he release her gaze when he reached out to accept the drying towel.

After the meal, he joined his uncle to provide music. He sat on the ground with a *daira*, a small, thin drum he held upright between his hands. His uncle played a stringed instrument with a long fretted neck, balancing the hollow, gourd-shaped body between his knees. A toddler wandered in and out among the musicians and finally planted himself directly in front of the two men. A teakettle and cups of tea were scattered about on the floor, and people visited or listened to the music, depending on the topic being discussed and the song being played.

Nan felt completely at home, surrounded by a close-knit and trustworthy family. The dynamic was much like her own—fun and informal. She watched Kamila's brother play the daira, a faint sheen of perspiration on his face as he forgot everything around him except the music, his head bent over his instrument, the posture accentuating the wayward strand of hair falling over one eyebrow. He had loosened his tie, leaving his shirt collar open. She could not deny the attraction he held for her, or the connection between them. Even Jo teased her after one of their visits. "No wonder you're fascinated with each other," she said. "You two are exactly alike!"

The melody of the stringed instrument, coupled with the seductive rhythm of the daira pulled Nan into an even more flirtatious mood, and it was a feeling she did not take for granted. She was an American. She was safe. But it was a dangerous world for Afghan women, who could not dream of showing their feelings so openly.

She wondered how it would feel to have her freedoms taken away, if she wanted to marry Kamila's brother, for example, but was "sold" to someone else instead. And what if she *did* marry him? Would he be a loving husband? Would he take another wife? It was all conjecture, and yet,

Nan suddenly felt dizzy, as if she stood on the edge of a precipice, swaying, fighting desperately to keep her balance. In her mind's eye she dropped to her knees and crawled backward from the ledge, her body trembling, her breath coming in short gasps.

The women of Afghanistan had no choice. They were forced to jump, and there was no safety net.[65]

Chapter 27

THE BELL WILL CRACK

We passed the body of a soldier lying in the middle of the road. We were all upset, especially Ken.

—October 15, 1969

Communism. The word was rarely spoken in public. After all, who could you trust? The Communists had spies everywhere. Occasionally, over a second cup of tea, Mr. Hyatullah would speak of it, but still, he chose his words carefully.

"Yes," he admitted. "It's no secret the Soviets want to reform Afghanistan. Just look! Look at the new roads and bridges they are building—the laws they want passed to protect women. And I have to agree. It's good. Most of it's very good. But the Soviet dams and irrigation, the electricity—it all comes at a price." Mr. Hyatullah lowered his voice. "The Communists are godless. They have no regard for Islam. They're infiltrating the country. And now ..." Mr. Hyatullah set down his teacup. "Now they're training the Afghan army."

Jo had a sudden memory of the Soviet planes in Mazar-e Sharif, the deafening roar, the clear view of the Soviet insignia coming straight toward them. Once again, she wondered what the Russian presence meant for the future of Afghanistan.

At the same time she didn't need Mr. Hyatullah to point out the unrest within the country itself. Laborers were unhappy with poor working conditions, the long hours and low pay. College students were outraged at a government that dictated curriculum. By the late 1960s, both groups had begun to demonstrate openly against a corrupt government that restricted personal freedoms.[66]

Protests erupted across the country, beginning in Kabul and extending even to the little community of Baghlan. Students at the Vo-Ag School organized to condemn the rigid government control over the school. As far as they were concerned, the principal was nothing more than an extension of government oppression. They petitioned to have him fired.

The Volunteers were sympathetic to the students' cause, but in their role as Peace Corps workers they were expected to remain neutral. Nan, drawing on the ties to her home in Philadelphia, coined a clandestine phrase to use when talking in public. "The bell will crack," became a thinly disguised code for their support of the demonstrators. In the naiveté of youth and idealism, the Volunteers wanted to believe it was possible, that someday the bell of liberty would ring for Afghanistan.

It was one thing, however, to endorse the Afghans' growing desire for a fair and just government while talking in the safety of their own home—endlessly discussing the matter over dinner—and quite another thing to arrive at work one morning and encounter the Vo-Ag students assembled in front of Baghlan Hospital.

A young man came over to the women and explained the situation. A classmate had been admitted to the hospital, and they were calling attention to his poor, substandard care. They had organized to demand reform of a corrupt health care system. The students moved aside, allowing the women access to the hospital, and Jo emerged from the crowd only to be stopped again, this time by uniformed guards, blocking the hospital entrance. One of the guards nodded, indicating the Volunteers had permission to enter. Jo walked past, trying not to stare at the rifles cradled in their arms.

Dr. Wasel waited for them inside the door. "Four girls came to school this morning," he said. "If you're willing, you can teach as usual. I'll escort you to the classroom myself, but first …" His nervousness was revealed by the distracted way he buttoned and unbuttoned his jacket, by his eyes darting from the students to the armed guards.

Always reluctant to intervene, even with his own staff, Dr. Wasel had perfected the art of avoiding conflict. Jo anticipated that he would simply ignore the demonstration, just as he ignored almost everything else in the hospital. With that in mind, she was amazed when he abruptly and without explanation turned away, striding purposefully through the open door as if he had suddenly made up his mind about something. He walked past the guards and approached the demonstrators. Jo could see him clearly as he spoke to the student leader, and although she couldn't hear what was being said, she saw Dr. Wasel clasp the young man on the shoulder and shake his hand.

She could hardly believe it. Whose side was he on? It was his hospital they were condemning, after all. Did he really support the students' rebellion over a corrupt health care system? Or was he covering his bases, ingratiating himself with the demonstrators in case they were successful?

Whether Dr. Wasel felt pressure to initiate hospital reform, or whether he chose to do so on his own, Jo never knew. She did know one thing. All hell broke loose when he called the women into his office for an announcement a few days later. It was a bombshell the Americans never saw coming.

"The students will no longer receive compensation for attending school," Dr. Wasel said. "That is, not unless they keep up scholastically. And it's my opinion the girls are not doing well enough to continue." He pulled at the sleeve of his suit jacket. "If things don't improve dramatically, I can't guarantee anything—not academic credit, or whether your program will be recognized by the Ministry of Health."

Jo felt the hair on the back of her neck rise straight up. Her heart pounded erratically, squeezing her chest, making her breathless. With a few offhand remarks, Dr. Wasel was wiping away almost two years of work, to say nothing of the emotional investment she had put into the school and her girls.

Dr. Wasel pressed on. "One more thing. The ambulance will no longer be used to pick up the students in Fabrika."

Relatively speaking, it was a minor issue, insignificant, really, compared to the discussion of academic credit, but it pushed Jo over the edge. She was outraged. "It's not right! The girls from Fabrika deserve the same chance as the girls from Baghlan."

Dr. Wasel shifted uncomfortably. He looked at the women, considering what to say next. "You should know one thing," he said finally. "I have been paying the ambulance driver myself." He held up his hand. "And I'll send it to Fabrika for ten more days, but only as a favor. A special favor. As for the rest ..." He shrugged. The meeting was over.

Jo left the hospital furious with herself. She had allowed the issue of transportation to dominate the meeting, and in effect, sabotage the entire discussion of accreditation. What had she been thinking, for God's sake? Transportation didn't matter, and Dr. Wasel had used it to his advantage. She saw that now. Dispatching the ambulance to Fabrika was the least of their problems. She thought about the Peace Corps office in Kabul. This was going to be disastrous news, and someone would have to tell Ken.

That evening, the women had dinner with Rick and Kathleen. Almost as soon as they sat down, Rick started with news of his own. "The students at the Vo-Ag School have been successful," he said. "They've managed to get the principal fired."

Jo was unnerved. Mr. Areff? Gone? She remembered playing checkers with him the day of Mr. Muktar's picnic, and recalled how his little girl had been transfixed by their Christmas tree, pointing at the ornaments, one by one. Was everything falling apart?

She leaned back from the table to absorb Rick's information, knowing that inevitably, she would have to make her own announcement. "That's not all," she said finally. "We met with Dr. Wasel today." Jo swallowed hard, food and words stuck in her throat. "He doesn't know if the school will be recognized by the Ministry of Health."

It was Rick's turn to be nonplussed. He set down his fork and regarded the women somberly. "What will you do?"

"Meet with Ken," said Mary. "See if he can help us." She looked over at Nan and Jo. "We'll all go."

Nan shook her head. "No. It should be you and Jo. I'll stay here. Keep the school operating until you get back."

It was a small group that met in the conference room at the Peace Corps headquarters in Kabul a few mornings later. Ken was there, along with Jo and Mary, and representatives from the Ministry of Health and the Ministry of Education. The Afghan officials were dressed in Western-style suits and ties, and Jo entertained a brief glimmer of hope the discussion would be in English, but it was soon apparent they spoke only Farsi. A feeling of nervousness came over her. If she had to present her case in Farsi, they were doomed.

She tried to study the faces of the Afghan officials without being obvious. They have no idea what the school is like, she thought, or the work that has gone into it. They have never seen the classroom, nor have they met any of the students. They have no understanding of Malia's persistence to finish her education, nor can they fathom Habiba's disappointment. But here they are, with the power to endorse the school or destroy its credibility.

The men talked among themselves, some of them leaning back in their chairs in a manner that indicated they were waiting for something, or someone, before getting started. Jo looked away and played with her pen, waiting with everyone else. And then a movement in the doorway caught her attention. A young Afghan entered the room in a slight rush. "*Mota' asefam.*" —Sorry. He took a seat. "I'm a government aid. I've been sent here as a translator for the Americans."

The meeting started. The Afghan officials were lavish with their praise of the Peace Corps in general and the nursing program in particular, making it clear the Volunteers had their unconditional support and gratitude. The translator relayed the message.

The Peace Corps officials thanked their Afghan hosts, reiterating how vital their cooperation had been, indicating it was only by working together that progress could be achieved. The translation followed.

With the formalities concluded, both groups got down to business. Jo and Mary answered the questions posed to them: questions about the curriculum, how well the girls were doing, and whether the Volunteers judged the students capable of functioning as nurses.

The issue of accreditation was addressed to the Peace Corps officials, and Jo strained to hear the words that would certify her program. After many clarifications and reiteration of policy, she was reassured her girls would be endorsed as nurses. More importantly, they would be accepted to midwifery school in Kabul if they wished to attend.

For the Afghans it had been another routine meeting on government policy. For the Peace Corps workers it was a monumental relief, a cause for celebration. Ken took the women to lunch, and when they had finished, he impulsively decided he would come to Baghlan with them. "It will be a break," he said. "Besides, we can stop at Puli-Khumri on the way. I'm long overdue for a visit there."

They left Kabul that afternoon. Jo was euphoric when she climbed into the taxi. She slid across the seat to make room for Ken and Mary, anticipating the pleasure of telling Nan the good news.

The driver turned north on the Salang Road, toward the foothills of the Hindu Kush. About fifty miles from Kabul, they approached the outskirts of Charikar. Not yet into the town itself, they traveled on a road free of traffic, the driver relaxed, passengers chatting. And so it came as a complete surprise when he slammed his foot on the brake pedal and turned the wheel sharply. Jo was thrown up against Ken, who sat next to her. The taxi careened to the side, skidding to a stop. With everyone else, Jo turned around to see what had happened. She caught a glimpse of a large, uneven mound in the road, covered with the tattered remnants of a military uniform. The driver had barely avoided running over the body of a dead soldier, left in the roadway.

The driver quickly shifted into first gear and turned the car back onto the road. He pressed the accelerator, clearly anxious to leave the scene as quickly as possible. Jo didn't have time to distinguish whether the soldier was Afghan or Russian, and with every second that passed, the dusty heap receded further behind them. She was incredulous. How could they abandon a human body? Leave it to rot? Become pulverized by traffic?

"Stop. We should stop!" Distraught, she looked to Ken for help.

Ken faced straight ahead, the color drained from his face. The only time she had seen him this upset was the day of Nan's accident.

"We can't stop." Ken spoke in English, so softly that Jo strained to hear. "Any one of the Afghans in this car could be sympathetic to the Soviet Union, or a member of the PDPA." He didn't have to explain. Jo was familiar with the organization—the Marxist People's Democratic Party of Afghanistan.

Ken avoided eye contact with Jo, and his lips barely moved as he gave her a final warning. "You have to let the matter drop. If we get involved, we could be arrested. End up in jail."

Jo hardly remembered the rest of the ride to Puli-Khumri, or how they met up with a group of vaccinators stationed there. She only knew it had been a very disturbing experience, and yet, as they had a few drinks and something to eat with the Puli-Khumri Volunteers, the incident became daring and exciting—a story with overtones of international intrigue. They thrilled to the sensationalism of it all, and repeated the story again and again, each time with more braggadocio and swagger. A few more drinks, and they were making jokes and laughing.

Jo was well aware their behavior was irrational, even bizarre, but as she eventually wrote in her journal: *It was just a release after the tragic event that left us feeling so guilty.*

They arrived in Baghlan late that night, where Nan waited up for them. Restless and agitated, they talked about everything—the soldier, the ever-increasing Soviet presence, the demonstrations, and the poverty in the outlying provinces.

They talked about the progress they saw in Kabul, Afghan women shopping in Western clothes with their heads uncovered, the libraries, the record stores. They wondered if the improvements would continue, and discussed how difficult it was to work in Afghanistan. No one could read or write ... there was corruption at every level.

"Sometimes I wonder if things will ever change," Ken said. "I have to admit, it's hard to keep going, day after day, when it seems like we're not making any progress at all."

Jo impulsively spoke up, "Maybe the people aren't ready to accept change, but how long will it take to wait for that? And what about the meantime—who will help them prepare for change?"

She was a little self-conscious after her remarks. She had not meant to reveal such personal feelings, but then, it had been a very strange day.

Chapter 28

LIFE IN BAGHLAN

I took so much cough medicine I almost fell in the juie.
—February 1, 1970

On the nights Jo couldn't stop shivering under the pressing weight of quilts, when she couldn't get warm in spite of the hot stone at her feet, she wondered if her second winter in Baghlan would ever end. On the days her chest hurt with every deep breath and her joints ached, she wondered if she had contracted tuberculosis, after all.

When the spring rains began and the roof leaked, when the fleas returned and her dysentery was as bad as when she first arrived, she wondered if she would feel completely well ever again. She wondered briefly if she was going crazy.

She could barely remember the night they talked with Ken—the night she had reaffirmed her commitment to the Afghan people. Since then, everything about the country had become tiresome: the summer heat and dust, the frozen mud in winter, and now the prospect of another spring thaw and dripping ceiling.

She had professed her desire to help the Afghans prepare for change, but during the intervening months she had taught day after day, explaining the same lessons over and over. Help the Afghans prepare for change? It's a joke, she thought, like trying to empty the ocean with a teaspoon. Nothing ever changes. Even the same damn rooster crows at the same damn time every damn morning.

She locked the gate on the outside, climbed over the wall, and escaped into sleep more and more frequently. She dreamed strange dreams, whether from her illness and fever, or because she was assimilating the Afghan world, even in her subconscious, she didn't know. She dreamed she was a nun at the hospital until someone in the dream said, "No, I think the nun is really a Muslim."

She was discouraged, bone-weary, and homesick. And yet, she refused to acknowledge the extent of her illness, afraid that if her friends knew, they would intervene and force her to quit working. She had become fixated, almost obsessed, on a single-minded goal, and that was to finish her assignment. She was so close. Final exams and graduation were only a few months away.

The last thing she wanted to hear was that Dr. Cole was coming for a visit. It nearly sent her into a panic. She tried to come up with a plan, a way to hide her symptoms, but she knew it was useless. Dr. Cole was too perceptive. He would know immediately that something was wrong. If he takes one look at me and sends me home, she thought, I'll just refuse to go.

Mary took Dr. Cole aside almost as soon as he arrived. "Jo's been coughing for weeks," she said. "Working much too hard." Mary shook her head. She had come to know Jo as a very determined individual—bordering on stubborn—nevertheless, she had a great deal of affection for her young friend. She looked up at Dr. Cole. "Well, you know how Jo is. She takes everything to heart. Refuses to give up."

Dr. Cole knew exactly how it was. He had seen it before—Volunteers who took their responsibilities too seriously, refusing to admit that even though they did the best they could, sometimes it still was not enough.

At the first opportunity, he spoke to Jo alone, asking about her lingering cough. He got her to admit that yes, her chest hurt, especially when she took a deep breath, and yes, she occasionally had heart palpitations. He took in the dark circles under her eyes, the way her shoulders slumped with fatigue, and didn't give her an option. She was coming back to Kabul with him for an exam and a chest X-ray.

But Jo was not happy, and vented her frustration with a particularly long and rambling entry in her diary:

> *Dr. Cole came to the hospital and then Mary filled him in and he came back for some friendly persuasion. He wants me to go to Kabul with him and spend a few days with his family because my friends are concerned. Everyone gets discouraged, I said in my defense. He mentioned that I said I was thinking about quitting and he was right and everything he and Mary said is true and I know what they say is best but I hate Kabul and I will not go at all.*

Eventually she ran out of arguments. Two days later, she was sitting on the edge of an exam table, awaiting Dr. Cole's verdict.

"Pneumonia," he said, looking at her over the top of his glasses.

So she wasn't crazy. Hadn't gone off the deep end. The diagnosis came as an unexpected relief. She agreed to a penicillin shot, and promised to see him again in the morning, before she returned to Baghlan. When she left the office to do some shopping and run errands, it occurred to her that oddly enough, she felt so much better, just knowing she was sick.

She spent the night with Peaches in her apartment, and in the morning as promised, she stopped by the Peace Corps headquarters. She didn't plan to stay long—a quick thank you and she would be on her way.

Dr. Cole came out of his office. He greeted her warmly, and reaching out, took the overnight bag from her hand. "You're staying with us. Mrs. Cole is expecting you. I'll bring your bag home this evening."

Jo blinked. Unless she wanted to make a scene by holding on to her bag, she had to let go. Her fingers gripped the handle. She was needed in Baghlan. Didn't he understand? She was in charge and had responsibilities.

After almost two years, it all came down to the suitcase. Jo had been taking care of everyone else, and now it was time to let go. He gently but firmly pulled the bag toward him. She relinquished her hold.

Riding in the taxi to Dr. Cole's residence, she sat in the back seat with her arms folded. She was fuming. She glared at the back of the driver's head, not caring how she appeared to the rest of the passengers. Everybody wants to tell me what to do, she thought. As if I'm not capable of making my own decisions. My job here is hard enough. Why can't everybody just leave me alone? The thought of how she would have to thank Mrs. Cole, and appear grateful for something she didn't ask for and didn't want, only added to her frustration. She sighed and turned her face to the window, at first not seeing a thing, then slowly taking in the quiet, residential streets of Kabul. The rows of houses and trees were calming somehow, peaceful and serene. Jo felt her anger subside. There wasn't much she could do, except acquiesce to Dr. Cole's orders.

Gradually, her irritation faded. And when the driver stopped in front of a welcoming two-story house, she was surprised at how relieved she was to be there, how free and unencumbered she felt when she stepped from the car without a bag.

Mrs. Cole met her at the door and took her to an upstairs bedroom. "Make yourself at home," she said. "Take your time and settle in."

Jo kicked off her shoes and stretched out across the top cover of her bed. She could hear Mrs. Cole downstairs, doing something in the kitchen. She sighed deeply, with the unaccustomed but pleasurable sensation that someone was taking care of her. It was her last thought before falling asleep.

For the next week, Jo napped every day. She had dinner with the Cole family every evening, took her medicine, and pondered her life in Afghanistan up to this point. She had been so busy, so engrossed with her work in Baghlan, there had been little time for introspection. Now, with her responsibilities taken away, she had nothing but time. Time to think. Time to reflect on the tragic, comic, crazy, and illogical things that happened every day.

In her two years in Baghlan, she had seen it all: the well-meaning physician who broke a baby's neck during a delivery, the sound sickening in the silence of the delivery room. The toddler who drowned in the juie. The mothers who died in childbirth. The women in *purdah*—not allowed to be seen outside their compound walls. Bibi Deeba. A government that sprayed the hospital with DDT for lice. Rumors that the Americans were spies, and carried tape recorders in their purses. The show of "dancing boys" she and Nan inadvertently stumbled upon, almost causing a riot because they were the only women in a tent filled with men.[67]

But life in Baghlan was more than a string of tragedies in a desperately poor and corrupt country. Neighbors brought little gifts: embroidered handkerchiefs, a watermelon, a Christmas tree. They came with invitations to family affairs. Served endless cups of tea. Mr. Hyatullah took them to Kunduz so they could take pictures of the countryside, driving his Jeep for sixteen hours even though it was Ramadan and he was fasting.

Anorgul brought hard boiled eggs to school and gave them to Jo, afraid her teacher would go without lunch. Jamila invited the Americans to her wedding, and asked them to be part of the henna ceremony. The village elders asked Mary to help judge a baby contest during Jeshen, the Afghan Independence Day.

The kebob vendor at the bazaar wouldn't let Jo take his picture until he had gone home to change into his best tunic. Neighbors and half the Vo-Ag School helped them move, and Jaleal lost his temper every time they were late getting home because he was worried about them.

Afghanistan is a paradox, she thought one day. It's a miracle we haven't all gone crazy. The Afghans are mired in poverty, yet generous to the point of embarrassment. The men are courteous and respectful toward us, even protective, keeping an eye out for our safety, but those same men turn a blind eye to the suffering of their wives, sisters, and daughters.

Afghanistan was not the malleable entity she had envisioned, ripe for change and improvement. It was unyielding, as impermeable as the massive

Hindu Kush itself. There were no easy solutions, no simple answers. And yet, she had been like Sisyphus, rolling the same heavy stone up the mountain every morning. In spite of mounting evidence to the contrary, she had clung to the belief that if she worked hard enough, she could reform an entire country—or at the very least, make a difference. In the end, she hadn't changed Afghanistan as much as Afghanistan had changed her. It had become a part of who she was.

If the day was warm enough, she liked to sit in Dr. and Mrs. Cole's garden. Sometimes she read. Sometimes she watched the birds, twittering back and forth on the compound wall. Other times she set her book in her lap, enjoying the peace and solitude. One such afternoon she leaned her head against the back of the chair closed her eyes in gratitude. It was in that moment, in the stillness and tranquility of Dr. Cole's garden, that she made the startling observation: *During my entire time in Baghlan, I was never alone.* And with that thought, Jo's ponderings—her reflection on her time in Afghanistan—came to an abrupt halt. It was so obvious. So simple. How had she missed it?

She had always been somewhat of an introvert, happy spending time by herself. So what part of living in a communal society had she thought she would like? It had been fun at first, but when visitors continued to ring the bell at all times of the day and night, she began to feel surrounded by people and constant conversation. She tried to recall the first time she had locked the gate on the outside and climbed over the wall. That should have been a clue, she thought. I need quiet time to myself, and I live in a house with a revolving door.

The list of visitors was staggering. Rick and Kathleen. The girls, especially Kamila, Mastura, and Zakhara, usually with little brothers and sisters. Mr. Muktar. Mr. Hyatullah. The German Peace Corps boys, Hans and Gunther. The American Volunteers in Puli-Khumri. Mary's English student, Jon Momad. WHO vaccinators, explaining they just happened to be in the area. The personnel from Kabul—Ken, Peaches, and Dr. Cole.

Mr. Arsala came over to collect the rent, repair the well pump, water the garden, or bring little food items one of his wives had made. Sometimes he came for conversation and tea, sometimes for no reason at all. The Afghans thought nothing of staying with the Americans for hours at a time. If they came for tea, it was for the entire afternoon; if they invited the Volunteers to their own homes for dinner, it was understood the meal would extend late into the evening.[68] Voices demanded her attention every waking moment, from the time she called class to order in the morning to the time she said goodnight to Mr. Muktar at the end of another working day. No wonder she had become exhausted.

When Jo left the Cole family, she thanked them all, but she especially thanked Dr. Cole. "You were right all along," she said. "I needed some time away from Baghlan."

"And your cough?"

Jo smiled. She knew Dr. Cole was interested in more than just her recovery from pneumonia.

"Almost gone," she said.

On the taxi ride home, Jo looked out the window. The snow receded as they descended toward Baghlan, and little tufts of green appeared on the outcroppings of rock. She bent over and retrieved her journal and a pencil. Holding her elbows close to her body, with an Afghan pressed next to her on either side, she wrote: *I feel like a drowned man revived. Bright blue skies, white puffy clouds, and bright sunlight illuminating the green fields and delicate hues of the mountains.*

Had the corruption at Baghlan Hospital always been this transparent? Or had she simply been oblivious to it before now? Jo was home only a few days when the latest development in Baghlan unfolded. The hospital staff was going through the building like a SWAT team, fanning out to every room, looking for the missing case of Sego. Twenty-four cases of the canned nutritional supplement had been delivered by WHO just that morning. Now a case was missing. Moussa was beside himself.

Moussa—the auxiliary nurse in charge of supplies—had inventoried the delivery and stacked the cases himself. He made a striking impression, his dark, clean-shaven features accented by a spotless white shirt. Moussa supervised all the deliveries that came to Baghlan Hospital, and meticulously kept track of the supplies going out, every bandage, every roll of gauze, and every dose of penicillin. It was Moussa who held the keys, literally and figuratively. The keys to power. The keys to the storeroom.

As chief of staff, Dr. Wasel had a key, and likewise, the Volunteers had also been issued a key; regardless, nothing left without Moussa's approval. He epitomized Afghan thinking—that is—if you have it, then you have it. If you use it, you no longer have it. His goal was to have it. His philosophy contrasted sharply with Western thinking: if you have it, you use it, with an expectation it will be replaced, most likely with something newer and better.

Everyone in the hospital was aware a shipment had come in that morning. The WHO truck was immediately recognized among the Afghan vehicles, and news of the delivery spread through the hospital on the ever-efficient Afghan pathway of communication.

Moussa's eyes had gleamed as he helped unload the truck. He stacked the cases in the storeroom, gratified at the sight of his shelves filled with rows of Sego. And then, Jo came with her students and took the first couple of cans to dispense to the patients. With every can that left, Moussa became more despondent. The students were taking his precious supplies. Soon he would *have* nothing. So when he unlocked the storage room that afternoon and found an entire case missing, he was wild. "*Dozd!*" he shouted. —Thief!

He closed the door and started through the hallways of the hospital, walking as fast as he could without breaking into a trot. "*Ma râ dozd zada!*" —I've been robbed!

He eventually brought everything to a standstill: patient care, teaching, exams, IV infusions, and treatments. Moussa would have stopped surgery if he thought he could get away with it. He would find the missing case of Sego if he had to shut down the entire hospital.

The Volunteers swept through the exam rooms and the OB/delivery room; the girls split into groups and looked into every patient room; the teachers opened their classroom for scrutiny. By the end of the day there was one room left. Dr. Wasel's office.

Moussa hesitated. Dr. Wasel was the chief of staff, and to enter his office was to cross a line of authority, but … Moussa was in agony. He threw up his hands in despair. "An entire case is missing!"

It was Mary who offered to intervene. She was, after all, the *muy safad*, the person of respect, the one person who could pass through the doorway to Dr. Wasel's office unannounced. She nonchalantly stopped by for a friendly visit with the good doctor.

She took a seat in his office and casually leaned back in the chair, crossing her legs. "Oh, my," she noted. "Why, there's a case of Sego under your desk, Doctor."

"Oh, my," said Dr. Wasel. "What a surprise! We have found the missing Sego. Here it is!"

"Well, well," said Mary. "We can put it back in the storeroom."

"Well, well," said Dr. Wasel. "But of course! I'm so glad we found it."

⌒∩⌀∩⌒

"It's a no-brainer," said Nan as she set out plates for dinner that night. "Dr. Wasel was going to sell it."

Mary opened the door to Roxanne and brought out the butter. "Sure—a nice way to supplement his income. A little subsidy from the World Health Organization."

"At the expense of the patients," added Jo.

"Well, it's a way to survive." Nan set out the silverware. "The government stipend barely pays the docs a living wage. No wonder they sell whatever they can get their hands on—or extort money from their patients. But there is one good thing." She took her seat at the table with a mischievous smile. "The docs have to treat all their patients in front of us, whether they can afford a bribe or not."

"Yep." Jo returned the grin. "We put a damper on their system of payment."

"Well, anyway," said Mary, closing the discussion. "It was a moment to remember. There we were, just me and Dr. Wasel, eyeball to eyeball, and all the time I knew that he knew that I knew—he had stolen the Sego!"

The uproar over the missing Sego eventually died down. Moussa demanded all the storeroom keys, and while the Volunteers surrendered theirs, Dr. Wasel kept forgetting to turn his in. Jo didn't care. It was spring, and she refused to waste her time thinking about Dr. Wasel. The rains were over, the air was dry and warm, and on a billowy, blustery day the women took down the plastic from the windows, spaded the garden, and cleaned out the yard.

Jo breathed in the sweet, clean air as she ripped the last few tatters of plastic from the window frame. The Hindu Kush rose in the distance, the snow cover melting to reveal delicate hues of brown and a gauzy mantle of green, barely discernible among the crevices and folds of the mountainsides. A flock of swallows spiraled above her. Back from Africa, they disappeared into a transparent blue sky then swooped back into view, flying as if from sheer joy, happy to be home again.

When Jo had gone to see Dr. Cole, she felt as if her time in Afghanistan would never end. Now suddenly it would be ending very soon, and she wanted to remember every detail: the sound of Jaleal cleaning out the bokhari, the Hindu Kush ever present on the horizon, and the women working in the compound with her. Nan hummed under her breath as she washed the newly exposed glass. Mary leaned on her spade, the skirt of her dress alternately swelling out full and taut, then clinging to her legs in tight little ripples as the gusts of wind changed direction. Jo turned her face to the sun and closed her eyes. Her assignment was almost completed. The next time she left Baghlan, it would be for good.[69]

Chapter 29

ENDINGS AND NEW BEGINNINGS

I cried as we boarded the gaudie and we were off bag and baggage.
—July 16, 1970

Jo never expected it would be Mr. Muktar who left first.

She had been surprised when he told her, and yet she quickly agreed—he would be foolish to pass up such an opportunity. After all, how many Vo-Ag teachers had the chance to study for an advanced chemistry degree at the American University in Lebanon?

She had been genuinely pleased, full of questions about his new venture. In turn, he put aside his own excitement and brought Jo's attention back to the matter at hand: the last few lectures, the review, and final exam. "There's plenty of time," he said. "We'll get it done before I leave."

He came every night as usual, only now he came directly from his teaching job. Mary or Nan made dinner while he worked with Jo, and after a break to get something to eat, they resumed the translation process until they were too tired to continue.

And then one evening Mr. Muktar came to the house in a suit jacket. The review had been translated, the final exam questions written. He wasn't there for a lesson. He was there to say goodbye.

Mary brewed tea and they gathered around the table. Jo pulled up her chair. How many times had they done this? So many times she had lost count, and now it was odd to think they were doing it for the last time. They discussed Mr. Muktar's impending studies, and speculated how the girls would perform on the final exam.

They finished a second cup of tea, and a third. They had talked easily and freely almost every day for the past two years, and now they awkwardly came to the end of a conversation. Jo was cast into limbo—that uncomfortable place where Mr. Muktar was still with them, yet already gone.

She walked with him down the worn path. There was a time when their daily Farsi lessons were drudgery; now all she could remember was the shared feeling of accomplishment, the private, little jokes they laughed at, the family stories they exchanged, and the day she had to turn away to keep from laughing when he blushed and stammered over the lesson on women's health.

Her every sense was attuned to an almost palpable bond between them. Sounds faded into the background; the evening birdsong came from a distance, and crickets chirped from somewhere far away. The house and compound wall reflected a hazy pink light from the setting sun, but she didn't notice. All that mattered was the immediate sound of their footsteps in the dust, and the bent head of Mr. Muktar as they walked side by side.

He opened the heavy gate, and as always, stepped back so that Jo could go first. She came out of the compound, stopped at the juie bank, and turned to face him. What to say? She studied his fine features and soft brown eyes. Most likely, she would never see him again. Not once had they spoken of their affection for one another; it was understood. She embraced him, feeling his compact body, the fabric of his suit. She barely had enough breath to say the words. "Goodbye, Mr. Muktar. Good luck in Lebanon."

"Goodbye, Jo." Mr. Muktar stepped back and looked into her face. "Someday you will marry."

Taken off guard at such an unexpected comment, Jo laughed, some-what relieved to have the solemnity of the moment broken. She resorted to the comfortable banter they had exchanged over the past months. "Oh, you think so?" She cocked her head, smiling. "And maybe I will never marry. What if no one wants me?"

But this time Mr. Muktar was serious. "You will. And when you do, I want a complete picture of your husband."

Jo immediately regretted her flip remark. In his own way, Mr. Muktar was telling her that he cared about her. He wanted her husband to be kind, and he wanted her to be happy. She nodded. Blinked, hoping the tears would not fall until after he left.

Mr. Muktar formally shook Jo's hand with a little bow, then crossed the juie and walked along the dirt road. He turned back once to wave goodbye.

It seemed everyone had already left, or was in the process of leaving. Hans and Gunther had long since gone back to Germany. Peggy Cannon was back in Ireland. Even Jaleal was no longer with them. His malaria symptoms had worsened and he had returned to his home to recover. In his place was a bacha named Khan.

Kathleen and Rick had returned to the States soon after finding out they were expecting their first child. The Afghans had pressed countless little gifts on them before they left: carved wooden toys, and tiny, embroidered tunics—things for the "Peace Corps baby."

And then Nan finished her assignment. Jo saw her off at the taxi bazaar on May 5, 1970.

The driver stowed her luggage in the trunk, lifting the bags easily. Nan had given away most of her clothes to the girls. He closed the trunk, came around to the driver's side and slid in behind the wheel. He was ready to go.

"Write to me," said Jo. "Let me know you're okay."

"You know I will." Nan looked around at the taxi bazaar for the last time. "I can't believe it. I can't believe I won't be coming back with supplies." She turned to face Jo and held out her arms. The two women embraced. "Be safe," she said. Then she climbed into the taxi. Jo watched as the driver pulled out of the bazaar. She stood waving until she couldn't see the car anymore.

It was time for all of them to go home, but Jo had agreed to stay an additional six weeks in Baghlan, and Mary had agreed to stay with her.

She began a comprehensive review with her students, amused when Kamila appeared in one of Nan's sweaters, tugging at the sleeves and hem, stretching it to fit her ample frame.

A few weeks before the exam, Ken came for a visit and asked if Jo would consider extending even further. He could use her expertise in Kabul, he said, helping train the new Volunteers. Jo turned down his offer without a second thought. She was ready to go home. "In any case," she explained, "I want to remember Baghlan, not Kabul."

Dr. Cole came with four new Volunteers, and Jo did her best to keep from smiling when they tiptoed through the little house not touching anything, as if they wondered whether or not they could live in such a place. She commiserated with them when they returned from the police station incensed at the expected bribe; she nodded sympathetically when they criticized Ghulam's bossiness, and offered flea powder when they complained of fleas.

Alex understood it all—the new people in his house, the flurry of activity, and trunks and belongings everywhere. It meant only one thing: Jo was leaving.

One of the new Volunteers had become enamored with the idea of having a dog and offered to keep him, but Alex wanted no part of it. He was a wild juie dog, after all, and if he couldn't have Jo as his master, he didn't want anyone. He began to jump the compound wall at night and run through the streets of Baghlan, often not coming back until morning. He occasionally limped into the compound with his fur dusty and dirty from fighting with other dogs. He pulled clean laundry off the clothesline and dragged it through the dirt. He growled when Jon Momad came too close to Mary.

Jo gave the final test over two days, and finished the last part on July 13, 1970. She chose to ignore the fact that Dr. Wasel and Ghulam had come into the classroom to help the girls with their answers. She didn't care. Never had the phrase *"parwâ na dâra"* meant so much to her. It simply didn't matter. She had done the best she could.

Eight students of the original thirteen finished the program: Jamila, Paregul, Anorgul, Kamila, Mastura, Zakhara, Malia, and Sedika.

After the test, Jo turned over her lecture notes to the new Volunteers. She didn't need her teaching materials anymore, nor would she walk into her classroom ever again. She attended teas and dinners in her honor, and after a ceremony at the hospital, she wrote in her diary: *July 15, 1970: Went to the hospital for a farewell tea. Dr Wasel said training a nurse was more important for the people than building a city.*

She had her girls over for lunch, even though a part of her simply wanted to leave quietly and avoid the heartache of a prolonged goodbye. The few things she might have taught them in a classroom paled in comparison to what she had learned. The girls had allowed her to become part of their lives, and she was the richer for it. Over the past two years the dynamic had been much more than teacher and student, lecturer and listener. They had argued, joked, laughed, cajoled, cried, and explained. They had shared rites of passage, and in a sense, they had grown up together.

On the day of the lunch, the girls crowded around the table, laughing and talking as always, but Jo was in a daze, stupefied to think they would never be together in this way again. The conversation flowed past her unheeded; jokes were incomprehensible. She took bites of food that tasted like sawdust.

When the girls prepared to leave, she embraced each one individually: Kamila, Malia, Jamila, Paregul, Anorgul, Mastura, Zakhara, and Sedika. They left in a group, walking along the footpath. They were almost to the compound door when Anorgul turned and called back, *"Bâmâni khodâ, mu'alim jân!"* —Goodbye, dear teacher! Jo waved, but when they were out of sight she closed the door, sat down on the floor, and cried.

Over the next couple of days, she would attend a termination conference in Kabul with Mary, and then, after two years and four months in Afghanistan, she was going home.

The night before Jo left Baghlan, she and Mary painted their names and home addresses on their Peace Corps trunks. They stayed up late reminiscing about their days at the Sugar Hotel, Nan's accident, and Alex chasing the turkeys in a circle around the house. They talked about their homes, their families, the last gaudie ride they would take in the morning.

"The last time we sit on a hard wooden bench," said Jo with a little smile.

"The last time we share a taxi with eight people," answered Mary. "Or brush our teeth over a back stoop."

Jo finally crawled into bed and lay on her back, her hands folded over her chest. A chapter of her life was nearly at an end, and she was awake for a long time. No one had told her about this part, she thought. No one had warned her of the attachments she would make—not just to Nan and Mary, but to the Afghans, and to the country itself.

She envisioned Anorgul making comments from the back of the room, and Jamila in her wedding gown. She thought about all her girls; their open displays of affection, their lack of sophistication, their innocence.

She thought about her own family, and how much she had missed them over the past two years. It was a strange night, that night before she left: a time of in-between, and she wondered how it was possible—that she could be homesick for the United States and homesick for Afghanistan at the same time, even before she was gone.

She anticipated the emotional rush she would feel when her plane touched down on American soil, the long awaited, crushing embrace from her father. And yet, she was filled with doubt. Could she really step into her previous life as if nothing had changed? She turned over and tugged at the pillow. In the dark and stillness of her room, she acknowledged what she had been avoiding, what she had most likely known all along. Her old life was gone. No matter how desperately she wanted everything to be just as she had left it, deep down she knew it would never be the same again.

306

Nothing is permanent, she thought. Nothing remains unchanged forever: not relationships, places, circumstances, or even myself. She wondered if given the chance, whether she would go back to the person she had been two years ago. She would never have seen the Hindu Kush—the snowcaps expanding in winter, and the massive, jagged summits deep brown against the sky in summer. She would not have known Mr. Muktar, never laughed with Nan, never cried for Bibi Deeba. She had stepped across a divide, had reached across a wall of separation between herself and the Afghans she had come to know.

Jo stirred and repositioned herself, throwing an arm up over her head. Her eyes finally closed, and she wobbled on the fine line between wakefulness and sleep—the thin place where truth is sometimes found. We are all connected, she thought. Whatever happens to any one of us happens to all of us.

She fell into a dreamless sleep and did not wake until the familiar sounds drifted over the compound wall: a rooster's crow, nân boy's adolescent voice, the muezzin call to prayer. Her last morning in Baghlan. Khan bustled in the kitchen, making tea. A few remaining stars were barely visible in a turquoise sky.

Jo sat up in bed. Everything was packed and organized, her clothes for the day folded neatly beside her bed. She went through the motions of getting dressed, then went into the kitchen and had tea and nân with Mary, hardly aware of what she was doing.

She made a last sweep of the little house. Was there anything she had forgotten? Every room, every corner, every piece of furniture was imbued with memories: the table where she and Mr. Muktar had exchanged lessons, the tin bathtub, Roxanne. It would all be left behind. She remembered the house filled with company on Thanksgiving, the food and music. Now the rooms were strangely quiet. Their bags looked out of place, stacked up against the wall.

Khan had already left for the bazaar. It would not take long. He would return soon with a gaudie. Jo opened the door to the back stoop and called Alex for the last time. She slipped a rope collar over his head, knelt down, and brought his face up to hers. She looked into his eyes. "Be a good boy," she whispered. Then she led him to the shower room, tied him up, and locked the door. Even if Khan held him back, he might start to bark, or worse, break away and chase after the gaudie. She could not bear the thought.

Voices were calling. Khan had returned. Some of the neighborhood kids gathered around the juie crossing and watched as he hoisted the Peace Corps trunks onto the cart. Then Jo climbed up and sat on the narrow wooden seat next to Mary. The horse shook his head. The driver clicked; the cart jerked forward.

Remnants of dew sparkled on wispy blades of grass, but whether she stayed or was long gone, it didn't matter. An hour from now the grass would be dry. The horse broke into a trot, kicking patterns of dust into the air. Ahead of them, the road was striped with elongated, early-morning shadows, cast by a line of trees along the juie.

EPILOGUE

Shortly after returning home in 1970, Jo accepted an invitation to be the director of a medical-surgical unit at Riverside Hospital in Kankakee, Illinois, a single unit with as many patients as all of Baghlan Hospital.

She corresponded with Mr. Muktar for a while, but lost track of him when he left Lebanon. Mr. Muktar would have been pleased to know she eventually married—indeed, to a husband who is kind to her and a good father.

She never saw Mr. Hyatullah again.

Nan lived for several years in Australia, working in the lab at the Royal Prince Albert Hospital. Ever the world traveler, she backpacked through Iran, Turkey, Malaysia, and Singapore. Keeping a promise she had made to Kamila, she returned to Afghanistan in 1976.

She found Kamila as cheerful as always, working in Baghlan Hospital. Malia had divorced her husband and was happily remarried, living in Puli-Khumri. Habiba had two children. Anorgul was married with three children, but Nan was dismayed to note that her former student had a large, untreated thyroid tumor. Paregul, the middle sister to Jamila and Anorgul, had finished her studies to become a midwife.

When Nan returned home she completed her degree and became an information technology specialist with Siemens Laboratories.

Mary returned to Afghanistan in the early 1970s and worked for an additional eight years with the Peace Corps. She mentored her young student, Jon Momad, and facilitated his emigration to the United States, where he continued his education and became a successful businessman.

Mary passed away on October 1, 1988.

In the forty years since leaving Afghanistan, the women have reunited dozens of times. Before Mary's death, they gathered at her lake house in Michigan during the summers. They met at Nan's home in Philadelphia, joined by Peaches, Charlotte Budum, and others. They talked late into the night, repeating shared adventures, stories that became much like family stories over the years—more comical, amusing, and poignant with each retelling.

They laughed at how naive and young they had been. How they depended on each other, doing crazy, silly things because there was nothing else they could do. How they rode camels, traveled to India, let Mary pierce their ears one hot summer afternoon, and had the first tin bathtub made in the history of Afghanistan.

They reminisced over details that would have been forgotten, if not for the pages of Jo's diary. During her two years in Afghanistan she wrote every day without fail, even if only a couple of sentences. She made notes about the little things—the ordinary events of everyday life—what they ate, where they went, and the daily routine of teaching, never dreaming her entries would eventually become a significant historical account. Her journal has become a bittersweet reminder of the country she once called home, and her tiny handwriting describes a time and place that has since vanished. The American Peace Corps workers are long gone from Afghanistan, replaced by Soviet troops in 1979, mujahideen fighters ten years later, the Taliban in 1996, and the United States military in 2001, joined by NATO forces in 2003.[70] Afghanistan is no longer the name of a country; it is the name of a war.

At one time the Volunteers walked through the countryside with Mr. Muktar. Now those same rocks and foothills are peppered with land mines. Compounds where the Volunteers shared tea with Afghan families have been destroyed by Soviet bombing, and the girls who once sat in Jo's classroom are now forced to live under the strict Sharia law of the Taliban.

On November 6, 2007, a suicide bomber killed 74 people in Baghlan Province. Among the fatalities were 62 children—students who had been assembled to welcome government dignitaries to the sugar refinery in Fabrika. Jo wondered how many of the children were from the families she once knew.

Jo and Nan were most recently together on a sweltering day in July 2008, meeting for lunch at Jo's home in Illinois. They discussed the recent bombing, saddened at the violence and suspicion that seems to be everywhere, not just in Afghanistan, but in their own country as well.

"It's hard to believe, isn't it? Nan accepted more iced tea. "I mean, look at how much things have changed. We were the only Westerners and the only non-Muslims in Baghlan, yet we felt so comfortable. So accepted."

Jo set the pitcher of iced tea back on the table. "It's because the Afghans cared about us. Remember how they helped us move from the Sugar Hotel? How Mr. Arsala's wives brought us dinner?"

The intervening years had not erased the crinkle from under Nan's eyes. "All the unexpected little gifts …"

"The embroidered handkerchief from Wyhab when he got engaged."

"The Christmas tree from Mr. Hyatullah."

"The way Jaleal used to yell at us when we were late coming home."

Both women laughed at the sudden, vivid memory of their bacha. The conversation drifted to the day Jaleal ironed Mary's dress and burned a hole in it, the time he ran through the house chasing a rooster.

Jo and Nan finished lunch, and as Jo's husband cleared the table, the discussion turned to updates on their respective jobs and family news. It was well into the afternoon when Nan glanced at her watch. If she was going to make the evening flight out of O'Hare, she would have to leave soon, before the start of rush-hour traffic in Chicago. She carried her glass of iced tea to the sink, then gathered her belongings.

Jo walked with her out to the car, into the hot, muggy air of a Midwest summer afternoon. She helped Nan stow her bags in the back seat. "Just think of all the times we said goodbye at the taxi bazaar," she said. "And now, here we are, saying goodbye in my own driveway."

Nan laughed. "It was a long time ago, wasn't it? Sometimes I can't help but wonder. For all our work, for all the time we were there, what did we really accomplish?"

"We thought we were going to save the world," said Jo. "Instead, we stepped out of the box into another culture and it changed us forever. And if only a handful of people learn something from us, well, it was still worthwhile. After all, you can only work toward peace one person at a time, beginning with yourself."

ACKNOWLEDGMENTS

This book could not have been written without the generosity of Joanne Carter Bowling. She graciously and without reservation gave me her entire box of memorabilia, including photographs, tape recordings, letters, and her journal. During the ensuing months and years she reviewed her diary with me, patiently answering questions, filling in details, and clarifying what she had written. In the process she gave me more than factual information; she revealed the dreams and aspirations she had as a young Volunteer. Her personal reflections and insights were essential to this project. In the end, however, she gave me the ultimate gift of all: the freedom to write the story in my own way, trusting that I would remain faithful to her message.

I owe a special thanks to Nan O'Rourke, who cheerfully spoke with me by telephone every Sunday morning for months, reading passages from letters she sent home over forty years ago—letters an aunt had saved for her. I had the pleasure of meeting Nan for the first time in the summer of 2008.

I am indebted to my writing group, The Literary Writers Network in Chicago, for helping me navigate the early drafts. Anne Unger, Denis Underwood, Chad Peterson, Alexander Slagg, Willy Nast, Stephen Markley, April Galarza, Kate Hawley, Lindsay Tigue, and Noor Nasseer—your comments and suggestions were invaluable.

Theodore Beers, working with USAID in Kabul during the time I started this book, checked the early drafts for accuracy. My editors, Jane Albritton, Kate Hawthorne Jeracki, and Jordan Rosenfeld not only brought their expertise and respect for the craft of writing to the table, they were unfailingly courteous and helpful, long after the manuscript revisions were complete. I thank my reader, Mary Hazeltine, and I thank Carol Kelley, who painstakingly and judiciously read and marked the final draft. I thank Susan Brady for her technical support and guidance during the last stages of book production.

I thank the Peace Corps community itself, and the generous assistance I received from Terry Dougherty, Lawrence F. Lihosit, and Will Lutwick.

Mary Simpson's son, Joseph R. Simpson, encouraged me in the premise of this book, as did Dr. John Bing, and the family of Dr. Jack Cole. Georgia Joyal (Peaches) and Charlotte Otts (Budum) kindly shared additional insights and information.

I am most grateful to Dr. Michael Spath, professor of religious studies at Indiana University-Purdue University, Fort Wayne, Indiana, for his endorsement of the manuscript. I thank Jo's husband Roy, who remained steadfast and patient throughout this entire project. I value his friendship and support.

I thank my "Eleventh Hour Readers," Linda LaCosse, Debbie Hendrick, Phyllis Jensen, Dwilene Young, Judith Hemphill, Sharon LaMotte, Linda Lund, and Cheryl Trudeau. I was touched by the enthusiasm of friends and family: Keith, D'Ann, Margaret, Maxine, Mick and Jan, Paul, Meg, Sally, and Cathy.

Many thanks go to the Peace Corps Writers, specifically to editors John P. Coyne, and Marian Haley Beil. I am honored to have this book published under the Peace Corps Writers imprint. And of course, I thank my children, Caroline, Elizabeth, Matthew, Amy, Sarah, and Mike.

Lastly, my heartfelt gratitude goes to my husband, Ken. For nearly six years I spent every waking moment with this manuscript. Without complaint or discussion, he quietly took over the domestic chores of our household, allowing me to continue without interruption. He read early drafts, final drafts, and those in-between, marking passages, and often finding errors and inconsistencies others had missed. Thank you, Ken, for taking this journey with me.

ABOUT THE AUTHOR

Susan Fox has worked as a technical writer for a major consulting firm in the Chicago area, and is a member of the Literary Writers Network, currently serving as senior editorial assistant for their online publication, *10,000 Tons of Black Ink*. She holds a bachelor's degree in psychology, a nursing degree, and a certificate in technical writing from the Illinois Institute of Technology in Chicago. Fox has been a keynote speaker at The Indiana Center for Middle East Peace, hosted by Dr. Michael Spath, and has read excerpts from her book at one of Chicago's premier independent book stores, the Book Cellar. The opening pages of the book recently took honors in the nonfiction category at the Writers' Institute in Madison, Wisconsin.

Susan works at St. Mary's Hospital in Kankakee, Illinois, serves on the Human Rights Committee for Good Shepherd Manor in Momence, Illinois, and is a member of the Kankakee Valley Wind Ensemble. She lives in Momence with her husband Ken.

Additional information about the book can be found on the website:
www.littlewomenofbaghlan.com.

APPENDIX: JO'S GIRLS

Anorgul (Pomegranate Flower) was generally positive and happy-go-lucky. She liked to play the role of class clown. Typical of most fourteen-year-olds, she could be brash, with a know-it-all attitude, always ready with a comment. Anorgul was the youngest sister to Jamila and Paregul, and the youngest student in Jo's class.

Habiba was a ninth grader, but she was highly intelligent, and could read and write with more proficiency than most of the other students. School was easy for her.

Jamila was the oldest sister to Paregul and Anorgul. She was nineteen, and took her responsibilities seriously, sometimes wearing a modified chador. She was sensitive, with many conflicts. Unknown to the Volunteers, Jamila's father was in the process of negotiating a husband for her when school started.

Kamila had somewhat of a matronly appearance. She acted mature, but for the most part she was positive and fun. She was Malia's sister-in-law. Kamila lived in Baghlan on the same street as the Volunteers, as did Jamila, Paregul and Anorgul.

Latifah was not willing to work as hard as some of the other students. She attended only a few months.

Malia was the oldest student at age twenty. She was married to one of Kamila's brothers and had three children. Attractive and self-assured, she was a mother figure to the other students. She did not wear the chador. She worked hard but had a difficult time reading and writing. Her husband eventually took a second wife.

Mastura was sixteen and self-confident, with an engaging personality. Flirty and cute, she would try anything and do anything on a dare. She was Zakhara's best friend.

Paregul usually dressed conservatively, wearing plain, unadorned tunics. She was outgoing and a tomboy. Paregul was the middle sister to Anorgul and Jamila, and the most intelligent of the three girls.

Sedika found it difficult to express her thoughts. Kind and sensitive, she had a poor self-image, and never tried to impress the Volunteers. Although she was practical, and had a great deal of common sense, but could not read or write very well, and consequently struggled with school.

Signora took the entrance exam but attended only a few months. She died of tuberculosis in January 1969.

Tiara attended only a few months.

Torpika was quiet but hard working and observant.

Zakhara was sensitive and shy. She was serious about learning, and had a level of sophistication slightly above the rest of the students. She was Mastura's best friend.

BIBLIOGRAPHY

SOURCES

Carter, Joanne. "Afghanistan Journal, 1968-1970." Private collection.

Carter, Joanne. "Cassette tape recordings to Mr. and Mrs. James Carter, April 1968-December 1969. Private collection.

Jack Vaughn to Joanne Carter, November 21, 1968. Private collection.

Photographs by Joanne Carter. Private collection.

BOOKS

Albritton, Jane. Introduction to *Peace Corps Experience: Write and Publish Your Memoir*, by Lawrence F. Lihosit, Bloomington, Indiana: iUniverse, Inc., 2012

Armstrong, Karen. *Islam: A Short History*. New York: Random House, 2002.

Awde, Nicholas, et al. *Dari Dictionary and Phrasebook*. New York: Hippocrene Books, 2002.

Benard, Cheryl. *Veiled Courage: Inside the Afghan Women's Resistance*. New York: Random House, 2002.

DuPree, Louis. *Afghanistan*. Oxford, England: Oxford University Press, 1997.

Ewans, Martin. *Afghanistan: A Short History of Its People and Politics.* New York: HarperCollins, 2002.

Hoffman, Elizabeth Cobbs. *All You Need is Love: The Peace Corps and the Spirit of the 1960s.* Cambridge, Mass.: Harvard University Press, 1998.

Kakar, Hassan M. *Afghanistan: The Soviet Invasion and the Afghan Response, 1979–1982.* Los Angeles: University of California Press, 1995.

Lihosit, Lawrence F. *Peace Corps Experience: Write and Publish Your Memoir.* Bloomington, Indiana: iUniverse, Inc., 2012

Meisler, Stanley. *When the World Calls: The Inside Story of the Peace Corps and Its First Fifty Years.* Boston: Beacon Press, 2011.

Thomsen, Moritz. *Living Poor: A Peace Corps Chronicle.* Seattle: University of Washington Press, 1990.

Ong, Walter J. *Orality and Literacy.* London: Routledge, 2004.

Rice, Gerard T. *The Bold Experiment.* Notre Dame, Indiana: University of Notre Dame Press, 1985.

Samovar, Larry A., and Porter, Richard E. *Intercultural Communication.* Belmont, California: Wadsworth, 1997.

Storti, Craig. *The Art of Coming Home.* Boston: Nicholas Brealey, 2003.

Tanner, Stephen. *Afghanistan: A Military History from Alexander the Great to the Fall of the Taliban.* Cambridge, Mass.: Da Capo Press, 2002.

Trautman, Kathleen. *Spies Behind the Pillars, Bandits at the Pass.* New York: David McKay, 1972.

PERIODICALS

Widmer, Ted. "The Challenge of Imperialism." *Boston Sunday Globe*, July 15, 2007.

Zabriskie, Phil. "Hazaras: Afghanistan's Outsiders." *National Geographic Magazine*, February 2008.

CONGRESSIONAL HOUSE HEARINGS

Vaughn, Jack. Quoted during testimony before the House Subcommittee on International Development, September 8, 20, and 29, 1977. "Peace Corp: Purpose and Development," House Hearings, p. 33.

INTERNET

"Afghan Avalanche Toll Exceeds 165." *BBC News*. http://news.bbc.co.uk/2/hi/8506033.stm. Retrieved May 4, 2010.

"Afghanistan's Turbulent History." *BBC News International Version*, October 8, 2004. http://news.bbc.co.uk/2/hi/south_asia/1569826.stm. Retrieved February 10, 2008.

Aviation Safety Network. http://aviation-safety.net/index.php. Retrieved June 1, 2009.

Baker, Aryn. "A Dam Shame: What a Stalled Hydropower Project Says About Failures in Afghanistan." December 15, 2011. http://world.time.com/2011/12/15. Retrieved July 15, 2013.

Boettcher, Mike, and Schuster, Henry. "How Much Did Afghan Leader Know?" *CNN.com International Edition*, November 6, 2003. http://www.cnn.com/2003/US/11/06/massoud.cable/index.html. Retrieved April 26, 2008.

"Brzezinski Interview." *Le Nouvel Observateur*, 1998. Translated by William Blum and David Gibbs. http://dgibbs.faculty.arizona.edu/brzezinski_interview. Retrieved June 23, 2013.

Elliott, Michael. "They Had a Plan." *Time in Partnership with CNN*, August 4, 2002. http://www.time.com/time/magazine/article/0,9171,1003007,00.html. Retrieved April 4, 2008.

"Robert F. Kennedy." http://www.bobby-kennedy.com/index.html. Retrieved June 27, 2008.

Garwood, Paul. "Poverty, Violence Put Afghanistan's Fabled Kuchi Nomads on a Road to Nowhere." December 15, 2009. http://www.rawa.org/nomad.htm. Retrieved December 19, 2009.

Kennedy, John F., Massachusetts. "Imperialism—The Enemy of Freedom." July 2, 1957. http://www.jfklink.com/speeches/jfk/congress/jfk020757_imperialism.html. Retrieved June 20, 2011.

Kennedy, John F., Massachusetts. Campaign speech, Cow Palace, San Francisco, California, November 2, 1960. *The American Presidency Project.* http://www.presidency.ucsb.edu/ws/index.php?pid=25928#axzz1M4871hbX. Retrieved May 20, 2011.

United Press International. "Robert F. Kennedy Assassinated." http://www.upi.com/Audio/Year_in_Review/Events-of-1968/Robert-F.-Kennedy-Assassinated/12303153093431-3/. Retrieved February 13, 2013.

Women's Human Rights Resources—Women in Afghanistan. http://www.law-lib.utoronto.ca/diana/afghanwomen.htm. Retrieved June 1, 2010.

West, Andrew. "RFK Assassinated." *University of Maryland/Library of American Broadcasting*, June 5, 1968. http://jclass.umd.edu/archive/hearit-now/1968.htm. Retrieved February 18, 2013.

CONFERENCES

Shadow Summit for Afghan Women's Rights. Amnesty International. Swiss Hotel, Chicago, IL, May 20, 2012.

FILMS

Vickers, Jill, and Bergedick, Jody. *Once in Afghanistan*. Dirt Road Documentaries, 2008. 4409 Town Line Road, Bridport, VT, 05734

NOTES

CHAPTER 1: THE HINDU KUSH

1. Ironically, the Salang Road would prove essential for the Soviet Union's invasion of Afghanistan less than ten years later. Soviet troops crossed the border on Christmas Eve 1979 and marched south along the main highway to Kabul, securing the Salang Pass and Tunnel by the next day. The resulting Soviet-Afghan War lasted ten years, leaving a million Afghans dead and another five million as refugees. The USSR lost fifteen thousand troops and spent billions of dollars before they were forced to retreat—contributing factors that led to the breakup of the USSR in the early 1990s. The tunnel that Jo crossed through on that April day in 1970 is possibly the most strategic 1.7 miles in Afghanistan.

2. Travelers crossing the Hindu Kush in 1970 were essentially cut off from contact with anyone until they reached their destination. Wireless communication was not extended to the Salang region until October 2005.

3. An avalanche on February 10, 2010, caused 165 deaths.

CHAPTER 2: THE OTHER SIDE OF THE HILL

4. Not only Jo, but much of the world lost interest in a poor, non-literate country. There was a brief surge of global outrage when the Soviets invaded in 1979 (U.S. President Jimmy Carter condemned the invasion, and in a controversial decision announced a boycott of the 1980 Moscow Summer Olympics), but after the Soviets retreated, Afghanistan slipped into oblivion. No one took notice of the civil war following the Soviet withdrawal, or the emergence of two powerful groups: a fundamentalist sect known as the Taliban, promising law and order, and the Northern Alliance, led by a Tajik named Ahmed Shah Massoud. The press barely mentioned Massoud's desperate plea for help in his

fight against the Taliban, or the speech he gave to the European Parliament in April 2000. Other news stories took precedence over the warning he issued in that speech, a warning of the Taliban's connection to a little known organization of Islamic radicals and terrorists known as al-Qaeda, led by a Saudi named Osama bin Laden.

On September 9, 2001—just five months after his plea for help—Massoud was assassinated by two suicide bombers posing as journalists. The men were linked to al-Qaeda, and forty-eight hours later, al-Qaeda terrorists destroyed the World Trade Center in New York.

One of President Hamad Karzai's first official acts was to posthumously award Massoud the title "Hero of the Afghan Nation," and place his image over the blue-painted concrete arch on the damaged and crumbling north entrance to the Salang Tunnel—the same entrance that Jo had passed through so many years ago.

5. Although Kennedy directed his speech at resolving the issue of Algerian independence from France, he also acknowledged America's ambition to spread freedom throughout the Middle East, and cautioned it is impossible to achieve a lasting peace through imperialism or by using military options. ("Imperialism—The Enemy of Freedom." Senator John F. Kennedy, Massachusetts. July 2, 1957.)

6. Senator John Kennedy gave his speech at the Cow Palace in San Francisco, California, on November 2, 1960. He noted that almost 70 percent of U.S. Foreign Ambassadors were unable to speak the language of their host country, and furthermore, diplomats were often oblivious to the disease, poverty, and illiteracy surrounding them. He continued: "I therefore propose that our inadequate efforts in this area be supplemented by a peace corps of talented young men and women, willing and able to serve their country ..." (Campaign speech, Senator John F. Kennedy. Cow Palace, San Francisco, CA, November 2, 1960. *The American Presidency Project*.)

7. Established in 1961, the Peace Corps defined a generation of Americans. President Kennedy pushed for final legislation during the Cold War, and he

reminded Congress that the Soviet Union already had teachers, engineers, doctors, and nurses prepared to spend their lives abroad in the service of world communism. The United States did not have an equivalent organization, and he felt compelled to match the Soviets.

Idealists saw the establishment of the Peace Corps as an unselfish act to help humanity; political realists viewed it as a way to protect our interests, and cynics interpreted it as a calculated method for the United States to increase its power and influence around the world. But for the tens of thousands of young Peace Corps Volunteers, there was little or no ambivalence. They felt called upon to share their good fortune, and letters began to pour into Washington even before Kennedy's inauguration, inquiring how to join an organization that had yet to be created, asking to serve in countries yet to be contacted.

8. Letter to Joanne Carter from Jack Vaughn. Private collection. Reprinted with permission. Jack Vaughn succeeded Sargent Shriver as director of the Peace Corps in 1966.

CHAPTER 3: GROUP THIRTEEN

9. For over fifty years the Peace Corps has trained Volunteers to carry out its three-fold mission: first, help interested countries meet the need for trained men and women, second, promote better understanding of Americans around the world, and finally, help Americans gain a better understanding of other peoples in the world.

10. Farsi is also known as Persian, and is one of two official languages of Afghanistan. Known more recently as Afghan Persian, or Dari, it is the preferred language for business and government communication. Farsi belongs to the Iranian branch of the Indo-European family of languages, and is also spoken in Afghanistan's neighboring country Iran. Worldwide, the total number of Farsi-speaking people is estimated to be 40 million.

The other official language is Pashtu. The roughly 35 percent of Afghans who speak Pashtu live primarily in the southern provinces. About 11 percent of Afghans speak Uzbek and Turkmen.

11. Transliteration explains why the same word often appears with different spellings. It depends on how the word is heard in the original language, and the variations in phonetic spelling. The word could be *Muhammad* or *Mohamed;* *Kunduz* or *Kundoz, Koran* or *Quran.*

    An example of transliteration:

    السلام عليكم

    Asalâmu alaykum

    Peace be upon you

12. Of the seventy trainees who started with Group Thirteen, approximately twenty were eventually asked to leave. Most were sent home because of health reasons or underlying personal issues. Ongoing testing was designed to weed out the Volunteers who wanted to join the Peace Corps as a way to escape from problems, and simultaneously identify the individuals who would be most successful in adapting to a foreign culture. In reality, the Volunteers themselves often didn't know why they were deselected, and few explanations were given.

13. Employees of official government agencies in Afghanistan at that time had the privilege of shopping at the PX, the Army and Air Force Exchange Service, in Peshawar, Pakistan. Although the Peace Corps also represented the United States overseas, it was self-funded and autonomous, not affiliated with diplomatic service or USAID. An American Foreign Service worker and his family were assigned to Afghanistan in 1968—the same year as Jo, and his wife wrote the following:

    > ... this showed how well the Peace Corps fit into the country. I used to get a little annoyed at the indifference the American diplomats sometimes showed toward the Volunteers. I could understand why there was little social contact between the two groups—the Peace Corps didn't want to be identified with official diplomacy—but I couldn't understand why the value of their work wasn't always appreciated. The Volunteers lived off

the local market and spoke the language fluently and as a result were probably the best-informed group of foreigners in Kabul.

(*Spies Behind the Pillars, Bandits at the Pass*, by Kathleen Trautman MacArthur. David McKay Company, Inc. New York. Copyright © 1985 by Kathleen Trautman. Reprinted with permission.)

14. Completed in 1909, the Stanley Hotel is probably best known as the inspiration for Stephen King's book *The Shining*, which he wrote after staying at The Stanley in 1974. Listed on the National Register of Historic Places, the elegant hotel remains operational, although several multimillion-dollar renovations have been completed since Jo danced there in 1968.

CHAPTER 4: FIRST IMPRESSIONS

15. Approximately one-fifth of Afghanistan's population, the Hazara people have traditionally lived in the central highlands of Afghanistan. Their distinctive Asian features have been linked to the invasion of Genghis Khan in the thirteenth century, when Mongolian soldiers conquered the area and eventually intermarried with the local inhabitants. The Hazara people are Shiite Muslims living in an overwhelmingly Sunni Muslim country, and have been discriminated against for both religious beliefs and ethnicity for centuries. After U.S. forces drove the Taliban from power, many Hazara families moved to Kabul, hoping for a better life. The best-selling American novel *The Kite Runner*, written by Khaled Hosseini, depicts a fictional Hazara character.

16. Animals drink from the juies; farmers use them as irrigation, kids pee into them, and Afghans water flowers and gardens with juie water. On occasion, Peace Corps workers fell into them. Before the irrigation systems were destroyed by Soviet bombing, gardens and crops were planted in small fields on a level just below the surrounding area. Farmers would then open the juie and flood their crops and vegetables once a week.

17. The hippie trail started in Turkey, and meandered through Afghanistan and India, ending at Katmandu, Nepal. Thousands of young adults backpacked, rode busses, and hitchhiked the trail during the 1960s and 1970s. Some sought spiritual enlightenment; others sought drugs and escape.

18. Loosely resembling a beret, Pakol wool hats originated in the Nuristan region of northern Afghanistan. Ahmad Shah Massoud, the late Afghan leader who led the Northern Alliance against the Soviet Union, is often depicted wearing a Pakol hat.

19. In this narrative, *burqa* refers to the article of clothing that covers a woman's entire body, head, and face, with a small mesh opening for her to see through. The *niqab* also covers her head and body but leaves a thin slit open for her eyes. The *chador* covers her body, hair, and neck, but leaves her face exposed. Finally, the *hijab* covers only her hair and neck, much like a scarf.

20. The people of Kandahar speak Pashtu and comprise one of the most conservative ethnic groups of Afghanistan, parochial in attitude and generally opposed to change. Toward the end of 1994 the Taliban emerged in the city of Kandahar, promising to restore law and order in the chaotic aftermath of the Soviet withdrawal.

CHAPTER 5: KANDAHAR HOSPITAL

21. Pashtuns are the dominant ethnic group of Afghanistan, approximately 40 to 50 percent of the total population. Pashtun society in general remains highly parochial, independent, and resistant to outside influence. The Pashtunwali code of conduct emphasizes revenge, hospitality, and sanctuary. Although Pashtuns share a strong devotion to freedom and often carry hospitality to embarrassing extremes, they are ruthless as enemies.

22. The Karakul hat is peaked and folds flat when taken off the wearer's head. Afghanistan's president Hamid Karzai is usually seen wearing a Karakul hat.

CHAPTER 6: A LITTLE HELP FROM MY FRIENDS

23. The vicious *bad-i-sad-o-bist-roz* (wind of 120 days) is a seasonal natural phenomenon in southern Afghanistan. Caused by the differential in pressure between the northern plains and the southern and southwestern lowland deserts, the winds whip down a natural corridor along the Iran-Afghan border, stirring up violent sandstorms beginning in July and continuing through September. Velocities can exceed 100 miles per hour. Most likely, the sandstorm Jo encountered toward the end of March was the result of other strong, cold winds pushing out of the high-pressure areas south of Central Asia. Another phenomenon of the lowlands of Afghanistan is the *khabad* (dust wind)—small whirlwinds of sand that can be seen swaying across desert and semi-desert areas.

24. Lashkar Gah is the capital of Helmand Province and the site of the ancient city of Bost. Approximately eighty miles west of Kandahar, it became a key U.S. development project during the Cold War, as engineers and agriculture specialists constructed the Kajaki hydroelectric dam on the Helmand River in the 1950s. When the Soviet army invaded in 1979, the project was abandoned. The U.S. initiated a $128 million refurbishing project in 2002, and in August, 2008, NATO and British troops hauled a $3 million turbine 100 miles through Taliban territory. However, five years later, the turbine has yet to be installed. No one took into account the 700 tons of cement that would be needed to complete the project, and so the massive piece of equipment remains unused. In May 2013, the U.S. handed over responsibility for the dam to the Afghan government.

25. The original project included irrigation canals to raise crops, but the water is now used primarily for poppies, making Helmand Province the largest opium producer in Afghanistan. The area has long been a Taliban stronghold and the site of intense combat between U.S. forces and Taliban fighters. Ironically, Lashkar Gah means "place of the soldiers," referring to the fact that it was originally a riverside barracks for soldiers accompanying the Ghaznavid nobility a thousand years ago.

26. From its inception the Peace Corps has actively recruited African American Volunteers. It is hard to determine how many served in the Peace Corps, because the agency declined to categorize Volunteers by ethnicity. Sargent Shriver took particular pride in the fact that the Peace Corps application did not ask for a candidate's race. It is estimated that 1 to 5 percent of Volunteers were African American during the 1960s, when they represented roughly 11 percent of the population.

CHAPTER 7: SIX DAYS AND SEVEN NIGHTS

Although Afghans were proud of their fledgling airline industry, they also often referred to it as *Insha'Allah* Airlines. The Aviation Safety Network lists twenty-six "occurrences" for Ariana Airlines between 1959 and 2007, including seven crashes. Two of the crashes occurred when the planes ran out of fuel, one when a door opened in flight, one on landing, and two when the planes flew into a mountain.

27. Muhammad died in AD 632, and although he was never venerated as a divine figure, he was held to be the Perfect Man. His surrender to God had been so complete that he transformed a society.

28. According to the Quran, women and men stand equal before God. Women have divinely sanctioned inheritance, property, social, and marriage rights. The erosion of these fundamental, human rights in many Muslim countries is the direct result of legislation and subsequent enforcement of a code of behavior by male dominated societies, and does not reflect Islam's values.

29. The USSR poured billions of dollars in economic and military aid into Afghanistan throughout the 1950s and '60s, and as early as 1956 the Soviet Union was training Afghan military officers. King Zahir was overthrown by his cousin, Prime Minister Mohammad Daoud Khan, in 1973. Within five years Daoud himself was overthrown by the Afghan army and executed, along with his family. Muhammad Taraki assumed the presidency, backed by the Soviet Union

and the growing Marxist People's Democratic Party of Afghanistan (PDPA). Taraki had an agenda of modernizing Afghanistan and eliminating Islamic rules and traditions, and he was killed by Afghan rebels in 1979, with the explicit approval of the Soviet leader Leonid Brezhnev. Immediately, another pro-Soviet leader seized power—Hafizullah Amin. By then, however, thousands of Muslims had joined the mujahideen, whose members believed they were on a holy mission for Allah. They declared a *jihad*, a holy war, against the Amin government and, by extension, the Soviet Union. Amin asked for Soviet troops to assist in his fight against the mujahideen rebels, and the USSR complied with his request. On December 24, 1979, Soviet troops were deployed to Kabul. The Christmas Day invasion eventually led to the ten-year Soviet-Afghan War.

30. Sometimes called *maadar-e-shahr-ha*, the "mother of cities," Balk was first settled around 2,000 BCE when tribes from the steppes of Central Asia migrated to the area. In the early centuries AD, the city became a center for Buddhist monasteries. In the ensuing centuries it was conquered by Muslim Arabs, sacked by Genghis Khan, and rebuilt in the early sixteenth century.

31. Archaeological work has been limited, with Russia and France doing most of the excavating. Present-day looters, often so poor they are looking for anything to sell in order to feed their families, sporadically sift through precious bits of broken brick and pottery.

CHAPTER 8: JALALABAD

32. Predominately Pashtun nomads, Kutchi clans have followed the same migratory routes for hundreds of years, bringing their herds of sheep and goats to graze alternately in summer and winter pastures. Kutchies are proud of their nomadic tradition, believing themselves to be superior to those who stay in one place to work or farm. Kutchi women are instantly recognizable in their colorful patterned dresses, worn over turquoise tombans. Even the Taliban have respected the nomadic tradition of their Pashtun brethren and have not forced the Kutchi women to wear the chador.

33. Officials estimate that there are about 3 million Kutchies among 25 million Afghans, with perhaps 60 percent of them still following the nomadic life. A few itinerant tribesmen have settled down and prospered, but most of them have been pushed to the brink of poverty by war, landmines, and shrinking access to land. Modern communication and transportation have made the nomads obsolete: they are no longer needed for trade or to bring news and information to the villages. Most Kutchies feel they are a forgotten people, neglected by the government. Even if they wanted to settle down, the majority could not afford to buy or rent a house. Pride is also a factor. The nomadic way of life has been passed down for generations; it is all they know. Many feel if they give it up, they will in effect, turn their backs on a tradition that has been in existence for centuries.

CHAPTER 9: EXODUS

Quotations taken directly from a cassette tape recording Jo sent to her parents, Mr. and Mrs. James Carter, in April 1968. Transcribed and used with permission.

34. Between the years of 1962 and 1979, the Peace Corps sent a total of 1,652 Volunteers to Afghanistan. Shortly after the American Ambassador Adolph Dubs was kidnapped and assassinated on February 14, 1979, the Peace Corps withdrew the last group of Volunteers. The U.S. government did not replace Ambassador Dubs, and finally closed the embassy in 1989 as security in Kabul deteriorated. The position of U.S. ambassador in Afghanistan was not filled again until 2002.

CHAPTER 11: MR. MUKTAR

35. During the time that Jo was in Afghanistan, the educational system consisted of six years of primary school and six years of *lycee*, or high school. Education was compulsory and free, but Afghanistan lacked the resources, teachers, textbooks, and facilities to implement universal education. Functional literacy was well

under 10 percent. Volunteer foreign teachers from Britain and West Germany, as well as American Peace Corps Volunteers, helped to fill part of the gap. In the years 1969 and 1970 there were 2,940 schools in Afghanistan—2,556 for boys and 384 for girls. When the Soviets invaded in 1979, many of those schools were destroyed, along with other infrastructure. More schools were destroyed by the Taliban. Today there has been a push for education, especially for girls; however, the literacy rate in Afghanistan remains under 30 percent.

36. Alcohol in any form is strictly forbidden to Muslims. Water is generally not safe to drink unless boiled; hence, the copious amounts of tea.

37. *Atan*, a 7/8-meter dance, is considered the national dance of Afghanistan. It is performed by groups of ten or more to the accompaniment of the *dhol* and sometimes the *soma*, a double-reed pipe. The 7/8 beat is divided into two-measure increments with the main accents falling on 1, 4, 6, 8. The Atan begins with an announcement by the drum, and the dancers then move slowly in a circle. Speed builds gradually and accelerates as the dancers go through various attitudes and figures.

38. Andrew West, a radio newsman with KRKD, a Mutual Broadcasting System affiliate in Los Angeles, followed Senator Kennedy from the ballroom of the Ambassador Hotel in Los Angeles on the night of June 5, 1968. As the Senator exited through the kitchen, West heard gunshots, and instinctively turned on his tape recorder. His audio feed was picked up by KRKD and its affiliates. Whether his exact words were aired by VOA is unclear. In any case, Jo heard the news on the early afternoon of June 5, Baghlan time. (United Press International. "Robert F. Kennedy Assassinated.")

39. Robert F. (Bobby) Kennedy was shot by Sirhan Sirhan, a Jordanian nationalist who resented Kennedy for his support of Israel in the June 1967 Six-Day War. Kennedy most likely would have been the Democratic presidential nominee in 1968 and would have faced the Republican presidential nominee, Richard Nixon, in the November election.

CHAPTER 12: INTERNATIONAL RELATIONS

40. Founded in 1963, the German Development Service (DED) was modeled on the American Peace Corps, but with a few differences. The DED is a non-profit, limited-liability company owned jointly by the Federal Republic of Germany and the working group Learning and Helping Overseas. In the early years, German Volunteers were sent to work in specialized fields. In recent years a bigger percentage of Volunteers have been university graduates with administrative and social science backgrounds.

41. The Soviets in Puli-Khumri were civilian engineers who worked on the hydro-electric plant that had been built on the Kunduz River. American officials and CIA agents occasionally questioned the American Peace Corps workers for information about the Russians, but the Volunteers did not have much to offer. The few encounters they had with the Soviets were exclusively social.

CHAPTER 13: HOUSE FOR RENT

42. With a complete absence of women in society, Afghan men often turn to each other not only for companionship, but for sexual gratification as well. Whereas in most Western cultures homosexuality is generally accepted as gender identity—the deliberate lifestyle choice a person makes, in Afghanistan it is more often a temporary fix for coping with a strict, sexually repressive Muslim culture. The prohibitive cost of marriage also contributes to widespread homosexual behavior in Afghanistan. Prospective bridegrooms are expected to pay the wedding expenses in addition to providing gifts to the bride and her family, something that most young men simply cannot afford.

CHAPTER 14: THERE'S NO PLACE LIKE HOME

43. *Bacha* means "boy" or "son" in Farsi. Bachas were young Afghan men who worked for USAID families, the diplomatic corps, and, in fact, most Westerners stationed in Afghanistan.

CHAPTER 15: ROXANNE

44. The United States Information Agency (USIA) was an independent foreign affairs agency established in 1953 under President Eisenhower. Voice of America and the Fulbright Exchange Program are two of the better-known programs of USIA. It was disbanded in 1999 and absorbed into the Department of State as the Bureau of International Information Programs.

45. Government agencies such as USAID, the American Embassy, the diplomatic corps, and the USIA were all "officially" off limits to Peace Corps personnel. It had nothing to do with national security and everything to do with the mission of the Peace Corps. Personnel with government agencies interacted with representatives of the Afghan government. Peace Corps Volunteers were living among the people of Afghanistan, with the mandate they remain neutral on government issues. Unofficially, parties and social events often included local Peace Corps Volunteers, both American and those from other countries.

CHAPTER 16: CURRICULUM DEVELOPMENT

46. As early as 1953, when General Mohammed Daud became prime minister under King Zahir, a number of social reforms were instituted, including the abolition of *purdah*, the practice of secluding women from public view. In 1964 the Afghan government decreed that the old traditions and customs impeding the advancement of women should be eliminated. In a comment to the United Nations, the government went even further and advocated the implementation of affirmative action policies for women.

CHAPTER 17: BAGHLAN SCHOOL OF NURSING

47. For a complete list of students, refer to Appendix A: Jo's Girls.

CHAPTER 19: SAINT ELSEWHERE

48. The Afghan medical school in Kabul was staffed almost entirely by French doctors in 1968. Classes were taught in French, which meant the Afghan medical students had to have their lectures translated, adding to the difficulties of medical training.

CHAPTER 20: BIBI DEEBA

49. An Afghan born as recently as 2012 has a life expectancy of forty-nine years.

50. During Ramadan, the ninth month of the Islamic lunar calendar, Muslims around the world fast from sunrise to sunset, abstaining from food and water and all other physical needs. Ramadan is a time of reflection, during which Muslims practice self-purification and self-restraint, thereby gaining true sympathy with those who are hungry. They are also expected to refrain from evil actions, thoughts, and words, and to make peace with those who have wronged them. Ramadan is one of the Five Pillars of Islam, along with faith in the oneness of God and belief in the words of his prophet Muhammad, daily prayer, giving alms to the needy, and the pilgrimage to Mecca for those who are able.

CHAPTER 21: AUTUMN LEAVES

51. In 1969, Nixon instructed his Peace Corps director, Joseph Blatchford, to cut the Peace Corps administrative staff by one-third. In January 1971, he proposed the Peace Corps budget be reduced from $90 million to $60 million and the number of Volunteers reduced from 9,000 to 5,800. He also merged the Peace Corps, VISTA, Foster Grandparents, and all other Volunteer programs into one bureaucratic agency called ACTION. The Peace Corps did not regain its independent status until 1981.

52. In 1798 Edward Jenner demonstrated that inoculation with cowpox could protect against smallpox, and routine vaccination began in the United States

during the early 1800s. WHO launched a worldwide campaign to eradicate smallpox in 1967, eventually pushing it back to the Horn of Africa and then to a single last natural case in Somalia in 1977.

CHAPTER 22: HAPPY HOLIDAYS

53. The Roman calendar divides the year into twelve months without regard to the lunar cycle. The Islamic calendar, on the other hand, has twelve lunar months, resulting in 354 days a year instead of 365. Consequently, the holy month of Ramadan and the fast-breaking celebration of Eid-al-Fitr fall earlier every year by eleven days.

    During the last few days of Ramadan each Muslim family gives a donation of food to the poor to ensure the needy can have a holiday meal and participate in the celebration. On the day of Eid, Muslims gather early in the morning for the Eid prayer, then scatter to visit family and friends. They often give gifts, especially to children. The celebration traditionally continues for three days, and in most Muslim countries, the entire three-day period is an official government/school holiday.

54. The spacecraft Apollo 8 was launched on December 21, 1968, and made ten elliptical orbits around the moon. For forty-five minutes of each orbit, the astronauts passed out of contact with mission control in Houston, Texas, when the spacecraft disappeared to the far side of the moon, which until that time had never been seen by man.

CHAPTER 23: PESHAWAR

55. The name and identifying characteristics of the airman Jo met in Peshawar have been changed to preserve his anonymity. The salient points of her relationship with him are true.

56. The USAFSS (United States Air Force Security Service) commenced operations in Peshawar in 1958 and continued through July 1970 as a listening post

to intercept information about the strategic military capabilities of the Soviet Union. Specialized airmen with top security clearance gathered communications from the Eastern Bloc, Communist China, and the North Vietnamese governments. In 1968, the Peshawar base had an operating staff of eight hundred and a support staff of five hundred, plus a dependent population.

57. The Khyber Pass begins ten miles outside Peshawar, Pakistan, and ends at the Afghan border. It is the main connection between Afghanistan and the Indian subcontinent, and the main point of access to Central Asia. After 1980, it became a major route for refugees leaving and later returning to Afghanistan. During that time, Pakistan periodically closed the border crossing on the Afghan side to control the influx of unwanted Afghan refugees. Presently, the Khyber Pass is the principal route for supplies to American and NATO troops serving in Afghanistan.

CHAPTER 24: THE LONG WINTER

58. Hajj is the annual pilgrimage to Mecca, the birthplace of the Prophet Muhammad. Muslims who are physically and financially able are required to make the trip once in their lifetime. Often, male pilgrims wear special simple tunics that strip away distinctions of class and culture so that all stand equal before God. Hajj is one of the Five Pillars of Islam.

59. Even Mr. Hyatullah was safe, as they found out later. He had been trapped with his wife and children for two days by the avalanche, but they escaped without injury.

CHAPTER 25: LITTLE WOMEN

60. Jack Vaughn often pointed out that in twenty-eight languages of the world, the word for "stranger" is the same as the word for "enemy." (Jack Vaughn, quoted during testimony before the House Subcommittee on International Development, September 8, 20, and 29, 1977.)

61. The national sport of Afghanistan, *Buzkashi* (pronounced bush-ka-shee), literally translates as "goat grabbing." Players on horseback compete to grab the carcass of a goat, called the *boz*, and gallop away with it to a scoring area. The other players attack the rider and try to steal the boz. Many historians believe that Buzkashi originated with the Turkic-Mongol people. The horses that participate in Buzkashi must train for five years before making it to the playing field.

62. Trachoma is a bacterial eye infection. If left untreated, it usually leads to blindness, mainly due to corneal ulcers that form when the eyelids turn inward and eyelashes scratch the cornea. It is largely unknown in the West; however, trachoma affects more than 40 million people globally. It is easily treated with antibiotics.

CHAPTER 26: JO'S GIRLS

63. Most likely Jamila and her fiancé recited memorized verses. The Quran is written in Arabic, a language neither one of them would have understood. Had Jo's girls been able to read the Quran for themselves, they would have learned that according to Islamic teachings, men and women are equal before God. They would have known Islam grants women divinely sanctioned inheritance, property, social, and marriage rights, including the right to reject the terms of a proposal and to initiate divorce. Since the Prophet Muhammad's death in 632 A.D., women's rights in many Muslim countries have deteriorated, but this is a function of patriarchal legislation and not an expression of Islamic values. It is no coincidence that the country with the most appalling treatment of women is also the country that is the least educated. The general population of Afghanistan cannot read, and this often gives mullahs and imams free reign to interpret and enforce the Quran as they see fit. Few people are in a position to question their authority. It also explains the Taliban's relentless suppression of education, especially for women.

64. Afghan society has always been patriarchal, even before the Taliban takeover. However, within the home, women are often strong decision makers, not only in household affairs, but in financial activities as well.

65. The fate of Afghan women was intertwined with two events far beyond the borders of Afghanistan: the Vietnam War and the Cold War between the United States and the Soviet Union. The Vietnam War was exacting a high price in American lives, and when the USSR moved to exert its influence in Afghanistan, the United States supplied aid to Afghan extremists and fundamentalists, hoping to ensure the Soviets were likewise enmeshed in a long and costly war. No one understood the implications of this strategy better than Meena, the visionary founder of RAWA, the Revolutionary Association of the Women of Afghanistan. She threw her support behind moderate, democratic Afghans in their fight against the Soviets, but it was a group that was largely ignored by the West. When the radical fundamentalists drove the Soviets out of Afghanistan, they took control of the country, bringing with them values completely opposed to those of their Western backers, including, as Meena predicted, the severe and ruthless oppression of women. She believed that education was the best opponent of fundamentalism. Women—and men, for that matter—who had some understanding of the broader world would not be so vulnerable to the fundamentalists' narrow, ignorant vision. Meena did not live to see the Taliban perpetuate their horrific crimes against women. In 1987 she was assassinated in Quetta, Pakistan, by Afghan agents of the KGB. However, the movement did not die with her, and the work of RAWA continues to this day.

CHAPTER 27: THE BELL WILL CRACK

66. From April through June 1968, there were no fewer than fifty strikes by workers and students in Afghanistan, mostly in Kabul. Students demanded curriculum reform, graduate programs, and changes in admissions policies. Workers went on strike for better working conditions, health and medical insurance, and reduced working hours, especially for Thursday, the day before Juma. In general, the two groups supported each other in protesting the inequities in Afghan society. Ironically, the protests were against religious fanaticism as well as Western materialism.

CHAPTER 28: LIFE IN BAGHLAN

67. Dancing boys are prepubescent boys who are sold to wealthy or powerful men for entertainment. The young boys dress as women and perform sensual dances, inevitably becoming victims of sexual abuse. Although it has been outlawed by the Taliban, the practice continues, most predominately in the southern provinces, including Kandahar Province.

68. From the moment of birth, Afghans are never alone. Extended families live in compounds that are little communities, and daily life is conducted to a rhythm of social interaction. Because a visit from a friend or relative takes precedence over anything else, fixed schedules are not important. Indeed, most Afghans do not own a watch. In contrast, Western societies are regimented by the clock, and schedules take precedence over social interaction.

   Countries such as the United States, Australia, Great Britain, Canada, and the Netherlands have formed individualistic societies, with a core value that allows people to think for themselves and make their own judgments. And while individual freedom is the basis of liberty, democracy, and economic incentive, it can emphasize materialism and individual gain. Afghan society is communal, based on hospitality, generosity, courage, honor, and self-respect. Communal societies, however, can be provincial and resistant to change. Loyalty is to immediate family, extended family, and then tribe. There is little national unity in Afghanistan, apart from the bonds of Islam.

69. Jo made one additional, unexpected trip to Kabul before she left for good: the trip she took on April 21, 1970, to call her father.

EPILOGUE

70. U.S. President Obama and Afghanistan President Karzai, along with representatives from 27 other member countries of the North Atlantic Treaty Organization (NATO), met in Chicago on May 21, 2012, in order to negotiate the

withdrawal of U.S. and NATO troops from Afghanistan by the end of 2014. Discussion centered on continued humanitarian development, reconstruction aid, and police training. Conspicuously absent from the agenda was a serious conversation of how to protect women's rights in Afghanistan once the troops' are gone. "We were told the Chicago (NATO) summit has nothing to do with us women," said Mahbouba Seraj, a member of the Afghan Women's Network. In agreement was Manizha Naderi, Executive Director of Women for Afghan Women. "Women comprise 50 percent of the population, and they have not been consulted in any of this: not the transition, not reconstruction, not the negotiations. They haven't been consulted at all."

71. Participants at a Shadow Summit sponsored by Amnesty International addressed this very issue, and drafted an open letter to Presidents Obama and Karzai. Signed by former U.S. Secretary of State Madeleine Albright and Nobel laureate Shiren Ebadi, the letter calls for participation by women in peace talks with the Taliban, and institutionalized guarantees of women's rights in any reconciliation agreements with the Taliban. It remains to be seen if women's rights are forgotten, or bargained away. As Albright concluded, "Women's rights and women being on various groups is the best way to ensure a better life for everybody, not just for women, but for everybody."

Made in the USA
San Bernardino, CA
01 March 2016